Tax-Funded Politics

Tax-Funded Politics

James T. Bennett

Transaction Publishers
New Brunswick (U.S.A.) and London (U.K.)

Copyright © 2004 by Transaction Publishers, New Brunswick, New Jersey.

All rights reserved under International and Pan-American Copyright Conventions. No part of this book may be reproduced or transmitted in any form or by any means, electronic or mechanical, including photocopy, recording, or any information storage and retrieval system, without prior permission in writing from the publisher. All inquiries should be addressed to Transaction Publishers, Rutgers—The State University, 35 Berrue Circle, Piscataway, New Jersey 08854-8042.

This book is printed on acid-free paper that meets the American National Standard for Permanence of Paper for Printed Library Materials.

Library of Congress Catalog Number: 2004047899
ISBN: 0-7658-0235-X
Printed in Canada

Library of Congress Cataloging-in-Publication Data

Bennett, James T.
   Tax-funded politics / James T. Bennett.
      p. cm.
   Includes bibliographical references and index.
   ISBN: 0-7658-0235-X (alk. paper)
     1. Lobbying—United States—Finance. 2. Political activists—United States. 3. Nonprofit organizations—United States—Political activity. 4. Grants-in-aid—United States. 5. Administrative agencies—United States—Appropriations and expenditures. I. Title.

JK1118.B3938 2004
322.4'0973—dc22   2004047899

Contents

Preface	vii
1. Introduction: Stuck in the Lobby	1
2. Uncle Sam: Sugar Daddy to the Feminists	13
3. Workers (and Teachers) of the World! Apply for Grants!	53
4. Greens Scramble for the Green	85
5. Heart, Lungs, and the Big C: The Big Three Take Aim at Your Wallets and Your Liberty	109
6. The Black, the Brown, and the Old	139
7. Gravy Train Conservatives	161
8. Conclusion: As I Told the Subcommittee . . .	193
Index	197

Preface

Ludwig Von Mises's classic book, *Bureaucracy* (Yale University Press, 1944, p. 1), begins with the statements "The terms *bureaucrat*, *bureaucratic*, and *bureaucracy* are clearly invectives. . . . They always imply a disparaging criticism of persons, institutions, or procedures. Nobody doubts that bureaucracy is thoroughly bad and that it should not exist in a perfect world." The same may be said of the terms *propaganda*, *propagandistic*, and *propagandism*, for these also have opprobrious connotations, although the dictionary definition according to *Webster's*—"the spreading of ideas, information, or rumor for the purpose of helping or injuring an institution, a cause, or a person"—is much less negative. This book is about propaganda financed with taxpayers' money. When government becomes involved in advocating ideas and information, issues arise that do not exist when private institutions and individuals espouse a cause.

Americans have always viewed government with considerable suspicion. Government employees are termed *civil servants* or *public servants* in recognition of the fact that the powers of government derive from the consent of those governed who are, at least in theory, the masters of the state. From the time of the nation's founding, government was intended to serve the will of the people. However, when government promotes ideas, the master/servant relationship is turned on its head, for the power of government is used to *influence and create* the will of the people rather than passively serve that will. Moreover, relative to institutions in the private sector, the government, especially at the federal level, has very deep pockets to promote its agendas. Because federal law has long prohibited federal employees from directly engaging in lobbying and advocacy activities, nonprofit entities in the private sector are given grants and contracts by governments at all levels to proselytize on behalf of the programs of the agency or government department providing the funding. These private groups are widely viewed as "charities" that have only the "public interest" at stake. The halo of charity often disguises the blatantly political role of these organizations.

And, when we also observe that tax dollars are collected coercively, many people would be rightly indignant about the causes being advocated with their money. At root, the central issue in this study is *tax-subsidized speech*. Freedom of speech itself is not at issue, for that right is guaranteed to all by the U.S. Constitution. This book chronicles and analyzes in detail the links between taxpayers' dollars and nonprofit organizations that are actively involved in politics.

I have long had an intense interest in tax-funded politics and in the advocacy activities of "those who know what's best for the rest of us." Almost two decades ago, Thomas J. DiLorenzo and I co-authored *Destroying Democracy: How Government Funds Partisan Politics* (1986), which dealt with the same issues. More recently, four other books co-authored with DiLorenzo, all published by Transaction, deal primarily with how charities are actively engaged in lobbying and political advocacy with taxpayers' funds: *CancerScam: Diversion of Federal Cancer Funds to Politics* (1998), *The Food and Drink Police: America's Nannies, Busybodies, and Petty Tyrants* (1999), *From Pathology to Politics: Public Health in America* (2000), and *Public Health Profiteering* (2001). Thus, this book is another product of a research emphasis that has engaged my energies and attention for years.

This research would not have been possible without the generous financial support of the Sunmark Foundation and help from the Locke Institute. Research assistance was provided by Mattias Eng, Benjamin Powell, and Brian Rooney. Finally, I owe profuse thanks to my editor, Bill Kauffman, who made major contributions to this study and added some zingers of his own. I am most grateful to these foundations and individuals for their many contributions to this work.

James T. Bennett
George Mason University
Fairfax, Virginia

1

Introduction: Stuck in the Lobby

Thomas Jefferson, in the Statute of Virginia for Religious Freedom, declared, "To compel a man to furnish contributions of money for the propagation of opinions which he disbelieves is sinful and tyrannical."[1]

Now, it may not shock jaded Americans to know that sin and tyranny have their defenders, especially in Washington, D.C., but that doesn't mean that we have to let them carry the day. This Jeffersonian principle is so basic, so powerful in its logic and its appeal to justice, that it seems almost irrefutable. Very few of the organizations mentioned in this book would gainsay Jefferson's declaration. Instead, they just ignore it, or, with an Orwellian twist, they claim to be the partisans of free speech and liberty. Those who would cut off the flow of public monies to such groups are caricatured as mean-spirited right-wingers who would tape shut the mouths of YWCA directors and spunky old folks trying to knock a few bucks off the cost of their prescription drugs.

They will also protest that any criticism of them as "lobbyists" is errant. After all, such lobbying is against the law. Lobbying with federal monies *is* illegal, and has been since 1913, but the loophole in this law is wide enough for Al Gore to drive an SUV through. The relevant portion of the 1913 statute reads:

> No part of the money appropriated by any enactment of Congress shall, in the absence of express authorization by Congress, be used directly or indirectly to pay for any personal service, advertisement, telegram, telephone, letter, printed or written matter, or other device, intended or designed to influence in any manner a member of Congress, to favor or oppose, by vote or otherwise, any legislation or appropriation by Congress, whether before or after the introduction of any bill or resolution proposing such legislation or appropriation.[2]

Federal regulations governing lobbying since have consumed enough paper to fell the Amazonian rainforests, but the basic problem can be discerned with crystalline clarity. In the words of the *Nonprofit Lobbying Guide*, "Charities are prohibited from using any federal funds for legislative lobbying and electioneering. However, they are not restricted from using private resources to lobby."[3]

Which is to say that the ban on lobbying with federal funds is utterly meaningless. A charity's resources are fungible: money spent in one area may easily be shifted into another area. If, say, the Committee for a Smoke-Free, Alcohol-Free, Drug-Free (and, perhaps consequently, Liberty-Free) World receives a $200,000 federal grant for its anti-smoking programs, the Committee may then transfer $200,000 previously designated for those programs to its lobbying arm—which spends that $200,000 to lobby for additional monies so that it may drag the rest of us into its vice-less utopia.

The way this scam works was nicely illustrated in a Cato Institute "Policy Analysis" by John Samples, Christopher Yablonski, and Ivan G. Osorio bearing the provocative title "More Government for All: How Taxpayers Subsidize Anti-Tax Cut Advocacy."[4] The authors examined the members of something called the Fair Taxes for All Coalition, an ad hoc cluster of liberal interest groups and nonprofit organizations formed in March 2001 to oppose President George W. Bush's proposed $1.6 trillion tax cut. When Washington lobbyists use the word "fair," the wise taxpayer will clutch her purse close to her bosom. The Fair Taxes for All Coalition was not proposing that lower or middle-income taxpayers get a larger chunk of that $1.6 trillion in tax relief; what stuck in its craw was the very idea of tax cuts for anyone. Permitting Americans to keep more of the money they earn, warned the coalition, "jeopardizes our nation's ability to meet domestic and foreign responsibilities, threatens fiscal stability and security, and inequitably distributes its benefits."[5] In other words: shut up and pay up.

The Cato analysts found that almost three score of those groups belonging to the Fair Taxes for All Coalition were the recipients of federal subsidies. In all, "one-third of the first 170 organizations that publicly endorsed the Fair Taxes for All Coalition . . . received, collectively, almost $618 million in public money from 1996 through 2000."[6] These included such baldly partisan groups as the AFL-CIO, the NAACP, and the National Council of Churches as well as such ostensibly nonpartisan entities as the YWCA, the League of Women Voters, and the PTA. (How many members of the three lastly named groups know that their national leaders are as scrupulously apolitical as Ted Kennedy?)

In subsequent pages, we'll take a closer look at these grant-munching kine in the pasture of Big Government.

There is nothing illegal in what the coalition members were doing. They were not lobbying specifically for more government money for themselves. No, they were lobbying against a reduction in those taxes that fund their programs. And they were using "private" money. Or so the line goes.

* * *

By the mid-1990s, Congress finally caught on to the scandalous misuse of tax dollars by advocacy groups. Fresh from the startling Republican takeover of the House of Representatives in the 1994 election, the new GOP majority took direct aim at the political use of taxpayers' dollars—and learned a bruising lesson about what happens when idealistic young legislators poke around in hornets' nests.

Throughout the summer of 1995, Indiana freshman Rep. David McIntosh's Subcommittee on National Economic Growth, Natural Resources, and Regulatory Affairs held hearings on the "Abuse of Taxpayer Funds to Subsidize Lobbying and Political Activity." Rep. McIntosh kicked off the hearings in fine style as he announced his intention to expose "one of Washington's best kept little secrets— welfare for lobbyists. Yes, America, you heard it right. Your tax dollars are being used by special interest groups to lobby Congress for more tax dollars. This vicious cycle is taxpayer abuse; it is an outrage; and it must come to an end."

McIntosh predicted that "Americans will be shocked to know that taxpayers are paying special interest lobbyists to walk the Halls of Congress, executive branches, and even local town halls, trying to influence their lawmakers."[7]

Alas, Americans are beyond being shocked by much that goes on in Congress. Rep. McIntosh's hearings brought to light countless examples of lobbying by government-funded nonprofits. I would like to say that shining the light of publicity on these abuses made them go away. But it didn't. His efforts, and those of Rep. Ernest Istook (R-OK), another leader in the House in the effort to end political advocacy with taxpayer dollars, fell short of success when a companion measure died in the Senate.

Among those appearing before Rep. McIntosh's subcommittee was the wry veteran Senator Alan Simpson (R-WY), who had tangled with his share of special interests and had the welts to prove it. Simpson greeted his young colleague with a warning about "how the game is played in Washington, D.C." "Whenever any type of reform is proposed," lectured Senator Simpson,

> "and whenever there is a danger that someone, somewhere will lose their access to Federal money, they will find the most sympathy-provoking, heart-wrenching way of making the case that the money should keep right on flowing. I can assure you at this very moment the search is being conducted for the most laudable tax-exempt groups that have ever been organized, ever conceived in the mind of man. Tireless people, selfless, altruistic beyond mention."[8]

Simpson knew whereof he spoke. Liberal Democrats, both those on the subcommittee and those appearing ex officio, denounced McIntosh with all the fury that self-satisfied insiders can muster for a young heretic. Henry Waxman (D-CA) declared himself "deeply offended"[9] by the very idea of such hearings. Cardiss Collins (D-IL) charged that McIntosh and the freshmen Republicans were trying "to silence the voices of their political opponents."[10] New York Congresswoman Louise Slaughter (D), who is kept alive in a marginal Upstate district by huge infusions of union PAC money, dropped by the hearing to denounce the legislation as "unconstitutional" and to huff, "it is certainly apparent to me that you only want to shut up people you don't want to hear from."[11] Having been heard from, she waltzed out of the room. But not before having her card punched—metaphorically speaking—by the special interests that pay for her campaigns. Their taxpayer-provided privileges were under assault. Rep. Slaughter had shown the flag (not the American one); she would be thanked profusely by those whose privileges she had defended come the 1996 election. Democracy in action.

The Democratic critics of the GOP investigation were right on one crucial point. Rep. Henry Waxman, who never met a regulatory hassle he didn't like, chided McIntosh for ignoring the lobbying activities of those corporations that receive federal grants. Like a smokeless Ross Perot, Waxman brought along a series of charts detailing the massive subsidies that many large corporations receive from Uncle Sam. "These corporations spend tens of millions on lobbyists," Waxman protested. "But we're not investigating whether they abuse their Federal aid."[12]

Congress ought to do just that. Better yet, simply end the subsidies, thus obviating the need for any federal watchdog. (As the great 1950s libertarian writer Frank Chodorov once said when asked what to do about Communists who held government jobs, "Easy. Just abolish the jobs."[13])

When Rep. Istook sought to ban political advocacy by organizations subsidized by the federal government, he ran into a hailstorm of abuse. As his colleague J.D. Hayworth (R-AZ) observed, "Every member of this new majority has been treated to a ceaseless parade of epithets from those who see the gravy train about to come to an end."[14]

The gravy train rolled right over Congressmen Istook, Hayworth, and McIntosh. It was driven by Independent Sector, a coalition of philanthropic and voluntary organizations. Independent Sector chose the disingenuous (if highly effective) name of "Let America Speak!" for its coalition of state-subsidized charities fighting to protect their privileges. They successfully framed the issue as one of "free speech," as if refusing to parcel out taxpayer dollars to lobbyists somehow violates the First Amendment rights of those lobbyists.

As Representatives Istook and MacIntosh discovered in 1995, any effort to separate lobbyist from state will be met by hysterical over-reaction—or perhaps it's not overreaction, given that federal grantees guard their access to the trough like a mother werewolf protects her cubs.

How much less potent "Let America Speak!" might have been had it been renamed "Let America Lobby!" Those nonprofits subject to Section 1307 of Public Law 94-455, better known as the 1976 lobby law, may spend up to 20 percent of their first half-million dollars of annual expenditures on lobbying; they may devote 15 percent of the next half-million to lobbying, 10 percent of the next $500,000, and so on, until reaching the maximum of $1 million. (In a classic formulation of one who has spent a little too much time in Washington, D.C., veteran nonprofit lobbyist Bob Smucker wrote, "It took a full 14 years for the Internal Revenue Service to issue final regulations under the 1976 lobby law, but the regulations were worth the wait."[15])

Yet the very word "lobbying" troubles these organizations. They know the wretched reputation of lobbyists out in the great flyover country; they understand how it looks when recipients of government largesse turn around and lobby that same government. So what do they do about it? Why, refuse to use the word "lobby," of course. Instead, lobbying by such groups is "advocacy." When they took on the Reagan administration, and later Rep. Istook, they were defending "advocacy rights." Sounds so much less grimy than lobbying, doesn't it?

A decade earlier, when the Reagan administration proposed Rule A-122, which would have prevented federal grantees from including the cost of lobbying in their overhead costs, the subsidized set also blew its top. As Michael Horowitz, Reagan's general counsel at the Office of Management and Budget, recalled,

> "What our OMB proposal said was that you could not put into your overhead pool the time value and amount of money you spent lobbying to get more government money. The fury was staggering. Jack Brooks (D-TX), then-Chairman of the House Judiciary Committee, said that not since World War II had anyone managed to mobilize such a broad spectrum of opposition. The Ford Motor Company and Ralph Nader, the Chamber of Commerce, and the Red Cross were all out to get me fired, Brooks said at a hearing, for having proposed in effect that government monies could not be spent for lobbying for more government money. The overhead scam . . . was a way to rob university researchers and poor people, who are supposed to be the beneficiaries of the grant program, in order to provide basic operating expenses for organizations that get grants and cost-plus contracts."[16]

The Reagan administration lost this tussle, but the outlines of a longer-range strategy had become visible, even to advocates of nonprofit partisanship. Brian O'Connell, president of Independent Sector, told a 1987 gathering of charitable staffers that "There is a general sense that the institutions of the sector are on more appropriate ground when they are providing services, especially services to the poor, and that it is a questionable extension of tax exemption when such organizations use the privilege of their government-granted tax-free status to turn around and try to influence that same government."[17]

A wise analysis, even if it did fly in one ear and out the other of many of O'Connell's auditors.

One Independent Sector report noted ominously, "There is a pattern of rapidly emerging government regulation of philanthropy and independent organizations." The logical companion to that sentence—"There is a pattern of rapidly expanding government subsidization of philanthropy and independent organizations"—was conspicuous by its absence. "He who takes the king's shilling, becomes the king's man," is an adage which grantees of the federal government would be wise to learn. I shall have reason to invoke it throughout this book.

The Independent Sector report goes on, in high dudgeon (or what passes for high dudgeon in the soporific language of nonprofit bureaucratese), to warn that limiting taxpayer-supported lobbying "gives public officials unwarranted authority to limit the activities of such groups, particularly if the new groups are antagonistic to the officials. There is no greater danger to the preservation of our free society than giving the powers that be any great control over who their own reformers might be."[18]

There you have it. "Reformers"—but only reformers of a certain stripe, it goes without saying—are entitled to a free passkey to the public treasury, and any attempt to curb their ability to use public funds to demand a greater share of the treasury strikes at freedom's heart. This is equal parts arrogance and obtuseness, but the joke is on us, dear taxpayer, for we pay for the privilege of being both robbed *and* insulted.

Reading a shelf-full of books on nonprofit lobbying—an endurance test to daunt the contestants on "Survivor"—one is struck by the sad gap between the often-praiseworthy person-to-person activities of the nonprofits and the grandiosely abstract political ambitions of those same groups—often of those same people. For instance, one Eden Fisher Durbin, director of public policy of the YMCA of the USA, writes of his early work with abused preschoolers in Philadelphia. He and his colleagues "taught Lyndell to talk in complete sentences and maintain eye contact, helped Missy refrain from eating her hair, and gave Hector the skills to cope with his chaotic household." One might think that the glow of such accomplishments would warm Mr. Durbin's heart, but no, he soon found out that "my strengths were working on behalf of children, not with them."

In other words, it was not the very real, flesh-and-blood Lyndell and Missy and Hector who were close to Eden Fisher Durbin's heart, but rather the abstraction "the children." And we all know that when "the children" are invoked, money—and constitutional limits on government—are *never* an object.

"I grew dissatisfied with the microcosm that Lyndell and Hector represented and became eager to get my arms around the bigger picture,"[19] says Durbin, and the mixed metaphor is apt: when one's *arms* are around a picture, the faces of those pictured no longer matter. They can't even be seen. The individual disappears when in the grasp of the world-reformer. What does it matter if little Lyndell can't speak in complete sentences: we have a world to save, a system to create, *a program to fund. Fully* fund.

This elevation of vicarious do-gooding over the real thing—of lobbying for various welfare-state or nanny-state laws instead of tending to the health and welfare of real life, honest-to-goodness people—is a matter worthy of investigation by a school of (unsubsidized) psychologists. Take David Cohen, co-director of the Advocacy Institute, which has as its mission "to strengthen the advocacy capacity of social justice organizations to set their public agenda." (In bureaucratese, this does not translate to "protect personal liberties" or "cut taxes.") Mr. Cohen, in an almost charming admission, says, "Today many people disdain all lobbyists. But to me, being a public interest lobbyist is a career you can write home about and wear proudly at class reunions. My children knew I was a lobbyist. They were proud!"[20] One supposes that the rest of us should be pleased that Mr. Cohen's kids were proud of the old man, though a churl cannot suppress the thought that this filial pride was purchased at the cost of many millions of taxpayer dollars. How much cheaper for the rest of us if Cohen had pursued a career as a professional baseball player.

Nevertheless, the audacity of those who lobby with public monies should not be underestimated. They are virtuous, and if you raise even the mildest complaint against the spectacle of people who receive government money using that money to lobby the government for more money, you are *mean-spirited*! A McCarthyite! A reciter of Satanic verses! And probably a smoker as well!

Brian O'Connell of Independent Sector points out that there are more than 900,000 tax-exempt organizations registered with the Internal Revenue Service, a number that does not include "religious congregations or the local affiliates of many national organizations such as Boy Scouts and the American Cancer Society."[21] O'Connell estimates that all told, our country has more than two million voluntary and charitable groups. The number may be taken as a measure of the health of our civil society.

I want to make it clear that I believe that many nonprofits do a marvelous job in helping the indigent, comforting the bereaved or lonely, and otherwise strengthening the connective tissue that binds us together in our communities. They are fine examples of the voluntaristic communitarianism that Alexis de Tocqueville, among others, regarded as a hallmark of American society.

But even the best of these groups—and certainly the worst of them, which are mere fund-raising machines—should not lobby with public money. Jefferson called it sinful. It was then; it is now.

And we must not be unmindful of the consequences of such lobbying, which, as I shall explain, are often harmful to liberty. As Supreme Court Justice Louis D. Brandeis wrote, "Experience should teach us to be most on our guard to protect liberty when the government's purposes are beneficent. . . . The greatest dangers to liberty lurk in insidious encroachment by men of zeal, well-meaning but without understanding."[22] Men of zeal, well-meaning but without understanding: we shall meet their like many times in the pages that follow.

For more than two decades, I have been studying the "men of zeal" at the helm of our county's nonprofit sector. My view of this sector has been shaped by public-choice theory, which assumes that people act in what they perceive to be their own self-interest. This may sound like a truism; it is not. For years, economists and political scientists had treated public employees as if they were somehow different from the rest of us: self-sacrificing, unconcerned with self-aggrandizement or the consolidation of wealth or power. They were angels, sent from heaven to rule over us softly and benignantly.

Thankfully, that fairy tale has been retired, due in large part to the insights of the public-choice school of economic thought. Government agencies act to maximize their size and scope. So do nonprofit agencies. And when governments hook up with nonprofits, the treasury raid is on.

The treasury raiders come in all ideological colors. Before the Reagan administration, the political tilt of this network leaned left: recipients of government boodle who then turned around and lobbied for bigger government included the decrepit welfarist liberals of the Gray Panthers, the suit and tie environmentalists of Washington, D.C. (whose favorite green cause was the accumulation of rectangular green sheets printed by the U.S. Mint), and Jesse Jackson's scam par excellence, PUSH.

In time, Washington "conservatives" got in on the game, too. President Reagan's National Endowment for Democracy, which Rep. Bill Emerson (R-MO) had retitled the "Taxpayer Funding of Foreign Elections Act,"[23] became a prime slush fund for neoconservative intellectuals who are subsidized through the NED and who write very pretty apologias for the agency whenever its funding is threatened. This is called licking the hand that feeds you—a canine skill that also comes in very handy along the banks of the Potomac.

By the time the second George Bush assumed the presidency, the network of government-subsidized lobbies had become extensive and, in worst Washington tradition, bipartisan. Only the gutsiest gadflies on Capitol Hill would dare bite these sacred cows. The whole matter had become a scandal—with precious few politicians willing to cry "shame!"

In his best-selling lament *Death of the West*, Pat Buchanan proposed that "some courageous researcher should produce a listing of all institutions with an arm in the federal trough, and the White House and Congress should be asked to defund all of those, Left or Right, that play politics with tax dollars."[24]

What follows is a somewhat irreverent tour of those institutions whose arms, fists, and sometimes entire bodies are deep in the federal trough. Will Congress and the White House defund them? Don't hold your breath.

Before starting the tour, however, two additional points deserve mention. First, my analysis does not deal with the substance of *individual* grants to the nonprofits groups that I review. Rather, I note the amount of funding that each group received from government and discuss the group's political activities and public policy stances. A study that attempted to assess hundreds of different grants to dozens of different organizations would be inordinately long and boring. To use an environmental metaphor, convenience dictates that I study the forest rather than the individual trees in the forest. Moreover, investigating individual grants is not essential to the validity of my arguments, for as noted earlier in this chapter, money is fungible. To claim that tax dollars are spent only for purpose x and that only dollars from other sources are spent for political advocacy activities and lobbying is simply disingenuous.

Second, other scholars interested in nonprofits are also greatly concerned not only with the involvement of charities in politics, but also the growing links between government and charitable institutions. For example, in an important symposium on the "Third Sector in Transition" in the May/June 2003 issue of *Society*, Steven Rathgeb Smith at the University of Washington, observes that

> "the government and nonprofit organizations have become increasingly intertwined in the last 25 years due to direct government funding and new government regulations as well as the increase in overall government policy activity."[25] Furthermore, the "political activism of nonprofit service providers is a sharp shift from previous eras. . . . [and] now nonprofit agencies regard their future viability and sustainability as tied to public policy."[26]

Strings always come with government money, but the impetus to use government funds to get more taxpayers' dollars is irresistible.

In the same symposium, Mark E. Warren, professor of government at Georgetown University, writes

> . . . [W]hen governments give money to nonprofits—to universities and health care providers, for example—they help to bring interest groups into existence. The groups can then exercise enormous influence over government policy. The result is one in which the public pays, in effect, to generate a covert form of corporatism that is no more democratic than the sort practiced by the business sector.[27]

Many are likely convinced, however, that these interest groups to which Warren refers will champion the cause of the most vulnerable in society, i.e., those on the bottom rung of the economic ladder, the most needy. But Warren provides a very different—and highly disturbing—perspective: ". . . [I]t may be that the overall effect of nonprofits in American democracy is to amplify the voices of the wealthy and powerful."[28]

Certainly, the growing symbiotic relationship between government at all levels and nonprofits is cause for serious concern, especially when the nonprofits are engaged in political advocacy. This concern may have prompted the Bush administration to emphasize faith-based initiatives in public-private partnerships: faith-based groups are less likely to be politically oriented.[29] Voluntarism and independent charities play an important role in alleviating myriad social problems, and such actions deserve praise and approval; politics and charity, however, are like oil and water—they don't mix.

Notes

1. Thomas Jefferson, "Statute of Virginia for Religious Freedom," in Edward Dumbauld, editor, *The Political Writings of Thomas Jefferson* (Indianapolis: Bobbs-Merrill, 1981; first edition, 1955), p. 34.

2. 18 USC Sec. 1913.
3. Bob Smucker, *The Nonprofit Lobbying Guide*, Second Edition (Washington, D.C.: Independent Sector, 1999), p. 70.
4. John Samples, Christopher Yablonski, and Ivan G. Osorio, "More Government for All: How Taxpayers Subsidize Anti-Tax Cut Advocacy," Cato Policy Analysis No. 407, (Washington, D.C.: Cato Institute, July 10, 2001).
5. Quoted in ibid., p. 2.
6. Ibid., p. 4.
7. "Abuse of Taxpayer Funds to Subsidize Lobbying and Political Activity," Subcommittee on National Economic Growth, Natural Resources, and Regulatory Affairs of the Committee on Government Reform and Oversight, House of Representatives, 104th Congress, First Session, p. 1.
8. Ibid., p. 77.
9. Ibid., p. 4.
10. Ibid., p. 10.
11. Ibid., p. 174.
12. Ibid., p. 4.
13. Frank Chodorov, *Fugitive Essays: Selected Writings of Frank Chodorov*, edited by Charles H. Hamilton (Indianapolis: Liberty Press, 1980), p. 25.
14. *Congressional Record*, October 30, 1995, p. H11439.
15. Smucker, *The Nonprofit Lobbying Guide*, p. 51.
16. Quoted in Samples, Yablonski, and Osorio, "More Government for All," p. 15.
17. Brian O'Connell, *People Power: Service, Advocacy, Empowerment* (New York: Foundation Center, 1994), p. 84.
18. Ibid., pp. 85–86.
19. Smucker, *The Nonprofit Lobbying Guide*, p. 90.
20. Ibid., p. 94.
21. O'Connell, *People Power*, p. 2.
22. Justice Louis Brandeis dissenting, *Olmstead v. United States*, 277 US 479 (1928).
24. Patrick J. Buchanan, *The Death of the West* (New York: St. Martin's Press, 2002), p. 260.
25. Stephen Rathgeb Smith, "Government and Nonprofits in the Modern Age," *Society* 40 (May/June 2003), p. 36.
26. Ibid., p. 40.
27. Mark E. Warren, "The Political Role of Nonprofits in a Democracy," *Society* (May/June 2003), p. 50.
28. Ibid.
29. For a discussion of faith-based initiatives in the Bush administration, see Leslie Lenkowsky, "The Bush Administration's Civic Agenda and National Service," *Society* 40 (January/February 2003), pp. 7–12.

2

Uncle Sam: Sugar Daddy to the Feminists

The phrase "taxpayer-funded feminist advocacy" calls to mind images of hideous harridans, testosterone-haters who think that the only good man is a dead man, or at least a castrated man. The classic specimen was Valerie Solanis, the lady who shot and almost killed Andy Warhol (ironically that most asexual of men), as an outrageous act on behalf of her aptly acronymed group SCUM (Society for Cutting Up Men). But SCUM is too easy a target, and believe it or not, SCUM never received a cent of government money. Instead, we shall begin with a starchy association of middle-class ladies who are about as controversial as the Rotary Club: the League of Women Voters.

The League of Women Voters is "widely trusted" and "nonpartisan"[1]—just ask the none-too-modest ladies. Current League President Carolyn Jefferson-Jenkins uses these terms as matter-of-factly as her predecessors have, perhaps on the theory that if one says night is day long enough, the credulous will buy it.

The League's mission statement is as innocuous as the suburban streets of so many of its members: "The League of Women Voters, a nonpartisan political organization, encourages the informed and active participation of citizens in government, works to increase understanding of major public policy issues, and influences public policy through education and advocacy."[2]

"Education" is handled by the League of Women Voters Education Fund. In 1998, government grants accounted for $210,075, or 11 percent, of the LWVEF's total revenue.[3] And this "education" was anything but nonpartisan.

The one constant in the League's long history is hostility to personal liberty and a fondness for the expansion of state power. Now, you might think that the League of Women Voters was conceived in an antiseptic laboratory devoted to an absolutely germless non-partisanship. After all, its name is redolent of well-intentioned middle-class ladies who sponsor debates and encourage people of both sexes to vote—just vote; doesn't matter whom you vote for: Democrat, Republican, Green, Libertarian, Communist, just vote!

Well, it turns out that the League, as a corporate whole, does care for whom you vote. It doesn't endorse candidates—it never has—nor does it take to the hustings to campaign for parties or persons. But it cares very deeply about causes: causes that in the aggregate would lead—have led—to a vast expansion of state power and a corresponding shrinkage of personal liberty. In the eighty-plus year history of the League of Women Voters, it is virtually impossible to find an instance when the organization sided with liberty against power.

The League was a direct descendant of the National American Woman Suffrage Association (NAWSA), which achieved its goal of federally mandated woman suffrage with the ratification of the 19th Amendment in 1920. With victory in sight, NAWSA president Carrie Chapman Catt envisioned a "League of Women Voters to 'Finish the Fight' and to aid in the reconstruction of the Nation."[4]

The nature of this "reconstruction" was laid bare in 1920, when the new organization delivered a load of proposed planks to the platform committees of the Republican and Democratic parties. These planks included:

- Adequate appropriation for the Children's Bureau;

- The protection of infant life through a Federal program for maternity and infancy care.

- A Federal Department of Education;

- Increased Federal support for vocational training in home economics;

- Such Federal-regulation and supervision of the marketing and distribution of food as will tend to equalize and lower prices. . .

- . . . a continuance of appropriations to carry on an active campaign for the prevention of venereal disease and for public education in sex hygiene.[5]

The other planks evinced a similar infatuation with big government. Though the League remained officially neutral during the election, Carrie Chapman Catt was so disgusted by the nonprogressive qualities of Republican candidate Warren G. Harding, who had failed to endorse Woodrow Wilson's League of Nations, that she endorsed Democratic James Cox.

Cox lost in a landslide. Signally, the women of America cast their first vote in overwhelming numbers for Warren G. Harding. Thus, from the very start, an enormous gap existed between the League of Women Voters and real, live, actual women voters.

The new League, as its historian Barbara Stuhler has written, "attracted as members women who were well educated, middle-class, and progressive in their political thought."[6] Though it achieved an enviable name recognition early on, the League has never had all that many adherents. Membership peaked in 1969 at a modest 156,780—a peak that in retrospect looks of Everest-ian size.

As the twenties roared, the League of Women Voters roared right back. The League's members were appalled by the widespread contempt for and disregard of the Prohibition Amendment; they urged strict enforcement. They wanted tougher child-labor and compulsory school attendance laws, which, as Allan Carlson and other contemporary revisionist scholars have argued, were the entering wedge of a government intent on remolding the family. The League supported new bureaucracies, urging the creation of a "federal department of Public Welfare" to be headed by "a woman who is an expert on social problems." (Like most progressives of their day, League leaders wished to transfer decision-making power from ordinary men and women to "experts" who "know best.") Though its membership was concentrated in the East, the League supported federal provision of electric power to the South and even requested that "the National Government [do] everything possible for the women held in harems in the Near East."[7] Truly, there was nothing not within the realm of the wise men along the Potomac.

To any mossbacks or individualist radicals who carped at the League's capacious conception of government, long-time League board member Marguerite Wells replied in a 1926 address to the LWV's national convention. The speech is remarkable for its contemptuous dismissal of traditional American liberties and its defense of what many would call despotism.

"Nowadays everybody is grumbling about too much government," began Wells. "From the press, from magazines, from the platform, out of the air, ring the phrases: 'Too much government; too high taxes; too many laws; too much paternalism; too much centralization.' Into the ears of thousands of people these phrases pour and out of their mouths come back: 'Less government; lower taxes; fewer laws; no more paternalism; decentralization!' Into the ear and out of the mouth, by the shortest route."

The tone of the speech has been set: anyone who calls for lower taxes, less paternalism in government, or greater decentralization is a nitwit who is merely parroting what he has read in the popular press. (Oh, for the days when the popular press trumpeted such notions!)

What these constitutionalist morons do not understand, Miss Wells instructs her listeners, is that the "cause of expanded government is enlightened self-interest," or a "broader social consciousness." You see, "people demand a higher standard of living than can be secured by individual enterprise." Simple human decency demands a paternalistic—or maternalistic—government.

Moreover, as propagandists everywhere like to say, times have changed. The old verities are outmoded. "Centralization everywhere is an inevitable tendency," Wells assures us. It's time to face facts: "[W]e cannot stand meekly by wringing our hands over too much government. We cannot sigh for the good old days. We cannot invoke those great men of our early history whose rules and regulations were adequate for a little band of three million agricultural people, scattered among the wilderness of the Eastern seaboard, living under conditions that had not changed as much for them in five thousand years as they have for us since that day."[8]

The Founding Fathers, it seems, have as little to say to us moderns as do the Druids. The Constitution might as well be Stonehenge, for all its contemporary relevance. It's time to start all over again, said Miss Wells—and six years later, Franklin D. Roosevelt was elected president. He, she would be pleased to learn, did not meekly wring his hands over too much government.

Consistent with its enthusiasm for the welfare state, the League has also praised the warfare state—all the while muttering sweet nothings about peace. The LWV's founders were staunch internationalists in the Woodrow Wilson camp. As one historian writes of the League's founder, "Catt, although opposed to war in principle, had supported U.S. participation in World War I."[9]

This was rather like a serial adulterer who believes in the Sixth Commandment—on principle. The League is always for peace until the clouds of war mass on the horizon, at which time it cheerleads for war. The League took an interventionist stance on entry into the Second World War very early in the debate, and it would brook no objections from those who feared that war abroad might lead to tyranny at home.

"The challenge before the American public," declared Louise Leonard Wright, chairwoman of the League's Department of Government and International Operation, in July 1941, "is how to achieve unity among 130,000,000 private minds made up privately." The solution: "accepting the fact that this democracy must voluntarily achieve a single-minded purpose equal to that in a nation run by a dictator."[10]

Democracy is fine: as long as no one dissents. Louise Leonard Wright might easily have given her speech in, say, the Bulgaria of the 1950s. Even the Iron Curtain-era communists could have tolerated this kind of voters' league.

Fitting for an organization that fell in love with the League of Nations while still in the womb, the League of Women Voters has been an ardent fan of the United Nations. The League is always scolding the U.S. government for being so niggardly with its UN dues.

In 1948, LWV president Anna Lord Straus boasted that "the League has an enviable record for pricking the conscience of our public life."[11] Picking the public's pocket is more like it, Mrs. Straus.

Today, the League takes stands on everything under the Washington sun—which means everything. It smiles upon gun control and firearms confiscation, favoring measures to "protect the health and safety of citizens."[12] This might be done by arming them, as political scientist John Lott has demonstrated in his pathbreaking book, *More Guns, Less Crime*, but the LWV supports restrictions on ownership.

The League's starry-eyed love affair with the welfare state is no less ardent than that of other establishment-liberal dinosaurs. It wishes to "Promote social and economic justice, secure equal rights for all, achieve universal health care coverage at reasonable cost, promote the well-being of children, and combat discrimination, poverty, and violence."[13] Libertarians, conservatives, decentralists, and classical liberals have proposals to achieve many of those same ends, though one would never know it from League agitprop, which might have been dashed off by a Ted Kennedy ghostwriter on his day off.

The ideological slant of the League's quarterly magazine, *National Voter*, can be inferred from the titles in a typical issue: "DC Deserves a Fair and Predictable Federal Payment"; "Social Security Helps Reduce Child Poverty"; "The 107th Congress and the Disability Community."[14] The editor of *National Voter*, one Bob Adams, may be a voter but he is certainly no woman; the LWV has admitted men as full members, if you'll pardon the expression, since 1974.

In this typical issue, Adams reports from Capitol Hill on the good ("campaign reform" that violates First Amendment freedoms in the form of a ban on "soft money"); the bad (Congress isn't funneling money to the United Nations with sufficient alacrity); and the ugly (those nasty and brutish working-class and rural men of the—ick!— National Rifle Association are opposing "gun safety" measures). The League's failure to act as anything approaching an honest broker is exemplified by its use of the cant term "gun safety" when it means the government regulation or outlawing of the private right to bear firearms.[15]

State affiliates are up to assorted mischief, whether pushing for public funding of state legislature campaigns in Wisconsin or joining with the Women's Reproductive Rights Advocacy Project, the National Women's Political Caucus, and others in the Los Angeles Women's Appointment Collaboration to push for a gender-based divvying up of political booty.

Xandra Kayden, president of the Los Angeles LWV, argues that "Women make their decisions differently than men. Women tend to be pragmatic and inclusive. Men are very hierarchical in the way they make decisions." Sure, Xandra: ask the browbeaten subalterns slinking out of one of Senator Hillary Clinton's staff meetings. (The president of the Los Angeles Women's Appointment Collaboration, Minnie Lopez-Baffo, uttered a classic Freudianism when she told the *Los Angeles Times* that women "don't know how to penetrate the system."[16] A case of power envy, anyone?)

The League has been generally supportive of feminism, although the case of the Equal Rights Amendment makes for an interesting footnote. The League opposed the ERA from the 1920s until 1954. Like many of the so-called "social feminists," League members supported legislation to protect women workers; they suspected (correctly, in all likelihood) that enactment of the ERA would have invalidated such laws. But the League eventually climbed aboard the ERA bandwagon, just as it came out for legalized abortion in 1983. If there is an establishment-liberal cause that the League has resisted, I haven't heard about it.

League publications trumpet "diversity" the way Pentecostals shout "amen" in church. In 1998, Carolyn Jefferson-Jenkins became the League's first African-American president, an achievement in which the League took obvious pride.

Carrie Chapman Catt, however, was turning over in her grave. League founder Catt was a smug racist who, during the battle over ratification of the 19th Amendment, announced to listeners in Mississippi and South Carolina that "White supremacy will be strengthened, not weakened, by women's suffrage." When Iowa State University, Mrs. Catt's alma mater, named a building after her in 1995, the diversity gang saw red. The head of the Ames, Iowa, chapter of the NAACP demanded that Catt's name be removed from the building so that the university could declare, "I will not tolerate racism in any form or fashion."[17] The name stayed, after the usual groveling and cringing by the usual gutless college administrators.

The League's Education Fund has declared, if anyone is listening, that the twenty-first is to be the "Century of the Voter."[18] The people have bridled their enthusiasm over this one. After all, a "voter" is the most passive and often hapless participant in the democratic process. Except in the most local races, her single vote is almost meaningless; statisticians have calculated that the risk of getting hit by a car on the way to vote far outweighs the possibility that one's vote will make a difference. Despite all the "every vote counts" bromides to which we were subjected in the wake of the Bush-Gore 2000 Florida fiasco, no state's electoral votes (or U.S. Senate race) have ever been decided by a single vote in a popular election.

The League is for "campaign reform," by which it does not mean greater democracy and exchange of ideas—which might be achieved by, say, easing ballot restrictions on third parties and independents or removing government limits on the expression of political ideas—but rather the trendy sham "reform" associated with that blowhard Manchurian Candidate, Senator John McCain (R-AZ). League affiliates support public financing of state and local campaigns: members testify and rally on behalf of legislation that would compel taxpayers to pay for the campaigns of candidates whom they find repulsive.

The League's orientation is professedly "internationalist" and always has been. Even today, the LWV busybodies are preaching their suburban liberalism to the innocent women in the Balkans (the League of Women Voters is in Bosnia and Herzegovina) and Africa. In the latter case, the League is cooperating with the United States Information Agency, the propaganda arm of the State Department, to educate women in Sub-Saharan Africa in the glories of Western-style liberal feminism. The local Muslim population is likely not amused.

Despite its ceaseless advocacy of a smotheringly maternalist state, the League of Women Voters retains a largely moderate image, punctured only now and then by a burst of Beltway candor, as for instance when Newt Gingrich called it a front for the big spenders. Its hefty public subsidy draws nary a complaint from watchdogs of the treasury.

* * *

Most of the other feminist organizations that suck sweetly at the public teat are more forthright in declaring their sympathies. Let's consider a few of these worthies.

In browsing through the taxpayer-supported roster of the Fair Taxes for All Coalition, one's eye is drawn to the newer riders aboard the government gravy train. Amidst the dreary list of hoary old clients of Uncle Sam—such usual suspects as the AFL-CIO, the NAACP, the National Council of La Raza, and the National Council of Churches, we find a variety of groups dedicated to promoting . . . well, sexual variety. These include the NOW Legal Defense & Education Fund (which pocketed $1.168 million in federal subsidies between 1996 and 2000), Gay Men's Health Crisis ($428,835 over the same period), Feminist Majority ($115,440), the Ms. Foundation for Women ($75,000), and something called the Sexual Minority Youth Assistance League ($154,470).[19]

No doubt the Assembly of God churchgoer next door will be pleased to learn that her taxes are going into such worthy coffers. I hasten to add that feminists and gay activists are entitled to just as healthy a measure of outrage when their tax monies flood the treasuries of Southern Baptist churches or abstinence campaigns.

Jefferson's stricture against compelling a man—or womyn—to furnish contributions of money to propagate opinions which he or she disbelieves applies no matter how orthodox or unorthodox are the propagator's views on . . . well, propagation, for one thing.

Take the Ms. Foundation for Women—please, I shall not say, for Henny Youngmanesque jokes are emphatically frowned upon by this collection of viragos.

Government subsidy constitutes only a small percentage of the foundation's income—for instance, $24,975 out of a total revenue of $8.313 million in 1998.[20] But it's the principle that counts, and besides, there are ominous signs that the Ms. Foundation for Women means to dig ever deeper into the taxpayer's pocket.

Ms. magazine, and the Ms. Foundation for Women, illustrate nicely a dispiriting phenomenon: the way in which once-radical organizations—whose radicalism at least makes them interesting, and enables them to ask pertinent questions—age into dull establishmentarians who are about as countercultural as NBC News.

Ms. was founded in 1972 by a group of women writers and editors, most notably the comely and shallow feminist journalist Gloria Steinem. Its influence far outpaced its circulation; around it grew a legend that had little to do with its reality. Feminist intellectuals disdained it as hopelessly lightweight; most readers who sampled it found it hectoring, simplistic, anti-male, and, most damning for a magazine, boring. Yet it has endured, dragging along with it a Ms. Foundation for Women that battens not only on federal subsidies but also contributions from such corporate giants as American Express, Amoco, Exxon, Nynex, and Sara Lee.

Steinem's comrade in arms in those heady early years was Betty Friedan, who joined the Communist Party in 1942, well after most of the tiny number of American Communists had quit the party in disgust over Stalin's brutality. Feminist social critic Tammy Bruce perceptively notes that Friedan's *The Feminine Mystique* (1963), a cornerstone of modern feminism, was presented as the work of "a politically inactive housewife who simply had had enough of sexism."[21] If Friedan had been frank enough to reveal her communism, perhaps the book's reception would have been rather less celebratory. While the bored housewife who becomes a stripper is a B-movie staple, the bored housewife turned commie is not quite so saleable.

Marie Wilson has been president of the Ms. Foundation for Women since the mid-1980s. Her "biggest dream," she says, is to "broaden the meaning of feminism," presumably by making it wholly synonymous with statism. Under Wilson, the Foundation has increased its emphasis on lobbying for government-supplied medical services, or as a sympathetic media story put it, "protesting limited access to health care."[22] (Try finding an unsympathetic account of a New York-Washington-based feminist organization: now that would be news.)

What is most irritating about the puppy-dog soft coverage given *Ms.* and its leading lights is that whether or not the *Ms.* crowd is peddling bad ideology, it is certainly peddling bad numbers.

For instance, Clark University philosophy professor Christina Hoff Sommers quotes Gloria Steinem as writing that "about 150,000 females die of anorexia each year," a statistic also passed along by Naomi Wolf, another feminist polemicist not shy about showing off her comeliness. This is an absolutely startling statistic, and one that Ms. Wolf compares to the Holocaust. The authors derive this astonishing figure from the work of Joan Brumberg, who is a former director of the women's studies program at Cornell. There's just one problem: it's an utter fiction.

Sommers called the American Anorexia and Bulimia Association, source of Brumberg's assertion that 150,000 women die of these eating disorders each year, and spoke with its president. "We were misquoted,"[23] explained Dr. Diane Mickley. The actual figure is closer to . . . 100. Oh well. Let's not blame Mizzes Steinem, Brumberg, and Wolf: perhaps their inability to distinguish 150,000 from 100 is a consequence of the "math anxiety" suffered by young girls in our phallocentric educational system. (Hilariously, former Steinem flunky Amy Richard, coauthor of *Manifesta: Young Women, Feminism, and the Future*, writes of her boss, "Gloria is a consummate reporter, journalist, and fact checker, and this is what makes her work accessible, timeless, and valuable."[24] Feminism may have changed women's lives, but apparently kissing up to the boss is still a feature of the daily work life.)

The inability of *Ms.*-associated feminists to do simple math would almost seem to suggest that they are moles planted by nasty sexists who wish to perpetuate the discredited stereotype that women are innumerate airheads who substitute emotion for addition and subtraction. If only that were the case. For Sommers also exposes the role played by the Ms. Foundation in inflating rape statistics—a disreputable act that diminishes the very real and horrific crime of rape by defining it so broadly that women who were willingly sweet-talked into a night in the sack are afforded the same rape-victim status as are women who have been violently attacked.

The *Ms.*-ascription of rape was the product of feminist Kent State University professor Mary Koss, whose viewpoint is that "rape represents an extreme behavior but one that is on a continuum with normal male behavior within the culture."[25] In other words, a rapist is just a typical guy with a bit more gumption than the rest of us.

Koss and her researchers asked more than 3,000 college women about the degree to which their sexual experiences had been voluntary. Had the women ever "had sexual intercourse when you didn't want to because a man gave you alcohol or drugs?" Had you ever been violated by either a penis or other object because a man held you down or twisted your arm?

More than one-quarter of respondents (27.5 percent) answered yes to such questions. Yet only one-quarter of those women who had responded in the affirmative believed themselves to be victims of rape or attempted rape. About half—49 percent—chalked it up to "miscommunication."

Such nuances and complications do not register with orthodox feminists. The Ms. Foundation reported the Koss project as follows: "The Ms. project—the largest scientific investigation ever undertaken on the subject—revealed some disquieting statistics, including this astonishing fact: one in four female respondents had an experience that met the legal definition of rape or attempted rape."[26]

This is flatly false—three in four of those women deny that it was rape or attempted rape, and the Koss definition is not the legal definition of rape—but no matter. An urban myth was born. It has since been used as the justification for a vast expansion of the "rape industry," especially on college campuses, where anti-male busybodies find employment delivering stern lectures about another myth, "date rape."

More reliable estimates give the incidence of rape in America at about one in every fifty women—a number that in itself is disturbingly high. These victims are overwhelmingly lower-income and often black; they live on the mean streets of the cities, not in college dorms. But then as Sommers notes in her critique of Koss's work and its consequences, "privileged young women in our nation's colleges gain moral parity with the real victims in the community at large . . . [Expansive definitions of rape] justif[y] the salaries being paid to all the new personnel in the burgeoning college date rape industry. After all, it is much more pleasant to deal with rape from an office in Princeton than on the streets of downtown Trenton."[27]

But then American feminism has always been an upper-middle-class concern. Poor women may be useful tokens when one must burble on about "diversity," but the number of inner-city women who subscribe to *Ms.* is about as minuscule as the number who subscribe to *Foreign Affairs*.

* * *

On April 28, 1993, the Ms. Foundation launched "Take Our Daughters to Work Day," on which parents, especially mothers, are urged to take their children out of school and bring them along for a day on the job. This seems unobjectionable, except for the exclusion of boys, a deliberate oversight not corrected for ten years. But "Take Our Daughters to Work Day" rests on the materialist assumption that work-for-money is superior to work-for-love: homemakers, farmwives, and women who do volunteer work are invisible on this ersatz holiday. Given the anti-capitalist orientation of most *Ms.* feminists, this is a seeming inconsistency: shouldn't women who eschew the marketplace be honored, too? The more one examines the foundations of establishment feminism, the more one finds that its utopia has all the originality and appeal of a dreary gray cafeteria underneath a massive government building. As the irrepressible ecologist and anarchist Edward Abbey put it in his review of Steinem's *Outrageous Acts and Everyday Rebellions* (love that self-congratulatory title), "Steinem . . . concludes her revolutionary appeal by urging women to support Walter Mondale for president—and by condemning babies and little children to federally funded day-care centers while their mothers fulfill their human potential in offices, boutiques, boardrooms, army tanks, or coal mines. Outrageous."[28]

Take Our Daughters to Work Day was the brainchild of Nell Merlino, a New York public relations flack whose father had been a New Jersey Democratic political hack. As a former *Ms.* staffer recalled, the Ms. Foundation was initially reluctant to embrace the concept, as it seemed "insufficiently sensitive to homeless mothers

[and] women on welfare." The president of the foundation asked Merlino, "And are the daughters of prostitutes going to go to work with their mothers?"[29] (Capitol Hill observers report that, yes, female politicians do bring their daughters to the country's grandest whorehouse on the designated April day.)

Perhaps the nadir of *Ms.* feminism came during the travails of President Bill Clinton. Now, one might think that Clinton's caddish behavior toward women would prove a turn-off to feminists, who in any event are not easily turned on by men. Clinton was clearly a serial adulterer who groped and fondled women against their will; he was plausibly accused of rape by a woman who had no apparent score to settle with him. He admitted to having a young female intern service him in the Oval Office. No doubt he would love to take your daughter to work.

The women of *Ms.* didn't care. Marie Wilson of the Ms. Foundation for Women responded to the breaking of the Monica Lewinsky story with a mild, "we feel like there needs to be some cooling-down time"—with a post-coital cigarette, perhaps? Gloria Steinem, exhibiting a forgiveness not on display when Supreme Court nominee Clarence Thomas was accused to telling a few dirty jokes around the office, asked plaintively, "How can I require a leader to be blameless?"[30]

Steinem was similarly indulgent on the sticky matter of Bill Clinton and Paula Jones, the state government worker whom Clinton had requested to kiss his penis. A "clumsy sexual pass,"[31] pooh-poohed Steinem, who evidently has a remarkably high threshold for tolerating caddish behavior.

The young feminists Amy Richards and Jennifer Baumgardner, Steinem protégées, dismissed Juanita Broaddrick's rape allegation against Clinton as ancient history from twenty years back. Incredibly, they claimed, "This was during a time when forced sex among acquaintances—what is now called date rape—was excused as relatively inevitable, certainly not criminal, male behavior."[32] This sort of casual slur upon half the population—that forcing sex upon a woman was an "inevitable" consequence of having a penis in 1980— would be laughable were it not so offensive. But whereas Richards and Baumgardner apparently believe that rape was par for the course in the early 1980s, they are horrified by Clarence Thomas's "crass sexual overtures"[33] to Anita Hill in that same period.

As obvious payback for the craven bootlicking of Steinem and Wilson, the Clinton administration, in one of its final acts, on January 16, 2001 awarded a Presidential Award for Excellence in Microenterprise Development to the Ms. Foundation for Women. Such an imprimatur brings with it the promise of future sorties into the public treasury.

The award was presented by Treasury Secretary Lawrence Summers, who moved seamlessly from the Clinton administration into the presidency of Harvard. An outsider he is not; and indeed, the Ms. Foundation and the entire feminist establishment is about as close to an unassailable elite as one can find.

Does this sound like overstatement? Then count the number of feminist books published annually by the major and middle-range presses. Works challenging the feminist orthodoxy can be numbered on a single hand. As the economist Murray N. Rothbard wrote three decades ago in the new morn of "women's lib": "In all this welter of verbiage, not one article, not one book, not one program has dared to present the opposition case. . . . [T]he lack of published opposition negates one of the major charges of the women's lib forces: that the society and economy are groaning under a monolithic male 'sexist' tyranny. If the men are running the show, how is it that they do not even presume to print or present anyone from the other side?"[34]

Little has changed in the years since. For every brave or iconoclastic work challenging the regnant feminism—Christina Hoff Sommers's *Who Stole Feminism?*, Elizabeth Fox-Genovese's *Feminism Without Illusions*—a catalogue's worth of conventional dreck is published. And it's not like the feminists—even their stars—are brilliant stylists, coruscating wits, or even readable. To take one of the most-praised of their number, bell hooks (the lower-case orthography is hers) may be the single worst writer in America this side of computer-software installation manual composers. A randomly chosen sentence in her execrable *Feminism Is for Everybody* reads, "Positively feminist interventions called attention to the value and importance of male parenting both in regards to the well-being of children and gender equity."[35] Imagine that sentence repeated 1,000 times, and you have a book by bell hooks.

The Ms. Foundation for Women, though it is less heavily endowed by the federal government than some of its sister feminist organizations, is a fine example of why Jefferson's dictum about compulsory contributions remains pertinent. A survey of the foundation's activities uncovers several purely political functions. These include, in the Ms. Foundation's own words:

- "promoting state and federal policies that foster women's economic security" [Given that every one of these policies involves an expansion in the size and scope of coercive authority, they really "foster women's dependence upon the state," but that formulation is less like to attract corporate donors.]

- "address challenges from the right . . . and attempts to roll back gains made by the civil rights, women's, environmental, and gay rights movements" [Very well—but why must taxpayers of "the right" pay for such a campaign? Or is "mean-spirited" to even raise the question?]

- "protecting . . . reproductive choice" [Again, ought pro-life taxpayers be forced to subsidize political activity which they find morally repellent? And why do all the establishment feminists endlessly repeat the cant phrase "women's reproductive rights and health," which is a coward's way of saying "abortion"? If there is nothing morally troublesome about abortion, one wonders why its supporters have such difficulty uttering this simple three-syllable word.]

- "Oppos[ing] the nomination of John Ashcroft for Attorney General" [This was about as plain a lobbying activity as one can undertake. Whatever Ashcroft's merits or demerits, his foes—and his partisans—should have debated his nomination on their own dime.][36]

I don't wish to engage in—perish the thought—stereotyping, but the ladies of *Ms.* don't ever seem to have any fun. At times, the incessant whining becomes almost comic, as when Ms. Foundation for Women columnist Susan Wefald, beside whom your typical *Federal Register* regulation-writer is H. L. Mencken, decries the extraordinary fact that although "women suffer 64 percent of repetitive-motion injuries," they "are only 46 percent of the workforce."[37] The horror! The injustice! Carpal tunnel syndrome: the next Jesse Helms!

The Ms. Foundation for Women evinces occasional concern for poor women, at least rhetorically, though let some unemployed divorced husband miss an alimony payment and he is crucified as that most hideous and abhorrent of creatures: the deadbeat dad. Put him in jail! screech the feminists, in defense of a cruel and unusual punishment that most civilized nations discarded a century and a half ago: imprisonment for debt. But then, deadbeat dads are only men, and as such they get what they deserve.

The establishment feminist horror of men is on full display in the agitprop produced by the Family Violence Prevention Fund, whose name advertises its bias. A vastly disproportionate amount of "family" violence is perpetrated by boyfriends, not husbands and fathers, but the FVPF sees only the "millions of children whose fathers beat their mothers."[38]

Its director, Esta Soler, imagines a utopia in which "men routinely sent positive messages about the need to end domestic violence" and "fathers taught theirs sons never to threaten or harm the women they date."[39] An impossible dream, eh? Don't most of the men you know send "positive messages" about the need to perpetuate domestic violence? Don't the dads of your acquaintance teach their boys how to throw a baseball, change a car tire, and beat and threaten women? In her contempt for half the human race, Ms. Soler comes awfully close to committing a hate crime. (The Family Violence Prevention Fund also advocates severe gun control. Men mustn't be trusted with firearms—unless they are cops or soldiers, for the state is a gal's best friend. Nor should women take up arms to defend themselves, as the feisty ladies of the Second Amendment Sisters have done. Self-defense is not part of the battered woman's arsenal, apparently; far better to call the cops and social service agencies and throw yourself upon the mercy of the bureaucracy.)

Thankfully, not all feminists are killjoy mopes enamored of the omnipotent state. In her feisty book, *The New Thought Police: Inside the Left's Assault on Free Speech and Free Minds*, Tammy Bruce, former president of the Los Angeles chapter of the National Organization for Women and an outspoken advocate of gay rights, takes on the liars, victimologists, and party-line drones of subsidized feminism, especially the National Organization for Women (NOW), whose Legal Defense & Education Fund took in $1.168 million in government grants from 1996–2000.[40]

NOW had been founded in 1966 by feminist activists, including the communist masquerading as just another bored housewife, Betty Friedan. Tammy Bruce became involved in NOW in the late 1980s when she was disgusted by the tactics of Operation Rescue, a militant anti-abortion group that picketed abortion clinics. In 1989, she was elected president of the Los Angeles chapter of NOW. Almost immediately, she ran afoul of the old guard.

As Bruce tells it, on her first visit to the NOW office she found "an office full of Democratic Party workers using the space as though it were Party headquarters."[41] Concerned that this activity endangered NOW's status as a nonprofit organization, she threw the hacks out. That was her first mistake.

Though Bruce was a registered Democrat herself, she had run on a platform of inclusion, by which she meant she welcomed "men, Republicans, the religious, and anybody else who was a feminist, agreed with us on the issues, and wanted to improve the quality of women's lives." This was mistake number two. Molly Yard, then-president of NOW and a woman for whom the ancient term "old battle-ax" would be an effusive compliment, called Bruce on the carpet.

"There seem to be a lot of men in your chapter. How do you explain that?" Yard interrogated Bruce. The questioning got rougher. Yard chastised Bruce for ejecting the Democrats from the NOW office. "Democrats are our friends, and that's who we are."[42] Yard demanded to know Bruce's party affiliation; the Los Angeles president refused to answer. For Tammy Bruce, it was the beginning of six years of burgeoning membership in her Los Angeles chapter and constant clashes with the national NOW leadership.

Even more than the women of *Ms.*, NOW was compromised by its acceptance of federal subsidies. Tammy Bruce found what can only be called the smoking gun: "I learned that in 1995, during Clinton's first term, NOW accepted federal money for the first time in its history. According to my source, California NOW was close to bankruptcy at the time. Meanwhile Paula Jones's sexual harassment case had begun to pick up steam, as she fought for her right to sue Clinton while he was in office. The President himself was gearing up for his reelection campaign the following year. Instead of taking on Clinton as we had taken on Clarence Thomas, NOW may have opted instead to take on some money."

According to the Grants Management Office of the U.S. Department of Health and Human Services, California NOW was awarded more than half a million dollars in a grant from—get this—the Centers for Disease Controls' Office on Smoking and Health. The grant was for what was termed "tobacco control." From the years 1995 through 1997—while NOW maintained its strange silence on Bill Clinton and on occasion actually issued a direct rebuke to Paula

Jones—California NOW received a total of $543,636 in taxpayer money from Clinton's government, specifically the Donna Shalala-headed Department of Health and Human Services.

For an organization that had absolutely no history of leadership in the health arena, the grant was, to say the least, out of the ordinary. On the other hand, if the California organization—NOW's largest and most successful state satellite—had had to file for bankruptcy, it would have sounded a death knell for National NOW, exposing the depth of its troubles, financial and organizational.[43]

Bruce also found that in 1998, the Year of Monica, the CDC grant was transferred to the National NOW. (Presumably NOW's newfound interest in avoiding the use of tobacco did not extend to the salacious placement of cigars.) Another grant to the national NOW followed in 1999: in those two years when the beleaguered Clinton called in his chits from his feminist courtiers, NOW pocketed a hefty $223,463, putatively for an anti-smoking campaign of which the prominent NOW official Bruce had been entirely unaware.

We might call these grants hush money, except that the money loosened the tongues of NOW bigwigs in defense of the gallant President Clinton. But let's give them their due: it takes a top-notch whore to make a cool quarter-million just for talking.

* * *

The Feminist Majority Foundation (FMF), another of the subsidized sorority, is a classic case of nomenclature as wishful thinking. For decades now, public-opinion polls have found that about one-quarter of American women describe themselves as "feminist." But then, as we have seen, feminists have trouble with math.

The Feminist Majority has acquired a certain cachet, thanks to the presence on its board of Mavis Leno, who achieved her money and prestige the old-fashioned way: she married into it. Mavis is the wife of Jay Leno, the politically correct comedian who is still trying to fill Johnny Carson's loafers. Her position in Hollywood has attracted to Feminist Majority the kind of demi-celebrities for whom NOW is too . . . then. For instance, Feminist Majority's Million4ROE campaign, one of those Internet petition scams which are designed not to influence policy but to attract members and donations, has as a spokeswoman *X-Files*' babe Gillian Anderson. Not bad, though Ms. Anderson is probably destined to spend the rest of her career underemployed, a victim not of male sexism but typecasting, Leonard Nimoy-style.

Anderson emceed a pro-Roe rock concert featuring the unavoidable lesbian singer Melissa Etheridge, has-been new wave band The Bangles, and other lesser satellites in the city of stars.

If Feminist Majority has a Hollywood tincture, at least it came by this superficial glamour honestly. The organization was founded in 1987 by Eleanor Smeal, the controversial former head of NOW, and Peg Yorkin, a rich lady who became so in the tried-and-true way of Mavis Leno: she married money. Her ex-husband, Bud Yorkin, was a producer of *All in the Family, Sanford and Son*, and other sitcoms, in partnership with Norman Lear, the Hollywood liberal who founded the vaingloriously named liberal pressure-group People for the American Way. When the Yorkins divorced, Peg soaked the old man for a $50 million settlement.

Peg Yorkin labors under the illusion that she became a "producer" on her own, but Mavis Leno admits that "there's no question that celebrity helps. It's what I bring to the table."[44]

Abortion is the sentimental favorite cause of most feminist organizations, as well as a most effective way of loosening donations from members. "Choice" is always threatened, every single moment of every single day, and the only way to hold back the dark ages is by writing a check to the Feminist Majority Foundation, Los Angeles, California. From 1996–2000, unwitting taxpayers wrote checks totalling $115,440 to the FMF.[45]

In addition to sponsoring rock concerts, the federally subsidized Feminist Majority has also "provided its expertise" to Women on Waves, a band of Dutch pro-abortion activists who sail along the Irish coast, offering "advice" to Irish women who desire abortions or contraception. This is European imperialism in full flower, as what even its supporters call a "floating abortion clinic"[46] sets sail for those coastal countries in which abortion is illegal or restricted. In the Feminist Majority world, we all pray to the same god, all adopt the same morality, and all live by the same laws—made by, and for, Western feminists. Dissenters: you have been warned.

Feminist Majority is obsessed with abortion, toward whose moral ambiguities it is as blissfully blind as the most stone-throwing right-to-lifer. In 1989, Eleanor Smeal and sugar-momma Peg Yorkin traveled to France in order to convince Rouseel Uclaf, the company that manufactured the "morning-after" abortion pill RU-486, to sell its wonder pill in the United States. Peg Yorkin put up $10 million of "her" money toward what became a long and tangled and ultimately successful lobbying effort to bring RU-486 to America.

Despite its ritualistic invocation of the word "choice," the FMF is predictably opposed to persons exercising choice with regard to their pocketbooks, guns, schools, and speech. The group denounced President Bush's meek 2001 tax refund (which returned no more than $600 to a family, no matter how hard-pressed) as part and parcel of a "far right" agenda. Like other donation-sucking lobbies, the FMF sought to enrich itself at the expense of credulous members. The organization held up as a shining example of selfless feminism one lady who—allegedly—wrote, "When my partner and I receive our money from the Bush tax cut, we are going to send it to the Feminist Majority."[47] How convenient for the Feminist Majority!

The ladies of the Feminist Majority were part of the pack of squealing groupies who cheered Bill Clinton through the Monica Lewinsky travail. "On women's issues, there is no comparison between Clinton and his predecessors, and that is what matters,"[48] explained Eleanor Smeal in a revelatory remark. Realpolitik rules; better a cad (or rapist) who panders than a virtuous person who will not give you what you want.

Smeal even had the gall to argue that "the situation involving [Clarence] Thomas doesn't even compare"[49] to Clinton's case. In one way, she's right: a boss making a few dirty jokes around the office and asking out an employee (and accepting her declination) doesn't compare with an affair with an intern and lying about it while under oath. But that's not what Smeal meant. To power-hungry feminists, treating a lowly aide as a pathetic sex object is fine—as long as the mistreater is pro-choice. (Not that an unwanted pregnancy is much of a danger in the Clintonesque form of copulation.)

Give Mavis Leno credit for one thing, though: she was far-sighted enough to jump on the anti-Taliban bandwagon before the bandwagon even had wheels. Leno and the Feminist Majority Foundation's Campaign to Stop Gender Apartheid in Afghanistan cleverly, if somewhat clunkily, linked the Taliban's repressive policies with South African racism, thus permitting the usual guilt-ridden liberals license to denounce a Third World government.

The FMF, to give credit where credit is due, was not a Jill-come-lately to the issue. Since 1996, it lobbied the Clinton administration to withhold recognition of the Taliban-led government in Afghanistan. When, after September 11, 2001, the U.S. went to war—or whatever we call it now that Congress, neglecting the Constitution, no longer bothers to declare war—the FMF was a loud voice urging . . . well, it's not clear what they were urging. In the interventionist tradition of establishment feminism, the FMF wanted the U.S. to overthrow the Taliban. Yet it shied from air strikes as the means by which to do so. Perhaps, with a nod to the tactics of the FBI at Waco, the armed forces could simply have parked an amplifier outside Kabul and played Eleanor Smeal speeches at ear-warping decibel levels.

The FMF's anti-Taliban activities have the expected taint of limousine liberalism: a fund-raising auction at Christie's in Beverly Hills featured European works from the collection of Gigi Guggenheim Danzinger.

The FMF supports the U.S. acting as a kind of politically correct global cop. "As the only superpower, the United States has a lot of leverage and we should use it," declares Katherine Spillar, national coordinator of the FMF. "We have a moral authority to use that influence."[50]

Yet Ms. Spillar has a curious notion of "moral authority." When Los Angeles NOW president Tammy Bruce was rallying Southern California feminists to protest the outrageous acquittal of O. J. Simpson, she received a phone call from the moral authority Spillar.

"She was vague but dramatic," recalls Bruce, who wrote that Spillar told her only, "I have to ask you not to say anything more about Simpson."

Bruce ignored Spillar's advice and denounced the Simpson verdict, but she did agree to meet with Spillar at the Feminist Majority office the next day. Bruce describes their meeting as "the most unexpected and the strangest conversation I've ever had in my life."

Upon arriving at Ms. Spillar's office, Ms. Bruce was put in touch, via speakerphone, with an NAACP functionary named Constance Rice. Rice harangued Bruce: "I don't know if you understand the damage you're doing to the black community with your vendetta against O. J. Simpson. . . . He's a role model for the black community. . . . He's important to the black male. . . . You're condemning young black men with your crusade." After ten minutes or so of this absurd pleading on behalf of a vicious murderer, Bruce had had enough. She explained to the disembodied voice over the speakerphone that the Simpson verdict exculpated an obvious killer, and that feminists, of all people, should take the side of the victim. To Bruce's shock, the moral authority Kathy Spillar began shouting at her, "You've just got to leave him alone! You've got to stop and leave him alone!"[51]

"Leave him alone" is not exactly a common phrase in the feminist lexicon. Feminists seldom wish to leave anyone alone, as they agitate for a network of regulations on economic and social activity that can only be called tyrannical. The exceptions, it seems, are abortion and uxoricides committed by men of the right skin color.

If the Feminist Majority Foundation is obsessed with abortion, what can we say of Planned Parenthood? That it worships the abortionist as the apotheosis of humanity? ("Abortionist" is a word that has gone the way of "garbageman" and "lamplighter." The term is now "abortion provider." Coming soon: "choice facilitator.")

The birth of Planned Parenthood had elements of the courageous and the vile. Birth-control advocates of the early twentieth century had to brave arrest and opprobrium in propagating their anti-propagation message; they stood on the front lines of the free-speech debate and acquitted themselves creditably. In defying the Comstock Laws, which prohibited the mailing of "obscene" matter—with "obscenity" defined so broadly as to make a Puritan wince—the early birth-control missionaries struck a series of blows for liberty.

On the other hand, Margaret Sanger, mother of Planned Parenthood, was a eugenicist whose views on the "unfit" would not have been out of place at a seminar of Nazi academics. She wrote in *The Pivot of Civilization* (1922), "More children from the fit, less from the unfit—that is the chief aim of birth control." These "unfit" included members of "dysgenic races," which she also called "non-aryan people." The way to achieve "a race of thoroughbreds," announced Sanger, was to "segregate morons who are increasing and multiplying."[52]

Nasty stuff. So it is no surprise that in the April 1933 issue of *Birth Control Review*, which Sanger edited, one finds an article titled "Eugenic Sterilization: An Urgent Need" by Ernst Rudin, founder of the Nazi Society for Racial Hygiene. Planned Parenthood really ought to have chosen its parents with more care.

One might think that an organization founded by a woman with such reprehensible views would be a nonstarter. One would be wrong. In the most recent year for which figures were available, the Planned Parenthood Federation of America had revenues of $57.208 million. Incredibly, $378,244 was from government grants.[53]

Now, if any case encapsulates the wisdom of Jefferson's belief that to "compel a man to furnish contributions of money for the propagation of opinions which he disbelieves is sinful and tyrannical," it is Planned Parenthood. A very good case can be made for keeping abortion and less controversial forms of birth control legal, neither prohibiting nor subsidizing their use. But how can one argue that taxpayers who believe that abortion is murder must be forced by the state to turn over tax dollars which are then lavished upon Planned Parenthood? Is there no place for conscience in such matters?

For all its ritualistic use of the shibboleth "choice," Planned Parenthood is notable for its opposition to choice—at least when one might choose not to pay for the abortions of others.

The mission statement of the Planned Parenthood Federation of America emphasizes "the fundamental right of each individual throughout the world to manage his or her fertility"—a proposition to which most probably would adhere, though the enforcement of such a "right" is bound to entangle large powers (the UN, the U.S.) in the affairs of smaller, more religious nations. It is noteworthy that Planned Parenthood does not denounce "imperialism," for imperialism is precisely what its program requires.

"All individuals worldwide" also have the right to contraceptives, sterilization, abortion, and fertility drugs, according to Planned Parenthood. These "rights" are to be not only protected by the state but promoted by it: "Public funds should be made available to subsidize the cost of abortion services"[54] for every human being on the planet. That these "public funds" accumulate via coercive taxation—the antithesis of "choice"—does not occur to the visionaries of Planned Parenthood, so raptly do they gaze upon an El Dorado in which we are aborting, rolling on condoms, and tying tubes as costlessly as today we breathe the air. It has been said that everyone is entitled to his own utopia. But must the attainment of that utopia be made a government entitlement? Do I have to pay for your utopia?

Among the other feminist organizations sucking at the public teat is the Older Women's League, which consumed $181,904 in tax monies between 1996 and 2000.[55] This Washington-based advocacy group styles itself "the only national grassroots membership organization to focus solely on issues unique to women as they age," though it is about as grassroots as most D.C. lobbies. It claims only 15,000 members nationwide—and given that interest groups routinely inflate their membership for press consumption, it's likely that one is more likely to be struck by lightning and survive than ever meet a member of the Older Women's League. Nevertheless, like the National Organization for Women, whose minuscule membership does not prevent NOW from proclaiming itself the spokesperson for over 100 million American women, the OWL presumes to speak for "the 58 million women who are midlife and older."[56]

OWL was conceived at a 1980 White House conference on aging. That's the Carter White House, which is why the organization is little more than a virtually member-less front group for Democrats.

The OWL professes to be interested in "the image of midlife and older women,"[57] though the image it projects is that of helpless nincompoops who are about as independent-minded as Soviet pensioners. To the OWL, older women need money—your money. It joined the Fair Taxes for All Coalition that opposed the 2001 Bush tax cut.

These are not feisty older women, Mother Joneses and Millicent Fenwicks, but rather whiny victims who seek the aid and comfort of the paternal state. "Women are dealing with the double whammy of sexism and ageism, and it's going to inspire a whole second wave of feminism," warns former OWL president Janice Blanchard. Now, one might think that older women have it better than older men—after all, women live an average of seven years longer than do their counterparts. But no, living has its drawbacks. As Blanchard says, "Women tend to be focused on others: our husband, children, community, church, synagogue. We tend to forget about ourselves and tend to think our husbands will take care of us. Well, our husbands don't always take care of us."[58]

That's right: they die. The thoughtless, self-centered bastards! The nerve of those . . . those . . . those men! Women spend their entire lives sacrificing for others while the men lounge around the pool and drink martinis, and then the heartless creeps have the unmitigated gall to die—just to spite their wives! It's a man's, man's, man's, man's world out there.

One cannot read the drivel coming out of OWL without hooting. For instance, we learn that "Heart Disease is a Special Threat to Women"[59]—even though men suffer and die from heart disease at a greater rate than do women.

OWL's seventy-five chapters around the country have organized conferences on matters ranging from incontinence to pensions. But the national group's real mission is supporting clichéd liberal causes. For instance, the Older Women's League endorsed the McCain-Feingold campaign-finance reform bill which sought to ban "issues advertisements" critical of incumbents. Just the sort of thing that is uppermost on the minds of most eighty-two-year-old widows!

Perhaps closer to home is Medicare. The OWL likes it. Wants it bigger. More expansive. More expensive. And if you penny-pinching churls out there ask if socialized health care and free prescription drugs for old people—including rich old people—is affordable, why, then you're just calloused mean-spirited Republicans who probably trip old ladies in supermarket aisles. "The Face of Medicare is a Woman You Know,"[60] declares the OWL, and the implication is clear: if you demand any restraint in the spiraling cost of Medicare, you spit in Mom's face.

OWL cooperated with the Clinton administration to protect Medicare from any invigorating reforms, and it cooed over Vice President Albert Gore's 2000 campaign proposals regarding Social Security while disparaging private retirement accounts.

The generals in the private-less Older Women's League are fond of saying that we live in a different world today than when Social Security was created. Why, back in the benighted thirties, women were little more than doormats who slaved over a hot stove all day and didn't even have shoes to wear as they waddled around the hovel perpetually pregnant. . . . Or at least that's how we are supposed to remember our mothers.

In fact, as Allan Carlson and other social historians have revealed, women whose work was in making a home performed a diversity of essential and even noble tasks that make the drone-work of your typical yuppie lawyer look like spirit-deadening tedium. In a functioning household, women kept farms running, educated children, cooked, sometimes oversaw small home-based businesses, such as roadside fruit stands, and otherwise supervised a vital and productive homeplace.

These homes were centers of production, not just consumption, as is so often the case today. Such critical jobs as education, food preparation, and childcare had not been taken over by the state; nor were they often provided by strangers for pay. They were done in the home, by men and women working in partnerships called marriages. These were fulfilling "jobs," and the recent revival of home-based education, home businesses, and small gardens is a sign that women have never really bought into the feminist lie that satisfaction is best achieved by becoming an imitation man and working from nine to five in an office lit by fluorescent lighting.

Nevertheless, the worthlessness of home and the wonderfulness of the office remains a tenet of establishment feminism. And the array of government-subsidized think tanks and pressure groups informed by feminism promote this bias—with a vengeance.

These groups carry such anodyne names as "Women Employed" and "Women Work!" The conceit is that anyone who differs from them must be a troglodyte who denies the social or intellectual equality of women. Inevitably, the organization's history begins in the 1970s with an inspiring story.

In the case of "Women Work!" it was hard-pressed divorced California housewives who began agitating for relief from the California legislature. They formed the Alliance for Displaced Homemakers and set up shop in Washington, D.C. Displaced no more, they had found gainful employ as . . . lobbyists!

The word "homemakers" seems to have been a drag on fundraising, calling to mind frumpy hausfraus who may have had reservations about, say, the lasciviousness of Bill Clinton. So in 1993, as Mr. Clinton was settling into the White House with a helpmeet who'd have thrown a frying pan at anyone who called her a homemaker, the group changed its name to Women Work! The National Network for Women's Employment. The exclamation point was a nice touch; an in-your-face to those millions of louts laboring under the impression that women sprawled out on the couch all day eating bon-bons and watching soaps.

Today, Women Work! acts partly as a liberal lobby for "women's economic equity," and partly as a consumer of governmental and corporate grants as it works to "increase women's preparedness for the 21st century job market."[61] In other words, it pushes women out of what might be productive homes and into rewarding nine-to-five office jobs as data-entry operators and assistant human resources directors. In this dubious venture it is assisted not only by generous cash infusions from Uncle Sam (a whopping $2.86 million from 1996–2000)[62] but also corporate benefactions from Philip Morris, Chase Manhattan Bank, PepsiCo, and Texaco.

The sneering tone that Women Work! takes toward motherhood is exhibited in a piece titled "The Price of Motherhood" from its newsletter "Network News": "Mothers and motherhood have long been embedded into the American psyche as the epitome of purity, righteousness and goodness."[63] The obvious inference is that this is a lie, and that motherhood is no more to be esteemed than is the discharge of any other biological function. It's too bad that the onus falls on women, but aggressive government intervention can mitigate the harmful side effects of motherhood, which include a lack of unemployment insurance and workman's compensation. Yes, that's just what the hard-pressed moms of America need: federal worksheets to fill out, federal time clocks to punch, federal doles to go on. If it weren't so venomously anti-woman, it might even be funny.

Like so many other government-funded organizations, Women Work! acts as a referral service for women seeking government aid. It also lobbies for statist programs such as "increasing minimum wage, attaining fair employment benefits, and enhancing training for women making the transition from welfare to work."[64]

The "training" that it claims to provide hundreds of thousands of women annually is not training to once again become a homemaker. The whole concept of "job training" has been effectively debunked (see chapter 3), but Women Work! rolled merrily along, growing fat on Clinton-era grants as it helped to administer the U.S. Department of Labor's Women in Apprenticeships and Nontraditional Occupations (WANTO). A "nontraditional" occupation is defined as one in which "individuals from one gender comprise less than 25% of the individuals employed in each such occupation or field of work."[65]

This is government as social engineer: using taxpayers' money to pay women to take traditionally "masculine" jobs in the building trades or computer science and other such fields. Now, government should not prohibit or in any way discourage women from taking such jobs—but should it really subsidize gender-bending behavior?

If men typically display greater aptitude for math and science and women for English, is it any business of Uncle Sam's? (Well, yes, alas, Uncle Sam has made it his business.)

The premise of the federal WANTO program, according to Women Work!, was that "employer's needs for information technology workers" could not be met by the market but needed the guiding hand of the U.S. Department of Labor. So much for the myth of the invisible hand. Alarmingly, Women Work! warns that it is "currently investigating ways to replicate and expand"[66] the project, which is another way of saying "expand our take of the federal booty."

As a member of the Coalition on Women and Training, Women Work! stumps for job training programs with all the clueless diligence of a faithful if dimwitted bureaucrat dreaming of the grand success of the next five-year plan. Indeed, no sacred cow of the welfare state escapes the curtsies of Women Work! The welfare system that predated the Clinton reforms was just grand, and Social Security is a virtual godsend to Women Work! A "Privatized System is Bad for Everyone" declares the Women Work! newsletter. It would be "risky," "expensive" (the only time in recorded history that Women Work! has expressed that concern about a government program), and "particularly bad for women."[67] After all, women have the bad fortune to live longer than the penis-burdened monsters who spend their miserable lives harassing women, beating them, and paying them only two-thirds as much as men make, and by dying so soon men have even managed to shortchange their widows from beyond the grave. What horrid, horrid creatures men are.

A statewide example of "job feminism" comes from Illinois, where the Chicago-based Women Employed Institute consumed $146,962 in government grants (out of a total revenue of $883,610) in its latest available report.[68]

Women Employed, founded in 1973, says that it seeks "to improve women's career mobility and earnings through improved private and public sector policies and programs."[69] Another way of looking at it is that Women Employed lobbies for a variety of government programs to remove women from the role of mother and turn them into obedient workers. Its legislative program is rife with the words "increase" and "establish": it lobbies for more government funding of education, more government funding of daycare (which subsidizes the removal of women from home to office), and a government-mandated "parental leave" program which, paradoxically, encourages women to place their kids in daycare by enabling them to spend a handful of postpartum weeks at home with the baby. The assumption is that this glimpse of full-time motherhood will satisfy most new mothers, who will then high-tail it back to the kind of labor for which one is paid in greenbacks, not infant screams.

Women Employed has criticized the Clinton welfare reform and pressured Illinois to beef up its own welfare state in response. It worships at the altar of "training," despite the mounds of empirical evidence that job training is a fraud and a lie. It uses the loaded phrase "family violence"[70] in seeking more government programs for abused women. (That they are most often abused by boyfriends—not husbands—and that children are far likelier to be mistreated by mom's lover than by dad is an inconvenient fact that "family violence" lobbyists prefer not to recognize.)

Women Employed is a mouthpiece of the establishment. For instance, it issued a minimum-wage study of dubious veracity that was funded by the Illinois Department of Employment Security.[71] The conclusion: not only should the minimum wage be raised, but the state needs to spend more on childcare, transportation, and other public services. In other words, the government of Illinois paid Women Employed to publish a study that concludes that the government of Illinois needs more money. That, in a nutshell, is the problem highlighted by this book.

The organization is also economically illiterate. Like other feminist pressure groups, it prattles endlessly of the "pay gap": the mythical canyon separating women's earnings from those of men. At last count, gapsters claimed that women made seventy-six cents for every dollar made by men; an advance from the sixty cents made famous by a generation of pinback buttons, but still "unconscionable," in the diction of the Washington speechwriter. As Tipper Gore, wife of ex–Vice President Albert Gore, told the audience at Women Employed's 25th anniversary luncheon in 1998, "While women make up one-half of the workforce, they still earn only 74 cents for each dollar a man makes."[72]

The gap is almost complete bunk, as every reputable economist knows. The difference between men's and women's earnings is a consequence of women taking time off for child-bearing and often working part-time after childbirth. For example, among childless men and women aged twenty-seven to thirty-three, there simply is no wage gap. But don't try telling that to the hysterics of Women Employed. They're too busy agitating for a *Federal Register* chockfull of new powers for our friend, the state. These include more punitive laws regulating wages, a higher minimum wage, government-promoted unionization of the workforce, an Equal Employment Opportunity Commission armed with powers the FBI would envy, and government-enforced affirmative action that would give women preferential treatment in traditionally male occupations.

Though Women Employed was critical of the Clinton welfare reform, it was otherwise as suctorial toward the administration of the Arkansas Lothario as were the other dewy-eyed feminists. For instance, in 1998, Women Employed Executive Director Ann Ladky was asked about Paula Jones, the woman who had had the exquisite experience of seeing Arkansas Governor Bill Clinton's member up close and personal—a foretaste of a future presidential erection, one might say—complete with the Governor-and-soon-to-be-President's unctuous instruction to "kiss it." Though Ms. Ladky is normally in a state of more or less permanent dudgeon over sexual harassment that takes rather tamer form than Clintonian pants-dropping, she replied to the *Chicago Sun-Times* reporter with a stirring defense of . . . Anita Hill.

Hilariously, the *Sun-Times* piece carried a sidebar in which Women Employed grimly announced that sexual harassment can take any number of forms, ranging from "verbal abuse or jokes" (e.g., asking who put the pubic hair in one's can of Coke, presumably) to "unnecessary touching" to "displaying sexually explicit or degrading materials" (tear the Playmate off the wall . . .) to "a physical assault or demand of sexual favors."[73] Apparently, whipping out one's willie and sticking it in the face of an employee with a peremptory demand for fellatio is not sexual harassment to Ms. Ladky. What a strong stomach she must have.

Then again, when Uncle Sam has grants to give out, the ladies of establishment feminism are happy to "kiss it" for a few bucks. Take the "nation's first feminist policy research organization," the Center for Women Policy Studies. Founded in 1972, the Center is almost a parody of feminist political correctness. Family violence, sexual orientation, women of color, AIDS, diversity, reproductive rights: no cliché goes unslung when this Connecticut Avenue coven gets started.

The Center is at least forthright: it has published "Making the Case for Affirmative Action," and does not even bother with the usual fig leaves to cover its statist agenda.

Yet the Center is as well connected as the sleaziest K Street lobbyist. Its fifty-nine-member Policy Council is studded, if you'll excuse the expression, with a variety of women whose names are preceded by the honorific "The Honorable," including such congresswomen as the late Hawaii liberal Democrat Patsy Mink and the defeated Maryland liberal Republican Connie Morella.

The Center sometimes ventures into realms economic. It has denounced the Clinton welfare reform as "promot[ing] traditional patriarchal family structures" for its encouragement of two-parent households. (Perhaps the mistake was in the welfare reformers assumption that two parents mean a father and mother. Had they encouraged lesbian dads, the Center would have turned its hisses into huzzahs.)

The Center also supports government-mandated "access to collateral-free credit for women-owned small businesses,"[74] which is not only an invitation to failure (exceedingly few businesspeople who have no collateral could keep a fledgling concern alive without a continual infusion of taxpayer aid) but also a frank and rank act of discrimination against the penis-bearing enemy. But at the end of the day, or at least at the end of the fiscal year, those dick-swingers come through. The male-dominated government keeps the Center for Women Policy Studies alive, paying its way as generously as an older gent might subsidize a tart-tongued younger whore. In the most recent year for which figures were available, government grants accounted for $468,195 of the Center for Women Policy Studies' total revenue of $815,241.[75] The things we do for love—or the Potomac facsimile thereof.

The Center is not the only "women's" think tank to rely on Uncle Sam as its sugar daddy. The Women's Research and Education Institute in Washington banks $121,579 of its total revenue of $549,301 from government sources.[76] The Union Institute of Cincinnati took in $425,370 of its total 1998 revenue of $22.342 million in government grants.[77]

The Union Institute, an "alternative" educational institution, was formed by several liberal arts colleges in 1964. In 1970, boosted by federal monies from the U.S. Office of Education, it created a "University Without Walls" program and became a pioneer in what is now known as distance education.

Among the projects of the Union Institute is its Center for Women, which describes itself as "anti-racist" and "anti-sexist."[78] Surely a profile in courage. The Center for Women seeks to link scholarly feminists with feminist activists. This may sound like a cross-cultural lesbian dating service, but it is rather more political: its various programs subsidize the publication of lesbian and feminist agitprop, train feminist activists, and even organize the lesbians of Bangor, Maine, on health-care issues. An ambitious agenda, which the Union Institute ought to thank the taxpaying public for underwriting.

Lesbians are everywhere, or at least the corporate media would have us think so. Ever since filmmakers and TV impresarios discovered that a not insubstantial percentage of men enjoy watching women in Sapphic poses, the screens have been filled with (decidedly non-butch) women loving other women. What a change this is from just thirty years ago, when in her feminist classic, *Sexual Politics*, Kate Millett could write, "the term 'homosexual' refers to male homosexual here. 'Lesbianism' would appear to be so little a threat at the moment that it is hardly ever mentioned. . . . Whatever its potentiality in sexual politics, female homosexuality is currently so dead an issue that while male homosexuality gains a grudging tolerance, in women the event is observed in scorn or in silence."[79]

They are silent no more, Kate.

Let us take leave of the ladies by quoting the late libertarian economist Murray N. Rothbard, who wrote in his entertaining denunciation of what then was known as "women's lib": "Throughout the whole gamut of 'liberation,' the major target has been the harmless, hardworking, adult WASP American male, William Graham Sumner's Forgotten Man; and now this hapless Dagwood Bumstead figure is being battered once more. How long will it be before the put-upon, long-suffering average American at last loses his patience and rises up in his wrath to do some effective noisemaking on his own behalf?"[80]

At this writing, Dagwood is still silent.

* * *

To the extent that a "gay politics" existed in the days when homosexuality was still the love that dare not speak its name, it was largely libertarian. Homosexuals were harassed by anti-sodomy laws, their bars were occasionally raided by policemen, their pornography was censored more vigorously than was that of heterosexuals. The demand of homosexuals might have been summed up in three plangent words: Leave us alone.

Alas, government did not leave them alone—and now they won't leave us alone. The "gay rights" agenda has become as statist as that of your typical D.C.-based interest group. Enact hate-crimes laws. Further regulate employment and housing through gay-rights bills. Promote public acceptance of homosexuality by rewriting the public school curriculum. Pour taxpayers' money into a variety of gay-related causes.

The culprit—the agent that changed gay politics from libertarian to oppressively liberal—was the AIDS plague. The AIDS outbreak in the mid-1980s changed the focus of gay demands from laissez-faire to give-us-more. AIDS became known as a "gay disease"—despite the politically correct balderdash that "AIDS doesn't discriminate," and the government-subsidized subway posters that suggested that an eighty-seven-year-old virginal Baptist spinster from Shreveport was just as likely to contract the virus that causes AIDS as was a Manhattan drag queen who spent his evenings engaging in receptive anal sex with a passel of anonymous partners.

Part of the response of the gay community to the devastation of AIDS was inspiring. Energized and determined to confront what appeared to be a remorseless killer, thousands volunteered to work in clinics, comfort the afflicted, nurse the dying, and instruct the living in what became known as "safe sex." Working through groups such as the Gay Men's Health Crisis in New York City, they were quintessentially American in their voluntary mobilization. As sociologist Philip M. Kayal wrote in *Bearing Witness: Gay Men's Health Crisis and the Politics of AIDS*, "volunteerism in AIDS represented yet another chapter in the long American tradition of problem solving at the local level."[81]

Yet the other side of the gay community's response to AIDS represented a less attractive American tradition: calling for the Great White Father in Washington to set everything right.

The Gay Men's Health Crisis (GMHC) was launched by fiery playwright Larry Kramer and friends in 1981, as the news of a "gay cancer" was just reaching the mainstream media. The early volunteers gave freely of their own money and collected outside of gay bars, discos, and other meeting places. The GMHC has since become a large bureaucracy with an annual budget of more than $20 million, of which a third has been expropriated from taxpayers at various levels. Employing about 300 people who are assisted by over 5,000 volunteers, the GMHC serves more than 11,000 people with AIDS yearly. The services include counseling, HIV testing, free condoms, meals for the indigent, and legal assistance "for fair treatment of people living with HIV/AIDS."[82] This "fairness" usually involves some claim on government services—not only health-related but also food stamps, housing assistance, etc.

Among the more controversial services provided by GMHC is the distribution of "free" condoms at gay bars in New York City. The group distributes about 500,000 condoms a year, though director of education Richard Elovich has complained that government funding of the rubber giveaway is too stingy.[83] Half a million freebies in one city may seem sufficient to the hopeless squares who foot the bill, but to the men of Manhattan, they barely cover a month of one-minute stands.

And if the GMHC was born in desperate straits, it has grown prosperous in its middle age. Even the *New York Times*, ever respectful of sacred cows, took notice of the relative opulence:

> Behind the swinging glass doors that welcome visitors to the Gay Men's Health Crisis is a world where H.I.V. is not just a deadly virus, but also a ticket to a host of unusual benefits.
> At the center, the nation's oldest and largest AIDS social-service agency, almost everything is free: hot lunches, haircuts, art classes and even tickets to Broadway shows. Lawyers dispense advice free. Social workers guide patients through a Byzantine array of Government programs for people with H.I.V., and on Friday nights dinner is served by candlelight.[84]

This is not your neighborhood soup kitchen.

The days of passing the hat at discos are over; the GMHC is now as establishment as Planned Parenthood, the Brookings Institution, the other riders on the government gravy train. From its plucky street-corner beginnings, the GMHC has metamorphosed into the sort of big-budget tax-gobbler that puts out instructions on "How to Lobby a Legislator." (Sample tips: "Dress appropriately . . . If possible, wear a suit and tie or a conservative dress. If not, avoid wearing a tee shirt and jeans.")[85]

"AIDS has always been a political as well as a health crisis,"[86] insists the GMHA. This is debatable. Politics did not create AIDS (no matter what the Minister Farrakahns of the world think), nor will it cure AIDS. There are those mingy souls who would use the coercive power of the state to punish people with AIDS; there are also those who would—who do—use the coercive power of the state to funnel a hugely disproportionate percentage of public monies to AIDS research and palliation. If AIDS is a political crisis, the AIDS lobby is composed of master politicians.

The GMHC publishes a Voter Guide to elections. The group does not endorse candidates—it is a 501(c)(3) nonprofit, after all, and partisan activity could threaten that status—but the organization makes clear its policy positions. These include:

- More public health insurance, including for immigrants.
- More government health clinics.
- "Significant City Tax funds must be committed to the construction of permanent housing for PWAs (people with AIDS)."
- "The city must commit its own tax dollars to HIV prevention funding."
- "[C]ity tax dollars must be provided for needle exchange."[87]

The GMHC has also lobbied against welfare reform in New York state on the grounds that "there are a lot of people with AIDS who are poor and depend on welfare."[88]

In a dog-bites-man shocker, every candidate for citywide office in the most recent New York City election parroted the GMHC line. Just why city taxpayers "must" provide welfare services to AIDS patients above and beyond those provided to people with, say, pancreatic cancer or congestive heart failure is never explained. But then it doesn't have to be. Gay Men's Health Crisis is a muscular bureaucracy, maintained in part by infusions of cash from the government, and if it turns around and calls for even more spending by that government, where's the harm in that? This is how the game is played in high-stakes lobbying, and the GMHC, in its tailored suits and no blue jeans, plays it very well.

So well, in fact, that the largest single chunk of GMHC revenues (32.59 percent) now comes from government grants. Events and fund-raisers account for 24.43 percent, "major donors" for 17.01

percent, and the remainder is from foundations, direct marketing, and perhaps the odd voluntary donation, a reminder of its humble but honest origins.[89] Between 1996 and 2000, GMHC battened on $428,835 in federal grants.[90]

Like many bloated bureaucracies, GMHC has been battered by internal quarrels. In 1999, executive director Dr. Joshua Lipsman discovered a $2.5 million budget shortfall. He started cutting, and soon enough Dr. Lipsman's head was on the chopping block. It didn't help matters that he had supported a 1998 New York law that required people being treated for HIV infection to report the names of their sexual partners—a gross violation of privacy, in the eyes of many AIDS activists.

Playwright Kramer, who helped found the GMHC, later broke with it and started his own group ACT UP (AIDS Coalition to Unleash Power), which engages in juvenile stunts, often directed at the Catholic Church, that would earn the label "hate crimes" if they were done to an organization that was not despised by the media. Kramer is contemptuous of the GMHC, which he believes has been bought off by government funds. "They have all been co-opted by the very system that they were created to hold accountable," says Kramer. The GMHC, he charges, is "staffed with a lot of people who have jobs at stake."

Other AIDS activists are honest enough to question the extraordinary visibility and privileges afforded those who suffer from the disease. Martin Delany of San Francisco's Project Inform said to the *New York Times*, "Why do people with AIDS get funding for primary medical care? There are certainly other life-threatening diseases out there. Some of them kill a lot more people than AIDS does. So in one sense it is almost an advantage to be H.I.V. positive. It makes no sense."[91]

Speaking of making no sense, the aforementioned Sexual Minority Youth Assistance League is a real puzzlement. Given that women constitute a bare majority in these United States—giving us a Feminine Majority, if not a Feminist Majority—one might think that a "Sexual Minority Youth Assistance League" is merely a prolix way of saying "Boys Club." Er, no.

The SMYAL, as its cheerful acronym has it, is only interested in a certain subset of boys. This is to say that it is not catholic in its preferences, though in the wake of the priest scandals perhaps that is no longer the correct word to use in such cases. According to its website, SMYAL "is the only youth service agency solely dedicated to meeting the needs of youth ages 13-21 in the metropolitan Washington, D.C. area who are lesbian, gay, bisexual, transgender, and intersex, as well as those questioning their sexual orientation or gender identity."

> Our mission is to support and enhance the self-esteem of sexual minority youth and increase public awareness and understanding of their issues.[92]

This is emphatically not the Boys Club. Or the YMCA, for that matter, begging the pardon of the Village People.

Even a brief exposure to SMYAL raises any number of questions: What is an "intersex" person? ("Intersects" might make more sense.) If one "questions" an "orientation," then isn't it a "preference"? How rigorously are age-of-consent laws observed when thirteen-year-old boys come a-calling? And, most pertinent to our task, why in hell does Uncle Sam take federal taxes from the paycheck of a an Assembly of God churchgoing farm worker and transfer that money to SMYAL?

This last question might be asked of all the feminist and gay-rights organizations mentioned in this chapter. Not that any of them would bother giving us an answer. They're too busy filling out government grant applications.

Notes

1. Carolyn Jefferson-Jenkins, "Preface," *How Americans Talk About Medicare Reform* (Washington, DC: League of Women Voters Educational Fund, 1999), p. 2.
2. "Our Mission," About LWV, lwv.org/about/index, June 14, 2001.
3. IRS Form 990, League of Women Voters Educational Fund, 1998.
4. "Carrie Chapman Catt's Speech to the Convention," in Barbara Stuhler, *For the Public Record: A Documentary History of the League of Women Voters* (Westport, CT: Greenwood Press, 2000), p. 24.
5. "Suggested Platform Planks By the League of Women Voters," in ibid., p. 35.
6. Ibid., p. xiii.
7. "The League's Legislative Program," in ibid., p. 46.
8. Marguerite Wells, "The Great Administration," in ibid., pp. 131–133.
9. Ibid., p. 190.
10. Louise Leonard Wright, "The Battle of Production," in ibid., pp. 206–207.
11. Quoted in ibid., p. xi.
12. "Promoting Democracy in America: Gun Control," www.lwv.org/where/promoting/guncontrol.html, June 14, 2001.
13. "Creating a Just Society," www.lwv.org/where/society.html, June 14, 2001.

14. *National Voter*, December 2000/January 2001.
15. Bob Adams, "Hill Bulletin," *National Voter* (December 2000/January 2001), pp. 26–7.
16. Susan Carpenter, "Banding Together to Give Women a Louder Voice," *Los Angeles Times*, April 26, 2000, p. E1.
17. "Suffragette's Racial Remark Haunts College," *New York Times*, May 5, 1996.
18. "Fulfilling the Promise of Democracy," *League of Women Voters Education Fund, Annual Report 1997–98*, p. 2.
19. Samples, Yablonski, and Osorio, "More Government for All," pp. 5–6.
20. IRS Form 990, Ms. Foundation for Women, Inc., 1998.
21. Tammy Bruce, *The New Thought Police: Inside the Left's Assault on Free Speech and Free Minds* (New York: Forum, 2001), p. 15.
22. Dana Micucci, "Harnessing People's Power," *Cleveland Plain Dealer*, March 3, 1998, p. 3E.
23. Christina Hoff Sommers, *Who Stole Feminism? How Women Have Betrayed Women* (New York: Touchstone, 1995), pp. 11–12.
24. Jennifer Baumgardner and Amy Richards, *Manifesta: Young Women, Feminism, and the Future* (New York: Farrar, Straus and Giroux, 2000), p. xxvii.
25. Sommers, *Who Stole Feminism?*, p. 210.
26. Ibid., p. 211.
27. Ibid., p. 220.
28. Edward Abbey, "The Future of Sex," in *One Life at Time, Please* (New York: Henry Holt, 1988), pp. 204–205.
29. Baumgardner and Richards, *Manifesta*, pp. 181–82.
30. Bob Herbert, "The Feminist Dilemma," *New York Times*, January 29, 1998, p. A23.
31. Quoted in Bruce, *The New Thought Police*, p. 135.
32. Baumgardner and Richards, *Manifesta*, p. 62.
33. Ibid., p. 20.
34. Murray N. Rothbard, "The Great Women's Liberation Issue: Setting it Straight," *Egalitarianism as a Revolt Against Nature and Other Essays* (Auburn, AL: Ludwig von Mises Insititute, 2000; first edition: 1974), p. 157.
35. bell hooks, *Feminism is for Everybody* (Cambridge, MA: South End Press, 2000), p. 82.
36. www.ms.foundation.org/issues.html, September 10, 2001.
37. Susan Wefald, "Bush Policies No Gift for Mother's Day," Progressive Media Project, May 8, 2001.
38. Family Violence Prevention Fund brochure, undated.
39. Esta Soler, "The Next Frontier: Engaging More Men in Efforts to Stop Domestic Violence," *FVPF News from the Homefront* (Fall/Winter 2000), p. 2.
40. Samples, Yablonski, and Osorio, "More Government for All," p. 5.
41. Bruce, *The New Thought Police*, p. 119.
42. Ibid., pp. 120–21.
43. Ibid., pp. 136–37.
44. Kathleen Kenna, "Hollywood's Cause," *Toronto Star*, November 22, 1998, p. E2.
45. Samples, Yablonski, and Osorio, "More Government for All," p. 6.
46. Tracy Sefl and Dvora Lovinger, "FMF Aids Women on Waves in International Effort to Focus on Illegal Abortion," *Feminist Majority Report* (Summer 2001), p. 7.
47. "Take Action with the Feminist Majority!" http://capwiz.com/ fmfl/issues/alert/?altertid, September 10, 2001.

48. Muriel Dobbin, "Feminists Continue to Support Clinton as a Policy Champion," *Minneapolis Star Tribune*, February 13, 1999, p. 23A.
49. Sam Fulwood III, "Women's Advocates Offer Clinton Support," *Los Angeles Times*, September 25, 1998, p. A19.
50. Kenna, "Hollywood's Cause," *Toronto Star*, p. E2.
51. Bruce, *The New Thought Police*, pp. 133–34.
52. Quoted in Michael K. Flaherty, "A White Lie," *American Spectator* (August 1992).
53. IRS Form 990, Planned Parenthood Federation of America, Inc., 1998.
54. "Mission and Policy Statements," www.plannedparenthood.org/ about/thisispp/mission.html, June 14, 2001.
55. Samples, Yablonski, and Osorio, "More Government for All," p. 5.
56. "OWL Praises Plan to Strengthen Social Security for Women," press release, April 4, 2000.
57. www.owlillinois.org, October 25, 2001.
58. Mark Wolf, "New Frontier for Women," *Denver Rocky Mountain News*, September 14, 2000, p. 4D.
59. "Women and Heart Disease: A Neglected Epidemic," www.owl-national.org/heart.html, October 25, 2001.
60. "The Face of Medicare is a Woman You Know," OWL 1999 Mother's Day Report.
61. "Women Work! The National Network for Women's Employment," undated brochure, p. 4.
62. Samples, Yablonski, and Osorio, "More Government for All," p. 5.
63. "The Price of Motherhood," *Women Work! Network News* (Spring 2001), p. 5.
64. "Women Work! The National Network for Women's Employment," undated brochure, p. 2.
65. "Policy Issues: Workforce Investment Act of 1998," www.womenwork.org/alerti.html, December 14, 2001.
66. "Women Work! Completes First Phase of RITA Project," *Women Work! Network News* (Summer 2000), p. 7.
67. "Social Security Reform: A Women's Issue," in ibid., p. 6.
68. Women Employed Institute Financial Data, Fiscal Year Ending June 30, 1999, www.guidestar.org/search, March 28, 2001.
69. "Advocacy," www.womenemployed.org/programs/index.html, December 19, 2001.
70. "Family Violence Option," www.womenemployed.org/ publications/winter_2000, December 19, 2001.
71. Francine Knowles, "Federal Poverty Level Out of Touch—Study," *Chicago Sun-Times*, December 4, 2001, p. 43.
72. Al Podgorski, "Women Employed Turns 25; Challenges Still Remain," *Chicago Sun-Times*, June 4, 1998, p. 50.
73. Adrienne Drell, "Women Get Mixed Message," *Chicago Sun-Times*, April 5, 1998, p. 6.
74. "Education and Welfare Reform," www.centerwomenpolicy.org/ programs/education.html, June 21, 2000.
75. IRS Form 990, Center for Women Policy Studies, 1998.
76. IRS Form 990, Women's Research and Education Institute, 1998.
77. IRS Form 990, The Union Institute, 1998.
78. "Mission Statement," www.tui.edu/OSR/missioncfw.html, June 23, 2001.
79. Kate Millett, *Sexual Politics* (Urbana: University of Illinois Press, 2000; first edition, 1970), pp. 336–37.
80. Rothbard, *Egalitarianism as a Revolt Against Nature and Other Essays*, pp. 158–59.

81. Philip M. Kayal, *Bearing Witness: Gay Men's Health Crisis and the Politics of AIDS* (Boulder, CO: Westview Press, 1993), p. xv.
82. "GMHC Programs and Services," in *HIV/AIDS Facts*, GMCH, August 2001.
83. David Kirby, "AIDS Fears Rise as Gay Bars Offer Fewer Condoms," *New York Times*, April 25, 1999, p. 6 (Section 14).
84. Sheryl Gay Stolberg, "New Challenge to Idea That 'AIDS is Special,'" *New York Times*, November 12, 1997, p. A1.
85. "How to Lobby a Legislator," www.gmhc.org/action/lobby.html, December 14, 2001.
86. "Become an AIDS Advocate! Make Your Voice Heard!" www.gmhc.org/action/advmain.html, December 14, 2001.
87. *GMHC Action Voter Guide 2002*, p. 1.
88. Benjamin Gill, "Action for AIDS," *Newsday*, February 9, 1997, p. A27.
89. "GMHC Annual Report 1999–2000," unpaginated.
90. Samples, Yablonski, and Osorio, "More Government for All," p. 5.
91. Stolberg, "New Challenge to Idea That 'AIDS is Special,'" *New York Times*, p. A1.
92. www.smyal.org, April 17, 2002.

3

Workers (and Teachers) of the World! Apply for Grants!

The late and very unlamented National Council of Senior Citizens (NCSC) was perhaps the most egregiously partisan example of tax-funded lobbying in all of Washington. The NCSC was a creature of labor unions, pure (or impure) and simple. It organized elderly voters in support of labor causes in return for union support of welfare for the elderly. In its heyday, the NCSC president was Jacob Clayman, past president of the AFL-CIO's Industrial Union Department.

Most would expect the NCSC to flourish only when sympathetic Democrats controlled the federal till. And, indeed, from 1978–81 the National Council of Senior Citizens received an astounding $154 million in federal grants.[1] The Jimmy Carter presidency was very good to the NCSC. But then Ronald Reagan swept into office, determined to get government off our backs and out of our wallets. Or so his publicists said. Certainly an arrant—and in Republican eyes, errant—lobby like the NCSC would have to go cold turkey once Reaganites were manning the spigots.

Er, no. Even in 1984, at the peak of Reaganism, when it was morning in America and former Vice President Walter Mondale was on his way to winning but a single state in his presidential bid, the National Council of Senior Citizens still received $1.15 million in federal monies.[2] In flush times and in lean, these guys seemingly had an in.

"For 40 years NCSC thrived—on the taxpayers' dole—as the lobby organization that labor unions used to mobilize retired union members,"[3] writes Ivan G. Osorio, editor of *Labor Watch*, a publication of the Capital Research Center. The use of the past tense might imply a happy ending to this story—but beware of the plot twist at the end.

The NCSC was born in 1960 as "Senior Citizens for Kennedy-Johnson." It was not so much a product of mixed parentage as it was a result of an almost incestuous union between, well, unions and the Democratic National Committee. Once Kennedy and Johnson were safely ensconced in power, thanks to legions of Chicago corpses who had done their posthumous civic duty in the wee hours of Election Night 1960, the group took the innocuous name of the National Council of Senior Citizens.

Politically, the group peaked early. In 1965, President Lyndon B. Johnson signed Medicare into law with the words, "Without the National Council of Senior Citizens, there would have been no Medicare."[4] In that same year, the group lobbied for the Older Americans Act, which set up government make-work programs for the elderly. And that was to be the ladder on which the NCSC stepped aboard the gravy train.

As Osorio notes, "Government funding consistently accounted for over 90 percent of NCSC's income." For instance, in 1995, $70 million of its $74.7 million in annual revenues came from the federal government.[5]

Of course, these grants were not earmarked for lobbying efforts. Their ostensible purposes were varied, though far and away the NCSC's largest money-raiser was its administration of the U.S. Department of Labor's Senior Community Service Employment Program (SCSEP), a Great Society-era program that provides government make-work to elderly people. The NCCS is a "National Sponsor" of the employment program; as such, it receives Department of Labor grants to provide part-time employment and training to approximately 9,000 elderly persons. This employment is typically in local government positions or with nonprofit organizations.

The SCSEP is a virtual slush fund for welfare statists. Besides the NCSC, other organizations receiving plump subsidies to administer this pork barrel include the National Urban League, the AARP, the National Council on the Aging, and an offshoot of the National Farmers Union called Green Thumb. The vast majority of SCSEP money (78 percent) is doled out directly to these liberal interest groups; the remaining 22 percent is allocated to state governments. Because Republicans hold a majority of governorships, the GOP generally favors distributing more of the SCSEP money through the states. Of course, a few principled Republicans support abolishing the program altogether, but they are derided as "idealists" by the hacks who set the party's tone.

Because the NCSC was a mouthpiece for labor Democrats, it was a fat target for the Republicans who took over the House of Representatives in 1995. Enraged by a Federal Elections Commission investigation of ways in which the NCSC had illegally assisted the 1994 re-election campaign of Senator Charles Robb against his Republican opponent, Oliver North, the GOP quickly passed the Lobbying Disclosure Act of 1995, which forbade nonprofit lobbying groups which are designated 501(c)(4) by the IRS from receiving federal funds. This was no big deal for the NCSC, which simply transferred its grant-managing to a 501(c)(3) organization which it called the National Senior Citizens Education and Research Center (NSCERC).

As well intentioned as the Lobbying Disclosure Act of 1995 may have been, its effectiveness is in doubt. Ivan G. Osorio notes that since 1996, the NSCERC has received at least $276.6 million in federal grants. Department of Labor documents reveal, for instance, that in the period from July 1, 1999–June 30, 2000, the NSCERC pocketed $65.112 million in connection with the Senior Community Service Employment Program.[6]

Audits by the U.S. Department of Labor were somewhat more problematic for the NCSC. The Department's investigators discovered "an incredible array of ingenious bookkeeping misallocations, overcharges, and misrepresentations that diverted at least $12 million in taxpayer funds to labor coffers," according to *Labor Watch*.[7]

The documents, which I obtained with Freedom of Information Act requests, tell a damning tale. For instance, in Final Audit Report No. 18-99-007-07-735 of claims for reimbursement by the National Council of Senior Citizens for costs incurred in the Senior Community Service Employment Program, Assistant Inspector General for Audit John J. Getek declared, "WE QUESTION $5.8 MILLION OF THE COSTS CLAIMED FOR REIMBURSEMENT BY NCSC FOR FYs 1993-1995."[8] (Capital letters in original.)

This audit, audits of fiscal years 1996 and 1997, and an audit of the National Council of Senior Citizens/Department of Labor Unemployment Compensation Trust covering the period January 1984–March 1998—all conducted by the firm of Myint & Buntua—reveal a pattern of waste and mismanagement so egregious that the NCSC makes the Enron accounting department look like the Amish. Irregularities pockmarked the health and liability insurance purchased by the NCSC and NSCERC. Fringe benefits were overestimated. Pension plan costs were misestimated. Starting in 1991, the NCSC paid "termination fees" of $75 or $100 to job trainees who quit the program—a cash payment that was not "contemplated when the [Unemployment Trust] fund was created," according to the auditors.

Tellingly, one improper reimbursement request singled out by the auditors was a FY 1994 expense of $72,603 run up by the NCSC for its political conferences, which paid tribute to such rank partisans as the Americans for Democratic Action, the Coalition of Labor Union Women, the Workers Defense League, and Citizens Action.[9] Your tax dollars at work.

So how did the National Council on Senior Citizens and its masters respond to these devastating audits?

With legal legerdemain and a timely change in nomenclature. As of January 1, 2001, the NCSC vanished. A casualty of the millennium, perhaps. But its "membership" was magically transferred to a new group, the Alliance of Retired Americans (ARA). While the ARA disclaimed kinship with the NCSC, the new organization happened to have the same president, George Kourpias. Kourpias, retired president of the International Association of Machinists, had also been a board member of the 501(c)(3) "charitable" entity that the NCSC had created to handle its government grants, the National Senior Citizens Education and Research Center. (AFL-CIO Vice President Linda Chavez-Thompson is president of the NSCERC, which was not disbanded when the NCSC closed up shop. It continues to soak up grants.)

The creation of the ARA was recognized on all sides as a frankly partisan act. "The move is aimed at improving the prospects for labor and its political allies, mostly Democrats,"[10] noted the Washington correspondent of the *St. Louis Post-Dispatch*.

The ARA has been utterly predictable in its political slant. But then what did you expect of an AFL-CIO front group: the unpredictability of an Amtrak train schedule? Its first lobbying effort was in favor of expanding Medicare to provide low-cost prescription drugs. Other items on the ARA wish list include socialized health care, the expansion of Social Security, and—shockingly—greater appropriations for the very senior citizens' employment program which the NSCS got rich administering.

Membership in the ARA does not exactly require running a gauntlet of qualifications. All one has to do is be a retired union member. And while ARA officials dismiss the AARP as an elephantine marketing gimmick, they are not reluctant to imitate the kings of greedy geezerhood. The ARA offers members discounts on eyewear, rental cars, and the like. If you can't beat 'em, rip off their ideas.

* * *

The National Education Association (NEA) began life in 1857 as the National Teachers Association, a professional organization for teachers and school administrators. It was very much an elite club whose members were leaders in the field of education. From the start, this group pushed for nationalizing the gloriously fragmented and ingeniously localized system of American education. The ominous murmurings of a "Department of Education" were heard at its founding meeting and amplified in the 1860s, though this consolidationist dream was not realized until more than a century later, when in 1979 the U.S. Department of Education was created as a payoff from President Jimmy Carter to the National Education Association.

In 1917, when a dispiritingly large portion of the American elite were looking to Washington to assert greater control over the lives of Americans—whether through war, prohibition of alcohol, or the collection of the brand new income tax—the NEA set up headquarters in Washington, D.C. The teachers had learned where the action was. The NEA fastened onto the war effort to create a Commission on the Emergency in Education, which produced a report calling for a "complete national plan for education."[11]

The NEA became a powerful lobby for the nationalization of education. It was for federal aid: anytime, anywhere, unless there was a private school within 500 feet of the proffered aid. In which case it was a ferocious foe of government giveaways. The NEA was a major force in the series of Cold War/Great Society measures which began the steady flow of federal monies to the education establishment. As the *NEA Journal* declared in September 1965, on the heels of the passage of the Elementary and Secondary Education Act of 1965, "NEA hopes that President Johnson was correct in his estimation that, once started, federal aid to education will never be stopped."[12]

Believe me, *NEA Journal*: LBJ was right.

Educational policy analyst Myron Lieberman, a former NEA consultant and author of *The Teacher Unions: How They Sabotage Educational Reform and Why*, writes that the NEA was basically "anti-union"[13] for more than a century. It was a lobby, a professional organization, a clearinghouse for ideas on how to expand the government's role in schooling, but it was not a union as such. Class biases may be have played a role in this self-perception: unions were for grimy working-class sorts grubbing for extra nickels and watching TV in stained T-shirts. But the 1950s and 1960s saw private sector union membership start to decline while public sector union membership rose. The white collars were organizing. And no one organized like the NEA.

Today, the NEA is the largest union in the United States, boasting 2.6 million members, and quite possibly the most powerful. The union ripped into electoral politics with a vengeance. As NEA executive secretary Sam Lambert vowed in 1967, "NEA will become a political power second to no other special interest group. . . . NEA will organize this profession from top to bottom into logical operational units that can move swiftly and effectively and with power unmatched by any other organized group in the nation."[14] If that has the whiff of ruthlessness about it, well, no one ever made an omelet without breaking a few eggs.

The NEA's domination of the Democratic Party would be funny were it not so pervasive. At recent quadrennial conventions, NEA members have made up almost ten percent of the delegates who nominate the Democratic Party presidential candidate. The Democrats would no more take a position contrary to NEA policy than they would vote to take FDR's face off the dime. As William McGurn has written in the *Wall Street Journal*, "Those of us who have long dismissed the National Education Association as a tool of the Democratic Party have been badly mistaken. Apparently it's just the opposite . . . it's the Democratic Party that is the tool of the NEA."[15]

Hilariously, NEA President Bob Chase says, "Education is neither a Democratic issue nor a Republican issue, but a human issue. And so today, when we look at a political contest, we have a simple test: Which candidate is best for children and public education?"[16] If that candidate happens always to be a Democrat, so be it.

The NEA has a legitimate role to play in representing teachers as a collective bargaining unit and assisting individual teachers in conflicts they might have with the administration. Alas, these aren't terribly sexy activities. They may help the junior high science teacher in Minot, North Dakota, but they do nothing for the NEA mandarin in Washington who is angling for an invite to the White House or a breakfast with glamorpuss Democrats in the Senate Dining Room.

So the NEA has branched out into affairs far removed from the professional concerns of the teacher in Minot. In 1969, in its first significant foray into the daily muck of politics, the union opposed Nixon Supreme Court nominees Clement Haynsworth and G. Harold Carswell for reasons having nothing to do with the classroom.

Explaining the NEA's new ultra-political stance, then-President George Fischer said in 1970, "Whether we like it or not we're getting into a lobby-mad, power-mad world. We are realistic enough to know that the great lobbies have power, and that if we're going to get a share of the pie, we'd better move in alongside of them."[17] Not exactly high-minded, but then Fischer was speaking the language of power. The NEA has since weighed in on such issues as gun control and the Equal Rights Amendment. There really is no need to tell the reader which position the NEA took on those issues; it has all the unpredictability of a Bulgarian peoples' assembly, circa 1954.

Unfortunately, the NEA has pretty much had its way in national education policy. The notion that education is a state or local matter is as outdated as the Charleston. In the 2000 election, Democratic candidate Albert Gore proposed that the federal government start paying teachers in urban areas: a transfer of power so stark in its centralizing implications that one might have expected a tidal wave of criticism. Of course, there was none. His Republican opponent George W. Bush upped the ante. Under President Bush, the federal government has taken a greater role than ever before in what was once a state and local responsibility. Yet the NEA still complains that the Republicans are pinchpurses and states' rights loyalists. If only.

NEA-speak is composed of the same infuriating idiocies and untruths that come out of all mouths, Republican and Democrat, when the subject turns to education. Giving Every Child the Opportunity to Excel. Leaving No Child Behind. If its purpose were simply to enrich its members and fill its coffers, we might forgive the self-interest. But a more sinister interpretation can be given the NEA's agenda.

For instance, at a typical convention (this one in 1998), the NEA called for "early childhood education programs in the public schools for children from birth to eight."[18] From birth? Unwittingly, the NEA has adopted a staple of dystopian fiction: the ceding of control over an infant from parent to state. In Ray Bradbury's classic, *Fahrenheit 451*, "the fire captain explains the key to the erection of a totalitarian state: 'Heredity and environment are funny things. . . . The home environment can undo a lot you try to do at school. That's why we've lowered the kindergarten age year after year until now we're almost snatching them from the cradle.'"[19]

Ray Bradbury's nightmare is the NEA's constructive proposal.

On social issues, the NEA takes positions that would surprise many of the conservative middle-class teachers who pay union dues. It supports "the right to reproductive freedom," which is a coward's way of saying "abortion." It urges AIDS education "as an integral part of the school curriculum." (This education does not include the perspective that anal sex between men, which is far and away the most common sexual means of transmission of the AIDS virus, is immoral or wrong.) It supports "sex education programs" which transfer yet another function of childhood education from parents and the church to the state. It encourages teaching students about the "diversity of sexual orientation," which is to say the acceptance of homosexuality as a legitimate lifestyle choice.[20]

That the parents of some of the children who act as a captive audience for NEA pedagogues might object to elements of the union's sexual worldview seems not to trouble the NEA. Those convinced of their enlightenment and the benightedness of those with whom they disagree seldom make allowances for dissent. But as with the other organizations dissected in this book, the NEA ought not get a single shekel to propagate its political point of view. Alas, from 1996–2000 it received $3.655 million in taxpayer monies.[21]

The NEA's rival teacher union, the American Federation of Teachers (AFT), long lagged behind the senior organization in membership, despite the enormous boost it received when in 1961 the teachers of New York City chose the AFT rather than the NEA to represent them in collective bargaining.

The AFT had been around since 1916, when, as the United Federation of Teachers, its first member had been the philosopher of pedagogy, John Dewey. With its New York City base, the UFT/AFT underwent the usual numbing struggles for control: Trotskyists, Stalinists, anti-Stalinist social democrats, the whole European leftist menagerie.

The AFT did not achieve a sharp public profile until the 1960s, when President Albert Shanker blended union militancy and friendliness toward neoconservatism. Shanker's skill at public relations won the AFT praise from some on the political right, though as Myron Lieberman writes, the two unions "overwhelmingly endorse the same candidates for public office, and adopt the same positions on legislative issues."[22]

The two unions do differ on occasion. For instance, the AFT has proposed that would-be teachers must maintain a B average in college and pass two standardized tests before entering the professional ranks. However—and there is always a "however" when a public-employees union suggests a reform—the rigorous testing ends the moment one becomes a teacher. Which is to say, the moment one becomes a member of the AFT. It's all very easy to call for others to pass tests and maintain standards, but it would be suicidal for the AFT to throw its own members to the wolves of competency.

An NEA-AFT merger—or the NEA's absorption of the smaller AFT—seems inevitable. Tentative steps toward merger have been taken, though personality conflicts and ancient rivalries may delay the combination. If the AFT is not quite in the NEA's league when it comes to securing government grants, it ain't bad: it pulled in $996,629 from 1996–2000 as it, like the NEA, served as a member of the Fair Taxes for All Coalition.[23]

If the NEA is a lightning rod organization, the PTA is a milksop. Who could possibly have a critical word for the Parent-Teacher Association? Aren't those the civic-minded moms and dads who pour coffee during school open houses and sponsor roller-skating parties for the third-graders? What kind of ogre objects to that?

Well, this is not your father's PTA. In fact, even its name is shrouded in murk. One can peruse mountains of PTA-generated literature without finding a reference to the organization's name; it puts one in mind of KFC banishing the words "Kentucky," "Fried," and "Chicken" to the Coventry of unfashionable words. The legal name of the PTA is the National Congress of Parents and Teachers; "Congress," it seems, carries the unmistakable whiff of Power.

And make no mistake about it: today's PTA is about Power. Power to the federal government, power to the President, power to the U.S. Department of Education . . . in fact, power to just about everyone but the parents who long ago gave this statist lobby its hot-dogs-and-apple-pie image. When the National PTA joined the Fair Taxes for All Coalition in 2001, it had collected $282,196 since 1996.[24]

What is now the PTA was founded in 1897 under the politically incorrect name of the National Congress of Mothers. Its mothers included Alice McLelland Birney and Phoebe Apperson Hearst, who was related to a certain newspaper magnate. Like the League of Women Voters, another group with an anodyne image, the National Congress of Mothers was politically "progressive" in the very worst sense: it never met an expansion of state power it didn't like. From the start, the Mothers pushed for a national health bureau and government-subsidized sex education in public schools.

In 1924, the National Congress of Mothers became the National Congress of Parents and Teachers. As the group spread, it became associated in the popular mind with bake sales and other wholesome activities. But it was never apolitical. The PTA was a major force behind the creation of the National School Lunch Act in 1946 and the Child Nutrition Act of 1966. By 1961, its high-water mark, the PTA had 12 million members.

The educational historian Myron Lieberman has stated bluntly that the PTA "has become a tool of the NEA." He's not exaggerating. In 1992, Lieberman challenged the PTA's legislative representative in Washington to come up with just once issue on which the PTA disagreed with the NEA. He couldn't. In fact, notes Lieberman, the NEA has "subsidized PTA space in the NEA building in Washington."[25] In California, the NEA supplied the money and the PTA supplied the manpower (a word no doubt verboten in PTA headquarters) to defeat a voucher initiative. There is no discernible difference between the positions taken by the PTA on political issues and those taken by the NEA—an extraordinary consonance of interests between parents and teachers, who might be expected to part company on matters once in a while.

Then again, how many of the 6.5 million parents who pay their five-dollar-a-year dues to the PTA understand what causes are being advanced in their name?

Before taking office as National PTA President in 1999, Ginny Markell bragged, "The old PTA is gone."[26] The National PTA's slogan is now "Every Child/One Voice," which has a nice totalitarian ring to it. The conceit that every single child in America has exactly the same interests and can be served by exactly the same political program is almost North Korean in the simplicity of its terror.

Funny thing is, this "one voice" with which American children sing sounds an awful lot like that of your typical suburban liberal.

Although the words which the acronym PTA stands for suggest the sort of small-scale cooperative effort which marked American education in its halcyon days, today's PTA "supports increased federal funding for education and child-related programs," according to its "Legislative Program." Indeed, federal expenditures on education, health, and "welfare" must be "increased substantially."[27]

PTA propaganda can be counted on to blather on about the importance of "parental involvement," but concrete examples of promoting parental involvement are rare. After all, calling in Washington to fund and administer what used to be locally run school systems is not exactly a prescription for returning power to the people. The National PTA's idea of making mom and dad active participants in school is to "Require the U.S. Department of Education to collect new data on parent involvement policies and practices."[28] If that recommendation doesn't indicate a bureaucratic mindset, I don't know what does.

Contrary to the "Parent" part of its title, the PTA now bills itself as "the largest volunteer child advocacy organization in the nation,"[29] a subtle shift of emphasis that suggests an unbridled welfarism. For "parents" might have an interest in holding schools accountable for the use of their hard-earned tax dollars. "Children," on the other hand, at least as defined in the playbook of liberal nonprofits, care only about having tax dollars steered to the tax consumers whose self-appointed role it is to guard their health, safety, and welfare.

After-school programs, which keep children away from their parents for the better part of the day, might be thought to be objectionable to the "Parents" who supposedly make up a healthy chunk of the PTA. Not so. In fact, the PTA vigorously supports making school a virtual home for America's children, with their real homes reduced to the status of a pit stop at which kids can consume microwave meals, watch a little television, and sleep it off before re-entering the rat race in public school on the next day.

Not only should children spend the post-three o'clock p.m. hours incarcerated in public schools, they should also spend the early morning hours in these childlife refuges. We must "expand the availability of high quality, affordable school-based before- and after-school programs," bleats the PTA. These "reduce crime by and against youth"—the only alternative to staying in school from dawn to dusk is running with Crips and Bloods, apparently—and "contribute to improved attitudes toward school"[30] by making school the only environment in which the child ever finds herself.

Ever ready with a program to meet every perceived problem, the PTA whines that only 25 percent of those children who need after-school supervision in various urban areas have it. This is one of those impressive-sounding statistics that invariably are marshaled whenever an expensive program is under consideration. In the ancient world of the American Republic, children had parents, grandparents, aunts and uncles, and neighbors to watch them in those blessedly plenteous hours when they were not in the custody of government officials. But to the National PTA, "urban" areas—which is really just an uptight suburban white euphemism for black neighborhoods—are breeding grounds of crime, depravity, and low SAT scores. How much better off these virtual orphans would be if locked down in the prison-like public schools that litter the ghetto!

In perhaps the biggest "duh!" poll result ever obtained, the Mott Foundation and JC Penney teamed up for a PTA-plumped 1999 poll that found that "92 percent agreed that there should be some type of organized activity or place for children to go after school."[31] Well . . . yeah. It's called home. One wonders just what the eight percent who disagreed were thinking. Or maybe they were tired of stupid public-opinion surveys.

Darcy Olsen, former director of education and child policy at the Cato Institute, suggests an alternative which would never occur to the busybodies at the National PTA: "There are already 760 federal education programs right now crowding out parental involvement. There are breakfast programs, lunch programs, after-school programs: you name it, there's a federal program taking parents' place. The answer to low parental involvement isn't another federal program; it's to end the ones we have."[32]

The PTA opposes school vouchers, which makes plain just who has the preponderant influence in the PTA, the parents or the teachers. Absurdly, then-PTA President Ginny Markell testified before Congress that "vouchers do not offer families a real 'choice,'" apparently because those who enroll in private schools have to fill out application forms before being admitted. They also "divert scarce resources from the public schools,"[33] and hoarding "scare resources" is what the tax-consumers of the NEA are all about. Heaven forfend that a stray tax dollar make its way into St. Agnes rather than the Lyndon B. Johnson Elementary School. The chief evil of vouchers, it seems, is that they might lead to a system of education which is "free of public control and oversight."[34]

In September 2001, National PTA President Shirley Igo opined, "Vouchers do not solve the problems faced by our nation's public schools or the students enrolled in them."[35] This is not quite true—by enabling those students to leave wretched public schools for higher quality private or religious institutions, they will solve the students' problems quite nicely—but Igo's lament illustrates the extent to which the PTA is wedded to the one-size-fits-all philosophy of the bureaucrat.

Predictably, the National PTA also strongly opposes tax credits or educational IRAs that may give some relief to parents who choose to send their children to private schools. The insidious purpose of these proposals is to "funnel public money to private schools." Never mind that this "public money" begins life as hard-earned money belonging to a citizen. Educational savings accounts are a form of theft, in the world of the PTA: "The government would lose revenue"[36] if families were permitted to keep their money. Mustn't have that, eh?

From the vehemence of the PTA's attacks on nongovernment schools, one gets the feeling that should we ever see a revival of a proposal popular in the 1920s—the banning of religious and private schools, a measure that actually passed in Oregon and was widely supported by the Ku Klux Klan—the PTA will be foursquare behind it, with lots of red, white, and blue bunting and advertisements featuring a carefully selected gallery of multicultural children and a lot of copywriters' gas about how outlawing private schools is a giant step forward for "true choice." As in Orwell's *1984*, peace is war, freedom is slavery, and choice is coercion.

If you think the PTA dislikes vouchers, just think of its indignation when the dread word "privatization" enters the discussion. These dastardly privatizers "seek to profit from learning itself."[37] The nerve! As if providing desired services to schools and parents should be a profit-making venture. The usual arguments are advanced—innovation is unfair to the slowest and the most unruly students, private schools might not teach state-approved doctrine—but it all seems perfunctory, as if the argument has gone on so long and with so little rethinking of positions that everything PTA officials say about this and other issues comes from a vending machine that hasn't been restocked since 1985.

"Block grants," which permit states and localities a bit of flexibility in deciding how to spend federal monies, are anathema to the PTA. After all, the yokels might not spend the loot in the way that Washington thinks best. The states, asserts the PTA, "currently enjoy sufficient flexibility in allocating federal funds,"[38] so quit your whining about mandates.

The idea that government control of decision-making might have any downside at all never seems to occur to those who run the National PTA. In a background brief on Charter Schools, the PTA legislative mavens remark, with a wonderment that others might use in discussing the belief that the Earth is flat or that the boogeyman exists, "The concept underlying charter schools is that regulations inhibit innovation or creative school reform efforts."[39]

Perish the thought! Regulations make the world go 'round—or at least they do from the vantage point of a Washington, D.C. lobbying office.

Were the PTA's bureaucrats to play a word association game, "children" would be no doubt be answered immediately by "funding." Even the most billingsgate-spewing truckdriver cannot match PTA wonks in their promiscuous use of a certain four-letter word beginning with f: in the PTA's case, "fund." So enthusiastic are they for funding, spending, and investing that they have gone well beyond their early advocacy of federal programs to feed school lunches to poor children and now advocate, incredibly, a "universal breakfast program, where school breakfast is provided at no charge to all students enrolled in elementary school who wish to participate." Step right up, Miss Cosby, Mr. Spielberg, Baby Gates: wealth is no object. Free breakfasts for all, rich and poor, middle class and more.

Anything, it seems, to take children away from their parents even earlier in the morning and keep them in school for as many hours as are in the day.

As if this prodigious waste of money weren't enough, the National PTA also supports the inclusion of "children between the ages of 12 and 18 who do not participate"[40] in something called "Child and Adult Food Care," which subsidizes meals and snacks. (Perhaps each bag of potato chips should have a label reading "Your Tax Dollars at Work.") In other words, every teenager in America should have his meals and snacks paid for by the federal government, regardless of his family's income or even if he wants to eat the food. This would make a New Dealer's head spin: but hey, hey, we're the PTA! Money and freedom are no object when it comes to doing good.

The PTA insists that the federal government "restore or replace outdated and occasionally dangerous infrastructure that may interfere with a child's ability to learn,"[41] which is another way of saying it wants more tax dollars spent to build schools, buy desks, and otherwise prime the pump of the educational industry. That a child might derive a real benefit from sitting in the seats occupied by his parents, using the same classrooms once utilized by his older brothers and sisters, never seems to occur to the crumbling infrastructure crowd, with their boundless zeal to destroy old buildings and construct ugly modern educational factories.

As heedless of the architectural value of old schools as the most philistine strip-mall developer, the PTA declares that the "need for modernization and new construction of school facilities is critical in school districts throughout the United States."[42] An avalanche of self-serving statistics by partisan organizations follows; spending is advocated. And the world turns. The organization is also enthusiastic about federal spending on technology, which is to say computers, which is to say the PTA is a fervent believer in taxpayer subsidy of the computer industry.

It need not be added that the PTA believes in "teaching tolerance,"[43] but I'll add it anyway. "Earth Day," now extended to "Earth Week," is also big. Inclusiveness, relevance, being proactive: no idiotic buzzword is absent from PTA literature.

And as for tobacco: well, the script is the same as with any set of sanctimonious suburban liberals. The rap is routine: First Amendment protections do not apply to the vile merchants of the noxious weed. The use of attractive models in tobacco ads exerts a hypnotizing effect on children, who clamor to stick cigarettes in their mouths without quite knowing just what they are doing. Tobacco advertisements that appeal in any way to those under the age of 18 must be prohibited—and since there is no way to ensure that advertisements seen by adults are not seen by children, what the PTA really wants is a de facto ban on tobacco advertising. The next logical step is a ban on tobacco: a Prohibition every bit as totalitarian, hateful, and counterproductive as that which a previous generation of paternalists stuck us with in 1919.

The National PTA supports "the preparation of youth for their responsible contribution to a strong national defense" (training them to be little soldiers or pliant order-takers?) while also supporting "diligent efforts for international cooperation and world peace."[44] Peace, militarism: if it enhances the power of the central state, you can count on the diligent support of the PTA.

But whereas the National PTA wants to train the tykes to be useful cogs in a strong national defense, its state affiliates have pushed such paternalistic proposals as raising the age at which one is eligible for a driver's license (Georgia). The National PTA has been a loud voice in support of government regulation of television content; if it had its way, the airwaves would be filled with excruciatingly dull and painstakingly P.C. "educational" programs of the sort that encourage children to turn off the idiot box and go play outside. Which, on second thought, might be the best thing the PTA could do for the pre-adult army it purports to represent.

The National PTA also supports civil rights for gays and lesbians, an issue of dubious relevance to its purported educational mission. Occasionally the sort of earnest dorkiness which one associates with the PTA surfaces—for instance, its school-bus safety program called "Be Cool. Follow the Rules."—but for the most part, the organization is just another liberal interest group, albeit one possessing a 24-carat name.

Parents have been dropping out of PTAs like pop flies out of a six-year-old outfielder's baseball mitt. Organization mouthpieces concede that membership has been "static" for some time—the claimed membership of over six million is perhaps best taken with a grain of salt. Millions of parents have opted out of the PTA for something called PTOs: parent-teacher organizations. The *Christian Science Monitor* has estimated that three-quarters of all school-based parent-teacher groups are now PTOs that have nothing to do with the PTA.[45] Members of PTOs don't like a portion of their dues money going to the PTA headquarters in Chicago or to its lobbying office in Washington; they prefer that their dues stay local, with people they know.

To wrap it all up in a neat (if expensive) package, the general thrust of the National PTA may be summed up in the first six words of a PTA handout explaining its legislative agenda: "National PTA supports increased federal funding. . . ."[46] It doesn't much matter which specific program comes later in the sentence; those first six words remain the same.

The first item in the PTA's mission statement does not even mention parents. Rather, it announces its intention "to support and speak on behalf of children and youth in the schools, in the community and before governmental bodies and other organizations that make decisions affecting children."[47] No children have ever asked to be represented by the PTA; not that that matters. The National PTA is a reliable voice for expanding federal control of education, subjecting Americans to an ever more extensive web of regulations, and increasing the tax burden on all citizens. A repellent agenda, at least to many of us—and the fact that it is pursued with a generous infusion of our tax dollars is nothing less than an outrage.

* * *

Unions of government employees are the largest and most potent political force for the expansion of government. If their desiderata were simply higher pay, shorter hours, and more pleasant working conditions, the harm they do would be relatively limited. Budgets might be busted and taxes hiked, but the damage to the rest of us would be confined to the pocketbook.

No such luck. Public-employee unions agitate not only for more money, but for a more intrusive and regulation-ridden state. Prison guards actively support the construction of more prisons, which will be filled by criminalizing acts that others may think should be legal. (For instance, smoking marijuana.) Teachers unions were a clamant voice for compulsory education and now support stricter laws against dropping out of school. They have also been a consistent voice against child labor, which in our day does not take the form a cute little eight-year-old "breaker boy" manning the coal chutes for ten hours a day, coming home sooty and with the beginnings of a "coal cough" that will claim his life at a tragically early age. No, the child labor against which the educators lobby is called "valuable experience" by employers.

Unions representing needle workers lobby for import quotas on textiles, which drive up the cost of clothing for Americans of all income levels and have a disproportionate impact upon the very poorest. Unions of automobile workers support import quotas and domestic-content legislation mandating that a certain percentage of a vehicle be manufactured within the United States; these also boost the cost of a car for American consumers. Unions of social workers advocate a more intrusive role for the state in family life; unions of child-care workers support a vast expansion of subsidized daycare, which takes children away from parents at an early age and is producing a generation of Americans who were raised not within homes of familial love but by strangers who are bound to the children by a cord as thin as a weekly paycheck.

No, the damage that unions do goes far beyond a mere raid on the treasury.

And need we add that this pernicious lobbying is done with taxpayers' dollars?

The educational unions have had an ambivalent relationship with the American Federation of Labor-Congress of Industrial Organizations (AFL-CIO), the federation of sixty-eight unions that since 1955 has been the loudest voice and most muscular presence in the world of labor. The American Federation of Teachers is a member of the AFL-CIO; the National Education Association is not, which has been a sore spot in intra-union politics. The NEA, after all, began its life as a professional association, and many in the 13-million-member AFL-CIO nurse the suspicion that the NEA haughtily refuses to join what was once a solidly blue-collar movement for class reasons.

The political biases of the AFL-CIO and the NEA are identical: heavily Democratic, and in favor of any and all government interventions that would prosper the union and, secondarily, its members. Although the AFL-CIO's member unions range from the Teamsters to the Air Line Pilots, from the United Auto Workers to the Machinists, from the Building and Construction Trades to the Screen

Actors Guild to the Plumbers and Pipe Fitters, they speak as one on matters political.

The "defunding of the left" which myth has it took place in the 1980s never seemed to affect the AFL-CIO. It raked in $6.648 million in taxpayer dollars between 1996 and 2000,[48] which were not enough to dissuade it from being a member of the Fair Taxes for All Coalition.

Although the AFL-CIO has modernized its rhetoric, its agenda remains essentially unchanged. It now claims to have four goals: "strengthening working families by enabling more workers to join together in unions, building a stronger political voice for working families, providing a new voice for workers in the global economy and creating a more effective voice for working families in our communities."[49]

You will notice that self-preservation comes first. The portion of the American workforce that is unionized has declined from a high of 35.5 percent in 1945 to less than 15 percent at the beginning of the twenty-first century. No wonder altering federal law to encourage unionization is Job One at the AFL-CIO. As for the fine print between those pretty phrases about "working families," the AFL-CIO supports a higher minimum wage, government-guaranteed medical care, and higher federal spending (and a greater government role) on everything from education to transportation.

Twenty-two percent of AFL-CIO members are registered Republicans, but the union acts as a virtual adjunct to the Democratic Party. In the 2000 election, the AFL-CIO spent $46 million on a "get out the vote" effort for Democratic candidate Albert Gore. (Had only a fraction of that sum been spent teaching South Floridians how to read ballots, the union would be in clover today.) Just why the Republican Party would fail to shut off the flow of federal funds to an organization whose primary political mission is the election of Democrats is one of those unsolved Beltway mysteries.

The percentage of American union members belonging to public employee unions zoomed from 21.5 percent in 1975 to 43.7 percent in 2001. To an alarming degree, the union movement has become an arm of the government. Its interests are merging with the interests of the state: as the government grows in size, so does the union movement; as the government takes on more power, so do the public employee unions. Although we are currently in a strange post-9/

11 moment in which government workers are lauded as heroes, this, too, shall pass, and we will soon be able to measure, in dollars and lost liberties, the costs of an enormous and unionized government workforce. (It should be noted that the inspirational heroes of September 11 were, overwhelmingly, employees of local and municipal governments.)

The second-largest union in the country is the American Federation of State, County and Municipal Employees, which is 1.3 million members strong. (The Service Employees International Union, with 1.5 million members, is larger than AFSCME in terms of membership, but it represents mostly "unskilled" and low-wage workers in the private sector.)

In a sense, most of AFSCME's budget—indeed, most of the dollars in the home budgets of its members—comes from government. A plurality of AFSCME members are city or county employees (40 percent), yet the union concentrates on the usual range of national issues: opposing any Social Security reform that injects a dose of private enterprise into the system; opposing tax cuts and supporting tax increases; supporting funding for all programs, everywhere.

Unions for private employees still exist, though they are taking on the sepia tint of an old photograph. They have become almost quaint in this age of the bureaucrat-as-union-member. Working stiffs are becoming as rare in the union movement as blacks are in the U.S. Senate.

Still, the old-line unions soldier on, hemorrhaging members, exuding irrelevance, endorsing Democrats as if by rote, calling for an expanded federal government, and trying to squeeze as many dollars out of that state as possible. If they are not as dangerous to liberty as the public-employee unions, they are no less desirous of taxpayer handouts.

Every union has its bugbear. For the Union of Needletrades, Industrial and Textile Employees (UNITE), which received $281,000 in government grants from 1996–2000,[50] it's trade. Doesn't matter whom the trade is with: it could be China, Guatemala, or Burkina Faso. Trade is trade, and it ain't good. Garments in foreign countries are inevitably made in "sweatshops" by "slave laborers," even if those laborers toil and spin in conditions far more salubrious than those enjoyed by 95 percent of their countrymen and women.

Half of this union formerly went by the politically incorrect moniker of the International Ladies' Garment Workers Union: a strange name, given that its long-time president was Sol "Chick" Chaiken, a man. (Perhaps the nickname was an attempt to put one over on the ladies.)

UNITE is fighting a losing battle. The manufacture of clothing has moved largely offshore. Although there remains great sentimental appeal to "Buy American," that is increasingly difficult to do. And it will be made even more difficult if UNITE's goal of dramatically boosting the number of federal-government workplace inspectors were realized. The cost to employers of complying with every jot and tittle of workplace law would be considerable—enough to close down many of the extant U.S. clothing manufacturers. Especially the nonunion ones—which is UNITE's point.

UNITE takes the usual stances on issues having nothing whatsoever to do with needles or thread. It opposed the modest Bush tax cut of 2001. It wants to "rebuild our crumbling schools and cut class size."[51] It calls for amnesty for illegal aliens, or "undocumented workers," as the euphemism goes.

Innocently uttering the phrase "illegal aliens" would be enough to get one thrown into a re-education camp in the National Association of Social Workers (NASW), a union that is a virtual parody of political correctness. The NASW, which took in $629,733 in taxpayer dollars between 1996 and 2000,[52] is 150,000 strong. (One wonders: is "strong" an offensive word, slighting as it does the strength-challenged?) Despite the usual high-minded talk found in self-described "professional" associations, the NASW has its snout right down in the trough, advocating vast federal subsidies to mental health and substance abuse treatment programs. Every neurotic and pothead in America would get a free ride at the clinic in the NASW's dream world.

If the NASW has a routine phrase, it is "NASW will continue to support a strong federal role in. . . ." The social workers, always in the vanguard of trendy causes, even support "strong federal policies" on the critical yet disgracefully ignored subject of "transgender persons."[53] The lack of federal subsidy and protection of she-males is a crime of historic proportions, and one that the NASW does not intend to countenance for one moment longer. How on earth such trivia became a matter of national import—a "federal case," as children used to say—is a matter almost too grim to contemplate.

Yet sexual politics have become a commonplace in the union movement. The guys on the assembly line might not know it, but even the United Autoworkers is "strongly supporting"[54] federal hate-crimes legislation that is the first tumble down a slippery slope toward the criminalization of "hate thought." The UAW has a policy on "sexual orientation" that would have Walter Reuther and the grizzled old boys of yesteryear's union spinning in their graves.

Of course, the UAW's chief concern is trade. Like UNITE, its position on trade achieves a kind of magnificent simplicity: it is agin' it. Yet the union's bosses are nothing if not compromisers. In 2000, UAW President Stephen Yokich put the weight of his 700,000-member union behind the candidacy of Democrat Albert Gore—despite having earlier accused Gore of "holding hands with the profiteers of the world"[55] after Gore endorsed expanded trade with China. Yokich also ignored Gore's environmental manifesto, *Earth in the Balance*, in which he treated the automobile as a virtual cancer on the face of the earth.

After Gore had his epic pillow fight with the second President Bush, the union wasted no time in throwing itself behind the once-reviled Bush's energy proposal, which set fuel-efficiency standards for vehicles at a much lower level than the UAW's liberal Democratic allies had preferred. As the *Washington Post* noted, the UAW "estimated that thousands of their best jobs would be lost if higher fuel efficiency standards prevailed because demand for SUVs would plummet."[56] The only green one finds within the UAW is on the color of the money it covets. Speaking of which, from 1996–2000 the UAW received $3.032 million in taxpayer support.[57]

That labor is in the pocket of its Democratic masters hardly bears mentioning, but for the fact that these unions receive government funds. Take the Communications Workers of America, whose president, Morton Bahr, in a typical gush of hyperbole called a Republican victory in 2000 a "doomsday scenario" for labor. "If elections on November 7 don't come out right for working families," Mr. Bahr told a gathering in Buffalo, "forget about it."[58]

Forget about what, one wonders? Invitations to the White House for CWA bosses? Or was he worried about government grants, which enriched CWA coffers by $467,000 between 1996 and 2000.[59]

Unions such as the CWA have demonstrated time and again that even when the Democrats disappoint them, they stand by their party with a dogged loyalty that Tammy Wynette would envy. When in 2001 Congress, thanks to a significant minority of Democratic votes, gave President Bush the authority to negotiate "fast-track" trade agreements without congressional input, the unions huffed and they puffed and they . . . endorsed Democrats en masse in 2002. Those Republicans who opposed fast-track—some on protectionist grounds, but others on the very solid grounds that it represented an unconstitutional transfer of congressional authority to the executive—were lucky to receive an autopenned thank-you note from union bigwigs before becoming once more the object of vilification.

The United Food and Commercial Workers Union has tried and failed to unionize the Wal-Mart workforce, so it has struck back indirectly through such proposals as one to ban municipalities in California from approving building permits for superstores—defined as stores that are larger than 100,000 square feet, with at least 15,000 feet of the store devoted to food and drugs. In practice, this means Wal-Mart, and though the measure is advertised as a bill to protect the little guys from Wal-Mart (which itself often receives subsidies from towns eager for the Arkansas superstore), in fact it is "really designed to pressure Wal-Mart to negotiate with unions," as the *San Francisco Chronicle* summarizes. The *Chronicle* reporter writing up this thinly disguised legislative blackmail concluded by slyly noting that the mouthpiece for the Assembly speaker, who supported the bill, "declined to comment on why big box stores are considered a problem but larger developments such as shopping malls are not."[60]

The UFCW predictably supports measures protecting its members. For instance, it opposes electronic shelf pricing in supermarkets. In a pathetic echo of the radical Industrial Workers of the World's cry for "one big union," the UCFW rather more timidly demands "a Single Food Safety Agency."[61] (How's that for a rallying cry?)

The UFCW takes the usual big-union line on political issues: opposed to tax cuts, which are derided as giveaways, as if Washington, in a fit of altruism, was mailing checks to indolent and undeserving citizens. Fast-track trade agreements are criticized not for enhancing the imperial presidency but for exposing American workers to the perils of free trade. The minimum wage should be boosted—even if economists of all stripes generally agree that minimum wages reduce employment opportunities for the young and unskilled workers who are most in need of the discipline of entry-level employment.

Although the union would like to cast itself as the doughty underdog defending the little guy against the big interests, its pipeline to federal government monies belies that image. For instance, in 2000, the United Food and Commercial Workers Union received a $95,000 grant from the Office of Special Counsel for Immigration Related Unfair Employment Practices. The money was to be used to provide "anti-discrimination training"[62] to workers in Nebraska meatpacking plants. Interestingly, the grant from the Clinton administration came just as the UFCW was trying to organize 4,000 mostly Hispanic workers in the Omaha meatpacking industry. No doubt the timing was purely coincidental.

The grant was the first of its kind, but is unlikely to be the last. The purpose of the grant, according to the UFCW, was to "develop a union network of workers and staff members trained to protect immigrant workers' rights on the job."[63] Interesting that the word "union" precedes "network": this was a $95,000 recruitment tool for the UFCW. All told, the union received $284,000 in taxpayer support from 1996–2000.[64]

Until the last decade, the union movement was a bulwark of the anti-immigration lobby. No more. As fewer and fewer white and black native Americans have seen fit to sign a union card, labor has shifted strategy. Whereas once such union bigwigs as George Meany decried the presence of undocumented immigrants lowering the wages of working Americans, now such unions as the United Food and Commercial Workers call for a vast legalization of illegal immigrants (who of course are never called "illegal") and their induction into the UFCW.

This shift on immigration is not the only way in which unions have become internationalized. In the 1990s, a new issue emerged at the top of the labor agenda: protecting the rights of workers in . . . other countries?

What altruists! How selfless of the unions: ignoring their own pressing needs in order to defend the dignity and basic rights of those on other shores.

Well, that's one way of looking at it. The other is that this is just a new gloss on the oldest game in union town: protecting members' jobs.

The issue of conditions in foreign factories has become a cliché of the college campus activist crowd. Workers in Nicaragua/Malaysia/El Salvador are sewing clothes in "sweatshops" at rates that seem incredible to we fat, happy, and complacent Americans.

In fact, as a few enterprising journalists have shown, average pay in most if not all of these "sweatshops" is higher than the average wage of non-sweatshop employees. In Nicaragua, as *Milwaukee Journal-Sentinel* reporter Doris Hajewski found, the average pay at the Taiwanese-owned Chentex factory, which analyst Ivan G. Osorio calls "'ground zero' for anti-sweatshop agitation," is about $120 per month, or $20 higher than the average monthly wage in Nicaragua.[65]

Although Nicaraguan foreign minister Francisco Aguirre-Sacasa accused the trust-fund college kid protesters of a "hatchet job"[66] in their criticisms of Nicaraguan textile and clothing factories, few if any listened. The cause is too cheap, too easy, to forego. It confers moral superiority on the protester, who risks nothing, who sacrifices nothing, who gets brownie points for making lazy and unsupported assertions about conditions thousands of miles away in countries about which he knows nothing. And he can be back at his dorm or apartment in time to order a pizza for dinner (and stiff the hard-working pizza delivery man on the tip).

The anti-globalization forces often demand that trade be restricted with nations that do meet U.S.-dictated labor and environmental standards. (These standards are putatively international, but in fact, it is the U.S. government that is calling the shots.)

Certain of these standards may seem reasonable: for instance, workers ought to have the right to organize and bargain collectively. Others, such as a ban on child labor, are problematic: in developing countries, a child's assistance is often essential to a family's economic well-being. (And is learning a trade really "worse" than attending a public school? Isn't this a decision for a child's parents rather than middle-class foreigners?) Yet other standards, such as those mandating acceptable levels of pollutants and domestic social policy, are obvious infringements upon national sovereignty.

And however finely or sloppily drawn the standards and trade sanctions may be, they will not work.

Daniel T. Griswold, associate director of the Center for Trade Policy Studies at the Cato Institute, explains, "Sanctions deprive poor countries of the international trade and investment opportunities they need to raise overall living standards. Sanctions tend to strike at the very export industries in less-developed countries that typically pay the highest wages and maintain the highest standards, forcing production and employment into less-globalized sectors where wages and standards are almost always lower."[67]

Griswold notes that withdrawing Western investment in these nations could have pernicious, even catastrophic, consequences. For instance, "The most likely alternative for a 13-year-old working in a garment factory may not be school but prostitution or heavy manual labor." As the President of Brazil, Fernando Henrique Cardoso, told the Summit of the Americas in Quebec City in 2001, "It would be an obvious mistake—a very serious mistake, indeed—to set given standards of social development as a prior condition for free trade. This would be tantamount to making development a prior condition for trade. . . . [It] would be putting the cart before the horse."[68]

American unions were undeterred. Sensing a winning issue, they pressed the case against "sweatshops." Their real motivation was captured by Kendra Okonski of the Capital Research Center: The unions support "environmental and labor standards that are supposed to prevent corporations from exploiting developing nations. In reality, though, such linkage is a convenient cover-up for trade protectionism."[69]

The Alliance for Responsible Trade, a key organizer of the anti-globalization and protectionist movement, counts among its members the AFL-CIO. The aforementioned Union of Needletrades, Industrial and Textile Employees (UNITE), which received government funding of $281,000 from 1996–2000,[70] is also a ringleader of the anti-sweatshop movement.

UNITE is a new union borne of a merger of two dying unions: the International Ladies' Garment Workers Union (ILGWU) and the Amalgamated Clothing and Textile Workers Union (ACTWU). In 1996, just one year after the merger, UNITE took aim at Kathie Lee Gifford. Now, countless television viewers would have liked to do the same to the maudlin Ms. Gifford, but UNITE's objections were political, not artistic. Kathie Lee's signature clothing was being manufactured in "sweatshops," which is another way of saying factories that were not organized by UNITE. Kathie Lee made an easy target; a cheap cause was born.

Thousands of college students whose earliest memories were of Kathie Lee telling the world about her bratty children and well-preserved if ancient husband turned on her in a fury. Students Against

Sweatshops organized on more than 100 campuses. What courage it took to be a Student Against Sweatshops! How brave the young scholar who took on the powerful lobby of Students For Sweatshops! The SAS had as its goal "to stop our school from purchasing garments or putting its name on apparel that was made in sweatshops."[71] And if that threw the thirteen-year-old Bangladeshi girl out of the "sweatshop" and into a whorehouse, so be it. The consciences of America's youth were more important than the well-being of some anonymous Third World kid.

(I have put off to the side the political battleground on which much of the anti-globalization struggle has been fought: the transfer from Congress to the President of significant authority over the shape of international trade agreements. Reasonable people can disagree on this issue.)

* * *

He who controls the language of a debate wins the debate. Who can be for a "sweatshop"? And closer to home, who can be against "job training"?

Job training is one of those shibboleths the mere utterance of which causes even the most parsimonious politician to hold his tongue. Who wants to criticize it? After all, it's not like this is welfare money being doled out to the indolent. The money expended under such programs as the Job Training Partnership Act is going to teach marketable skills to eager young people and older workers whose skills may be rusty. A small investment in such programs will be repaid a hundredfold down the road, as the trained products of the JTPA take their places as productive, taxpaying citizens.

That's the theory, anyway. In practice, the whole edifice of job-training programs is a sham, a waste, a sacred cow that cries out for slaughtering.

Before 1982, "job training" was the business of technical schools, colleges, shop class, and the market. The government's primary public jobs program was CETA (the Comprehensive Employment and Training Administration), which at its peak in 1978 subsidized 725,000 jobs in nonprofits and local governments. CETA had become a byword for no-show, makework political patronage; even its dwindling band of supporters conceded that it had become a machine by which Democratic mayors dispensed jobs for the boys.

The program was due to expire in 1982, and even most Democrats were willing to let it go quietly into that good night. But then came the recession. As the first midyear election of the Reagan administration drew near, national unemployment rates topped 10 percent. In hard-hit areas of Pennsylvania, Ohio, and other electoral battleground states, as many as one in five workers was out of a job. Something—anything—had to be done, or else Republicans were going to be swept out of House and Senate seats en masse come November.

Enter Senator Dan Quayle, the birdbrain from Indiana. Quayle, later to achieve risible fame as the first President George Bush's malaprop-bedeviled vice president, had gotten the less than choice assignment as chairman of the Senate Subcommittee on Employment and Productivity. It was up to him—or, more properly, his staff—to give the appearance that Republicans were responding in a suitably "compassionate" way to what Democrats were calling the Reagan Recession.

A massive government jobs program, á la CETA, was not an option. While President Reagan often backslid in his campaign against big government, he was not going to sign CETA II. But "job training": ah, that had a different sound. As Quayle aide Robert Guttman told labor economist Gordon Lafer, Republican senators "wanted to say 'we're doing something about unemployment.'"[72] And so the Job Training Partnership Act of 1982 was born.

Unlike CETA, which was based on the premise that there weren't enough jobs to go around, and that Washington should just create them out of thin air, the JTPA was sold as a response to a supposed gap that existed between the skills of unemployed men and women and the work skills desired by employers. It was as empty as its sponsor's head, but it provided excellent political cover. As Senator Quayle explained to Reagan officials, in a typically lucid exposition, the JTPA "would give people something to run on. It would help with the rich/poor thing; the bill helps do something about the poor. It would help with unemployment; the bill helps people without jobs. It will help with the whole compassion argument. It's a natural."[73]

The natural was approved by Quayle's colleagues by a 95-0 vote. By fiscal year 1985, the JTPA was training 955,411 young people and adults at a cost of over $2 billion. The program peaked at over 1 million participants annually between fiscal years 1986 and 1989 before hovering around half a million participants at just under $1 billion each year during the Clinton octennium. In 2000, the program morphed into the Workforce Investment Act (WIA), which promises to hold high the banner of federal workforce training for years to come.

Politicians were near-unanimous in praising the JTPA. As the second President Bush enthused, for "years now, the Job Training Partnership program has been equipping the disadvantaged . . . to enter the work force, to start that climb up out of the poverty trap. JTPA—it works."[74]

No, it doesn't. As Gordon Lafer documents in his book, *The Job Training Charade* (2002), the JTPA is an abject failure. As Lafer summarizes: "The primary evaluation of the program, a massive study mandated by the Department of Labor, tracked 20,000 people over a four-year period. The study examined multiple demographic groups and types of training services, comparing the employment and wages of JTPA participants with those of a control group of similar workers who were excluded from the program. For the majority of participants, the program had no statistically significant effects. For those aged sixteen to twenty-one, the program actually had negative effects, with JTPA trainees earning less than the control group."[75]

That's right: this heralded, ballyhooed program actually seems to reduce the wages earned by its participants in their post-program years. Despite these "anemic results,"[76] writes Lafer, the program and its successor enjoy nigh-unanimous bipartisan support. (Lest one think that Lafer is some kind of libertarian ideologue who began his study with a *parti pris* against job training, he is actually a leftish economist with a strong pro-union bias.)

If Washington, D.C., were an island of sanity, the National JTPA Study to which Lafer refers would have reduced the program to a national laughingstock. The study, which cost $25 million and was conducted by the "nation's premier program evaluation consultants," found the JTPA to be so ineffectual that even Dan Quayle would have been dissuaded from his support had he the inclination or ability to read the report. "[T]he lack of program effectiveness for youths was pervasive," the authors determined. "In fact, we cannot identify any group of youths who benefitted, in terms of earnings gains, from participation in JTPA."[77]

One problem may be that the program is predicated on an untruth. Employers are not crying out for better-trained workers. For instance, the 1990 Commission on the Skills of the American Workforce found that employers hiring from the bottom third of the labor market desired "a pleasant personality behind the service counter, physical stamina on the construction site or a steady hand on the wheel" rather than the trendy and yuppie-tinted skills which technocrats allege to be in great demand. As Lafer notes, "employers seem primarily concerned with workers' attitudes." Or as the Commission on the Skills of the American Workforce concluded, "Employers do not complain about an inability to do algebra or write essays."[78]

Nevertheless, the job-training charade continues, and it attracts the usual suspects. For instance, the inevitable National Senior Citizens Education & Research Center, the grant-managing division of the late NCSC and newborn Alliance for Retired Americans, has also been aboard the job-training gravy train, administering a JTPA Contextual Learning Demonstration Project grant in Tarrant County, Texas.

The National Senior Citizens Education & Research Center brings me back to where I started this chapter. One way or another, by hook or crook or *Federal Register* book, the piggies find the trough.

Notes

1. Bennett and DiLorenzo, *Destroying Democracy*, p. 278.
2. Ibid.
3. Ivan G. Osorio, "Labor's Shell Game with Taxpayer Dollars, *Labor Watch* (Washington, DC: Capital Research Center, September 2001), p. 1.
4. Ibid., p. 2.
5. Osorio, "Labor's Shell Game with Taxpayer Dollars," *Labor Watch*, p. 1.
6. U.S. Department of Labor, Employment and Training Administration, Grant No. D-7516-9-00-81-55.
7. Osorio, "Labor's Shell Game with Taxpayers," *Labor Watch*, p. 2.
8. U.S. Department of Labor, National Council of Senior Citizens Final Audit Report No. 18-99-007-07-735, p. 1.
9. Osorio, "Labor's Shell Game with Taxpayer Dollars," *Labor Watch*, pp. 3, 5.
10. Philip Dine, "Labor Leaders Launch Political Organization for Retired Workers," *St. Louis Post-Dispatch*, May 24, 2001, p. A2.
11. Samuel L. Blumenfeld, *NEA: Trojan Horse in American Education* (Boise, ID: Paradigm, 1984), p. 73.
12. Ibid., p. 91.
13. Myron Lieberman, *The Teacher Unions: How They Sabotage Educational Reform and Why* (San Francisco, CA: Encounter, 2000; first edition, 1999), p. 12.

14. Blumenfeld, *NEA: Trojan Horse in American Education*, p. 161.
15. Quoted in Joel Mowbray, "The NEA's Political Machine," *Labor Watch* (Washington, DC: Capital Research Center, November 2001), p. 6.
16. Percy Ednalino, "'New Unionism' Urged for Teachers," *Denver Post*, April 22, 2001, p. A26.
17. Blumenfeld, *NEA: Trojan Horse in American Education*, p. 164.
18. Lieberman, *The Teacher Unions*, p. 30.
19. Ray Bradbury, *Fahrenheit 451* (New York: Simon and Schuster, 1967; first edition, 1953), p. 66.
20. Lieberman, *The Teacher Unions*, p. 32.
21. Samples, Yablonski, and Osorio, "More Government for All," p. 5.
22. Lieberman, *The Teacher Unions*, p. 6.
23. Samples, Yablonski, and Osorio, "More Government for All," p. 5.
24. Ibid.
25. Lieberman, *The Teacher Unions*, p. 238.
26. Cathy Cummins, "The PTA in '90s," *Denver Rocky Mountain News*, January 4, 1998, p. 16A.
27. National PTA Legislative Program 2001–2002, p. 1.
28. Ibid., p. 2.
29. "Your Children, Our Mission," undated National PTA brochure.
30. National PTA Legislative Program 2001–2002, p. 3.
31. "Before- and After-School Care," www.pta.org/ptawashington/ issues/before.asp, October 23, 2001.
32. Karen MacPherson, "Getting Parents More Involved," *Pittsburgh Post-Gazette*, February 6, 2000, p. A16.
33. *National PTA Annual Report 1999*, p. 6.
34. "Vouchers," www.pta.org/ptawashington/issues/vouchers.asp, October 23, 2001.
35. "PTA and Washington," www.pta.org/ptawashington/index.asp, October 23, 2001.
36. "Tax Subsidies," www.pta.org/ptawashington/issues/tax.asp, October 23, 2001.
37. "Privatization," www.pta.org/ptawashington/issues/ privatization.asp, October 23, 2001.
38. "Block Grants," www.pta.org/ptawashington/issues/blockgrants. asp, October 23, 2001.
39. "Charter Schools," www.pta.org/ptawashington/issues/charter. asp, October 23, 2001.
40. "Nutrition," www.pta.org/ptawashington/issues/nutrition.asp, October 23, 2001.
41. *National PTA Annual Report 1999*, p. 6.
42. "School Construction," www.pta.org/ptawashington/issues/ construction.asp, October 23, 2001.
43. *National PTA Annual Report 1999*, p. 2.
44. National PTA Legislative Program 2001–2002, p. 4.
45. "Rethinking Parent-Teacher Ties," *Christian Science Monitor*, June 4, 2001, p. 8.
46. National PTA Legislative Program 2001–2002, p. 1.
47. "The Mission of the PTA," www.pta.org/aboutpta/ mission_en.asp, October 23, 2001.
48. Samples, Yablonski, and Osorio, "More Government for All," p. 5.
49. "AFL-CIO: A Voice for America's Working Families," undated brochure, p. 5.
50. Ibid.
51. "UNITE Issue Sheet: Taxes," undated.
52. Samples, Yablonski, and Osorio, "More Government for All," p. 5.

53. "Legislative Agenda for the 107th Congress," www.naswdc.org/advocacy/agenda.html, December 14, 2001.
54. "Civil and Human Rights," www.uaw.org/cap/01/issue02.html, December 14, 2001.
55. Susan Milligan, "Vice President Wins Backing of UAW," *Boston Globe*, August 12, 2000, p. A9.
56. Sarah Schafer, "Labor Pushes Some Democrats to Vote for Bush Energy Plan," *Washington Post*, August 5, 2001, p. A8.
57. Samples, Yablonski, and Osorio, "More Government for All," p. 5.
58. Fred O. Williams, "Labor Leaders Face Watershed Election Cycle," *Buffalo News*, September 4, 2000, p. 6B.
59. Samples, Yablonski, and Osorio, "More Government for All," p. 5.
60. Carol Emert, "Assembly Bill Threatens Supermarkets," *San Francisco Chronicle*, September 10, 1999, p. B1.
61. "We Need a Single Food Agency," www.ufcw.org/contact/internal, October 23, 2001.
62. John Taylor, "Worker Rights a Key in Immigration Effort," *Omaha World-Herald*, October 23, 2000, p. 1.
63. "U.S. Justice Department Funds Union Information Network on Immigrant Rights," press release, UFCW, October 23, 2000.
64. Samples, Yablonski, and Osorio, "More Government for All," p. 5.
65. Ivan G. Osorio, "The National Labor Committee: Leftist Foundations and the Money Behind the Anti-Sweatshop Movement," *Labor Watch* (Washington, DC: Capital Research Center, July 2001), p. 6.
66. Ibid., p. 7.
67. Daniel T. Griswold, "Trade Labor, and the Environment: How Blue and Green Sanctions Threaten Higher Standards," Cato Institute Trade Policy Analysis, (Washington, DC: Cato Institute, August 2, 2001), p. 1.
68. Ibid., p. 14.
69. Kendra Okonski, "Anti-Global Trade Protestors Become Global Force," *Organization Trends* (Washington, DC: Capital Research Center, July 2001), p. 1.
70. Samples, Yablonski, and Osorio, "More Government for All," p. 5.
71. "United Students Against Sweatshops," www.aflcio.org/sweatfree/students.html, February 9, 2001.
72. Gordon Lafer, *The Job Training Charade* (Ithaca, NY: Cornell University Press, 2002), p. 178.
73. Ibid., p. 156.
74. Ibid., p. 88.
75. Ibid., p. 5.
76. Ibid., p. 10.
77. Ibid., pp. 102–103.
78. Ibid., pp. 67–68.

4

Greens Scramble for the Green

The modern environmentalist movement, which in some ways was born in 1962 with the publication of Rachel Carson's *Silent Spring*, expands apace. Indeed, for a movement dedicated to a series of "no growth" propositions, it seems to grow beyond all reasonable limits. According to the Capital Research Center, which studies nonprofit foundations, the number of environmental organizations boomed from 1,802 in 1990 to 4,018 in 1998: this increase of 123 percent dwarfed the average increase (59 percent) in the nonprofit sector.[1]

It has become something of a truism to say that environmentalism is a substitute religion, but because a thing is said often does not make it any the less true. Environmentalism is a religion, a secular faith whose adherents are often far more zealous than are those "fundamentalist" Christians whom all good liberals disdain and regard as almost subhuman. To the environmentalist, Nature is the God, and His priests are the lawyers and bureaucrats of the regulatory state. But this may be giving the typical movement environmentalist too much credit. To say that Nature is his God makes him sound like a virile pantheist, a skin-wearing, spear-carrying warrior sacrificing virgins to Mother Nature. In the main, he is nothing of the sort. His complexion is pasty pale, as befits one who sits in an office, stares at a computer, and yaps on a telephone all day. He knows much about the minutiae of the Resource Conservation and Recovery Act but couldn't tell an oak tree from a pine tree. His true religion, more often than not, is statism.

While environmentalism may seem to be a fairly innocuous strain of statism—after all, who could possibly object to clean air or safe drinking water?—it has become more virulent in recent years. The culprit, oddly enough, is the triumph of capitalism over socialism.

The British economist Wilfred Beckerman, Emeritus Fellow of Balliol College in Oxford, writes in *Through Green-Colored Glasses: Environmentalism Reconsidered* of "the appeal of environmentalism to modern-day radical revolutionaries. Socialism now has been visibly discredited throughout most of the world. Everybody has been able to see that, instead of ushering in a society characterized by equity, justice, and comradely love, it led to the imposition of monstrous and incompetent regimes in many parts of the world. So the radical revolutionaries have turned to environmentalism as their rallying cry."[2]

Just why environmentalists would want such comrades (except the wealthy ones who write fat checks to nonprofits) is a mystery. In addition to being repressive, harsh, and economically malfunctional, socialism was the greatest enemy the environment has ever known. The nations of Eastern Europe and the former Soviet Union are ecological wastelands: polluted monuments to a wicked ideology that made men and women slaves to an abstraction.

Still, the socialists, once the rougher edges were smoothed away, fit fairly well into the environmental establishment, which often seems blind to the damage that government can do to the nation's air, water, and landscape. For instance, who can reckon the number of trees that were sacrificed as the federal government built that grand experiment in Republican public works, the 40,000-miles plus of the Interstate Highway System? Or, as it was originally styled in order to win support, the National System of Interstate and Defense Highways. Adding Defense—like adding Education or Children—makes a measure almost unopposable. What? You're against defense? Against education? Against children? You . . . scoundrel! You cur! You, you, you . . . libertarian!!

Although the knee-jerk response of the modern environmentalist is to look to Washington for a solution, the federal government has been a large part of the problem. Federal mismanagement of its land in the National Park System, the National Wildlife Refuge System, the National Forest Service, and the National Wilderness Preservation System has been conceded even by many advocates of a strong federal role in environmental protection. One trenchant critic of federal land management, Dr. Richard Stroup of Montana's Political Economy Research Center, points to the 342,000 miles of government-built and maintained roads scarring the national forests. These roads exist, in large part, because the feds subsidize logging on public lands. As Stroup writes, "These roads, primarily designed to facilitate logging, extend into the ecologically fragile backcountry of the Rocky Mountains and Alaska, where they are causing massive soil erosion, damaging trout and salmon fisheries and causing other environmental harm. In many cases, the costs of these logging activities far exceed any commercial benefit from the timber acquired; so this environmental destruction would not have occurred in the absence of government subsidies."[3]

The array of federal government subsidies that cause unwise or destructive use of public and private lands—whether for logging, irrigation, or farming that is unsuited to the local climate—ought to trigger a wide-scale reconsideration of the benevolence of state regulation. Alas, it has not. With, admittedly, some exceptions, the environmentalists who raise most of the money and hog most of the press attention are about as skeptical of government regulation as an intern in Al Gore's office.

Although a Republican president, Theodore Roosevelt, introduced the concept of conservation into the national political discourse, the major environmental groups are solidly aligned in the Democratic camp. In 2000, every single one of these organizations endorsed Albert Gore for president—even Friends of the Earth (FOE), which had supported former Senator Bill Bradley (D-NJ) in the primaries because Gore had faithfully served a Clinton "administration which has done significant international environmental damage." After Bradley's air ball of a campaign, FOE—a more honest acronym would be hard to find—cozied up to Gore. Its president, Brent Blackwelder, decried "the abysmal environmental records of Bush-Cheney" and gushed, "Only Al Gore and Joe Lieberman can vanquish that threat."[4]

Opinion polls have long found that the membership rosters of the big environmental organizations are crammed with Republicans. This encourages a certain deftness on the part of the environmentalist officials. For instance, in 1980, almost three quarters of the members of the National Wildlife Federation voted for Ronald Reagan, yet the NWF leadership lined up in the anti-Reagan camp. The Sierra Club has a considerable "conservative" membership, yet its leaders have yet to meet a Republican president they didn't scorn. Not that they don't try to profit from Republican policies. As the checks from the Bush tax cut of 2001 started flooding the nation's mailboxes, the Sierra Club sent out a clever plea for funds that read, in part: "Over the next few weeks, millions of 'advance payment' tax rebate checks will be sent to most American taxpayers. Yet the Bush administration is abandoning a long list of projects that would help protect the planet and result in immediate financial benefits for every citizen." What to do with these $600 checks? Ever so tactfully, the mailing suggests that the recipient might use this manna from Washington to "Fund the Sierra Club, which is helping to protect the planet and educate the American people about the overall environmental record of the Bush administration."[5] Now, that's taking green consciousness to an entirely new level.

At least the Sierra Club wasn't dunning for rebate checks using government money. At one time, the Club was a virtual vulture circling around taxpayer carrion. From 1978 to 1981, the Sierra Club received $790,746 in government grants.[6] This was the day in which the Club was particularly active in campaigning against nuclear power plants, which themselves benefit from government subsidies in the form of research and the limitation on liability fixed by the Price-Anderson Act. All sides of the issue, it seems, were paid for by the U.S. government. Only the taxpayer had to pay his own way.

In recent years, the Sierra Club has grown far less dependent on government subsidies, thanks in part to the Reagan administration's fitful efforts to "defund the Left." EPA administrator Anne Burford cut off the Club, cold turkey, from the agency that had been its single largest source of government funds. By the time the Sierra Club joined the Fair Taxes for All Coalition in 2001, its cumulative taxpayer support from 1996–2000 was a measly $5,000.[7]

Still, the Sierra Club, to its credit, has become far less dependent upon federal dollars since Anne Burford kicked the greens off the dole. The Sierra Club, founded by John Muir in 1892, is an interesting mixture of activities: it publishes beautiful and often eloquent books, it sponsors backpacking and cross-country trips, and it plays politics with the swagger and aggressiveness of the classic insider. This is not to suggest that the Sierra Club has been "wrong," at least from a free-market point of view, on everything. It was an early voice against the wasteful and environmentally destructive dam-building orgy of the first half of the twentieth century, and it has teamed with taxpayer watchdog organizations to go after such egregious pork as the Tennessee-Tombigbee Waterway and the Clinch River Breeder Reactor.

On the other hand, the Sierra Club was a leading—perhaps the leading—advocate of the creation of the Environmental Protection Agency, the National Wilderness Preservation System, the Endangered Species Act, the Clean Air Act, the Clean Water Act, and the whole panoply of laws and regulations that have come to define the relationship between state and land in our America. Its earliest role was as a promoter of the national parks system, particularly Yosemite, and it remains a ferocious opponent of oil drilling in the Arctic National Wildlife Refuge

The Sierra Club has no pretenses to nonpartisanship. Through its Sierra Club Political Committee (SCPC), it contributes to candidates in precisely the same way that the AFL-CIO and the NRA do. It even boasts of its "key role in [sic] election of pro-environmental candidates"[8]—yet all the time it hypocritically trumpets its support of campaign finance reform, that will-o-the-wisp of suit-and-tie liberals everywhere.

Like all massive lobbies, the Sierra Club tries, clumsily, to "involve" its more than 600,000 members. The most important aspect of this involvement is opening the checkbook at regular intervals and inscribing upon the checks numbers followed by as many zeroes as possible. Inevitably, however, some rosy-cheeked eager beaver will want to do more. So the Club offers him or her the opportunity to press the "Send" button on a computer and transmit a prewritten letter to congressmen and senators endorsing a variety of Sierra Club political positions. "Feel free to edit or add a personal comment,"[9] notes the Club's website.

As is often the case with organizations grown large, bloated, and Washington-centric, the Sierra Club has drifted into policy areas far from Yosemite. Opposing the Bush tax cut was one example. Another is the Club's support of government-mandated contraception. The Sierra Club urges members to inform their congresspeople that "Affordable access to family planning is critical to slowing population growth."[10] Therefore, the federal government should force private insurers to offer contraceptive coverage. The environmental link here is as thin as a Malthus-fed fashion model. But "reproductive rights" are a shibboleth of the organizational left, and the Sierra Club needs to keep its p.c. card punched. Interestingly, the Club has fiercely resisted an effort by one faction to endorse immigration restrictions. After all, the restrictionists point out, if "excess population" is a threat to the integrity of the American ecology, surely millions of immigrants are as dangerous as millions of new babies. Thus far, the Sierra Club hierarchs have held off the restrictionists, but the battle is far from over.

* * *

"Scarcity" is to environmentalists as sin is to fundamentalists: it is a baleful presence, always hovering, never far, and most useful for justifying intervention into the lives, economic and personal, of the unenlightened.

The myth of scarcity was effectively demolished by the Danish political scientist and former member of Greenpeace Bjorn Lomborg in his landmark work, *The Skeptical Environmentalist: Measuring the Real State of the World* (English translation published in 2001; first published in Denmark in 1998).

Audaciously, Lomborg uses as the epigraph to this work the puckish remarks of the late Julian Simon, who made it his life's work to refute the sky-is-falling canards of the doomsday left. Wrote Simon (as versified by Lomborg):

This is my long-run forecast in brief:

> The material conditions of life will continue to get better for most people, in most countries, most of the time, indefinitely. Within a century or two, all nations and most of humanity will be at or above today's Western living standards. I also speculate, however, that many people will continue to think and say that the conditions of life are getting worse.[11]

Using statistics and techniques that were easily available to anyone who wished to actually measure the truth of the environmentalist case, Simon demonstrated the utter fatuity of the myth of diminishing resources. As his friend, the political scientist Ben Wattenberg, nicely summarized Simon's key insight, "supplies of natural resources are not finite; they are created by the intellect of man, which is an infinitely renewable resource. (Coal, oil, and uranium were not resources until mixed well with intellect.)"[12]

Simon saw the glass as half full, not half empty. Moreover, he demonstrated why the water therein was cleaner and healthier than it had ever been before. From death rates to air quality, he insisted—and he had the numbers to back up his claims—that "almost every long-run trend in material human welfare points in a positive direction."[13] This was good news for most of us, if bad news for those who raise funds for the Big Green lobbies. They need dirty air and despoiled landscape the way liberals used to need Jesse Helms and conservatives needed Ted Kennedy: as bugaboos, as bogeymen, as crowbars with which to pry open the wallets of credulous donors.

Simon, by the way, had as his special foil Paul Ehrlich, the doomsiest of the doomsayers, and a man so consistently wrong as to inspire an odd sort of pity even in his foes. In perhaps the most famous wager of the latter half of the twentieth century, in 1980 Simon bet Ehrlich and Ehrlich's colleagues that the prices of any raw materials he chose (which turned out to be chromium, copper, nickel, tin, and tungsten) would drop by 1990. Ehrlich and friends responded to the bet the way a hayseed charges into a sidewalk game of three-card monte. "The lure of easy money can be irresistible,"[14] he boasted, and the pair drew up a contract. In October 1990, a decade of abundance later, with the aggregate value of the metals down by more than 50 percent, Ehrlich sheepishly wrote Simon a check for $576.07. He did not, alas, retire from the forecasting game. But that's because a sucker is born every minute, and enough of them buy gloom and doom books to keep even a critic of capitalism comfortable.

Paul Ehrlich, in his unintentionally hilarious Chicken-Little classic, *The Population Bomb* (1968), had sketched a future (now past) none of us recognize outside of the movie house: "The battle to feed all of humanity is over. In the 1970s and 1980s hundreds of millions of people will starve to death in spite of any crash programs embarked upon now."[15]

Well, Paul, not quite.

The Ehrlichian prognoses are alive and well in the world of environmental publishing, however, and even in the more mainstream green outfits.

Bjorn Lomborg's epigraph was a nice tribute to the man who had inspired his book. As Lomborg tells it, he was leafing through a copy of *Wired* magazine in a Los Angeles bookstore in 1997 when he came upon an interview with Simon in which the feisty iconoclast was castigating environmentalists for using specious statistics to promote a skewed view of the world. Lomborg, a statistician by trade, was intrigued. Though he suspected that "most of Simon's talk was simple, American right-wing propaganda,"[16] he and ten of his brighter students spent a semester scrutinizing the agreed-upon environmental statistics. Their conclusion: things are getting better, not worse. For instance,

> We are not running out of energy or natural resources. There will be more and more food per head of the world's population. Fewer and fewer people are starving.... [W]e have reduced poverty more in the last 50 years than we did in the preceding 500, and it has been reduced in practically every country.
>
> Global warming, though its size and future projections are rather unrealistically pessimistic, is almost certainly taking place, but the typical cure of early and radical fossil fuel cutbacks is way worse than the original affliction, and moreover its total impact will not pose a devastating problem for our future. Nor will we lose 25–50 percent of all species in our lifetime—in fact we are losing probably 0.7 percent. Acid rain does not kill the forests, and the air and water around us are becoming less and less polluted.
>
> Mankind's lot has actually improved in terms of practically every measurable indicator.[17]

Them was fightin' words. The fact that they came amidst a dense profusion of charts, statistics, and figures which no has yet refuted made Lomborg's book all the more annoying to the environmentalist establishment.

* * *

The major environmentalist lobbies have found their greatest success in harvesting the Beltway's kind of green: rectangular notes imprinted with images of dead Presidents and signatures of the forgotten hacks who have served sinecures as Treasurer of the United States.

The World Wildlife Fund (WWF), whose immodest goal is "to leave our children a living planet,"[18] seems determined not to leave our children a solvent treasury. Based in Washington, D.C., whose wildlife might be better off in captivity, or at least in a well-guarded zoo, the WWF is a moneymaking machine that even the cynical con-men of the other WWF, the World Wrestling Federation, would envy. In 1997, of a total revenue of $111.994 million, a cool $23.798 million came from government grants. In 1998, the comparable figures were $111.263 million and $20.076 million.[19] In 2000, the WWF has conceded that $23.4 million (21 percent) of its total revenue of $111.8 came from government grants. The majority of this—$16.8 million—was granted by the U.S. Agency for International Development.[20]

Among the world-saving activities undertaken by the WWF is the Conservation Action Network, which sends out e-mails urging WWF members and supporters to "communicate with the president, members of Congress, state legislators,"[21] etc. Now, this is the lowest form of activism: a kind of lobbying for couch potatoes. The WWF is far too huge and unwieldy and impersonal to offer the chance for members to participate in any meaningful way, so the Conservation Action Network offers them the illusion of action. So convinced is the WWF of the basic torpor and listlessness of its members that it actually writes the e-mail for you; all the inert WWFer must do is press the "Send" button on his computer.

This is truly pathetic. Taken singly, such e-mails are not worth the air they are printed on. But in the aggregate, they might conceivably matter. And what is most pertinent to our subject is that these constitute organized lobbying by an entity that receives massive infusions of taxpayer money.

The WWF has urged legislative action on matters ranging from the Florida Everglades to the Rhino and Tiger Product Labeling bill to the urgency of meeting the alleged threat of global warming. Although officially nonpartisan, the WWF is Democratic in all but name. It praised the Clinton administration's "impressive legacy of protection and rehabilitation of America's public lands," even adding Clinton Interior Secretary Bruce Babbitt to its board of directors, while the administration of President George W. Bush "turns its back on the climate" (a difficult thing to do, it would seem) while offering a "blueprint for more global warming."[22]

* * *

Every religion must have its holy days, and in the environmentalist calendar April 22, or Earth Day, is Christmas, Easter, and the Fourth of July wrapped into one.

The first Earth Day, in 1970, has been called "a hectoring mix of street theater, corporate p.r., and speeches by such paragons of self-restraint as Senators Ted Kennedy and Bob Packwood."[23] The idea's true father was Wisconsin liberal Democratic Senator Gaylord Nelson, a respected member of that not always respectable body. Nelson, it seems, had envisioned Earth Day as the opportunity for a national teach-in and dialogue about ecology. Boy, did he guess wrong.

The tendentious, propagandistic quality of Earth Day was on display from the very beginning. To coincide with this first Christmas of the aborning religion, the Sierra Club produced an ugly paperback titled *Ecotactics: The Sierra Club Handbook for Environmental Activists*. (Sierra Club mainstay Ansel Adams, the brilliant photographer of the American West, ridiculed the book as "two dimensional."[24])

Adams was too kind by half. The book is as one-dimensional and soporific as a Department of Energy press release. Although the editor notes with pride that more than half of the contributors are under thirty years of age, they are, in the main, young fogies: law school grinds, earnest liberals, and college newspaper journalists who take themselves far too seriously. In other words, these are the boys and girls who grew up to be the men and women who largely run this country, and reading their musings at a tender age is a depressing experience indeed. While some contributors—for instance, Ralph Nader—make salient points about the ways in which the federal government drives ecological destruction through corporate welfare, others intone the tedious mantras that have become the clichés of establishment environmentalism. For instance, the first item on the "activist's checklist"—that is, the single most important thing that a budding saver of the Earth might do in 1970—is to "return [bottles] to the store." That's thinking big! What a way to inspire a generation of revolutionaries! In fact, as I will get to shortly, recycling is a colossal waste of time and energy and may in fact be, on the whole, a net loss for the environment. But the important thing is to feel good about oneself; to feel virtuous, to know that you are superior to all those unwashed unbelievers tossing bottles of Coke into the trash instead of driving in your exhaust-reeking automobile to a supermarket (whose products are trucked in over the Interstate Highway System) to claim your measly nickel deposit.

Other items on the activists' checklist range from the innocuous to the harmful. Pester the Department of the Interior to set stricter standards for water quality. Report violators of pollution laws. (In other words, be a snitch, fourteen years before 1984.) Clean up a roadside. A nice idea, that, but here's the kicker: "Call the . . . newspapers, TV, radio, and tell them what you're doing."[25] In other words, do not perform this healthful civic act because it's a good thing to do, or because it may add to the aesthetic quality of the area; no, do it to get publicity. To get your mug in the papers or on the TV. I know that Baby Boomers are often criticized as narcissistic self-regarding preening publicity hogs, but this is ridiculous.

Senator Gaylord Nelson, in his remarks in Denver on the first Earth Day, speculated that "Earth Day may be a turning point in American history. It may be the birth of a new American ethic that rejects the frontier philosophy that the continent was put here for our plunder, and accepts the idea that even urbanized, affluent, mobile societies are interdependent with the fragile, life-sustaining systems of the air, the water, the land."[26]

Nelson was right in one respect. Earth Day rejected that aspect of the "frontier philosophy" that held that men ought to be self-reliant. For unlike Christmas, Earth Day is supported by a range of direct federal subsidies, e.g., a $30,000 grant in 1999 from the U.S. Department of Energy to Earth Day NY. Certain holy days, it seems, are eligible for public funding. Where is the ACLU when we need it?

If indeed environmentalism is a substitute religion for those who have lost their faith in the God of their fathers, then recycling must stand as one of the foremost sacraments of this new religion. Every public-school child in America learns a fourth "r" in the new curriculum: readin', 'ritin', 'rithmetic, and recyclin'. They read publications with such enchanting titles as "Inside the World of Trash."

The Beltway interest group called the National Recycling Coalition received government grants of $377,692 (out of total revenue of $1.699 million) in the most recent year for which an IRS Form 990 was available (1997). The coalition provides "educational materials related to methods and standards for recycling of natural resources"[27]: in other words, recycling agitprop written on dead trees.

Anything believed in so widely, promoted so fervently, enforced so zealously, must be complete bunk. And recycling is. In perhaps the most devastating refutation of environmentalist doctrine ever published in the mainstream media, *New York Times* writer John Tierney impolitely interred this fad in a June 30, 1996 *New York Times Magazine* cover story titled, "Recycling is Garbage: Rinsing out tuna cans and tying up newspapers may make you feel virtuous, but recycling could be America's most wasteful activity."[28]

Tierney's tour de force should be required reading at every school of journalism in America. (Alas, it is not: the budding Woodwards and Bernsteins are too busy learning the iniquity of gender-specific pronouns and the capital punishments dished out to any writer who permits either style or skepticism to creep into her prose.)

Drawing on voluminous studies, Tierney states what has become obvious to all who have bothered to look beneath the clichés: that while in some instances recycling is a worthwhile activity, in the vast majority of cases "the simplest and cheapest option is usually to bury garbage in an environmentally safe landfill."[29] This should not be taken to mean that an America free of the recycling nags would be dotted with reeking landfills: as Cato Institute analyst Doug Bandow notes, "A. Clark Wiseman of Spokane's Gonzaga University figures that, at the current rate, Americans could put all of the trash generated over the next 1,000 years into a landfill 100 yards high and 35 miles square. Or dig a similar size hole and plant grass on top after it was filled."[30]

This would seem to be a simple, sightly, even green solution. It is also a far sight cheaper than the alternative: New York City's recycling program—which is mandatory; when it comes to saving the Earth, choice is not an option—costs $200 per ton more than using a landfill would cost.

But burying garbage in a landfill does not make a body feel good, in the way that sorting bottles and bundling newspapers and placing them in garish blue boxes to be picked up every Tuesday morning makes one feel good.

After all, we are a disposable society, a people who consume more than anyone else on earth and throw our trash wherever we feel like it. At least that's the story we get from our national scolds. The truth is rather more complicated. As John Tierney wrote: "Plastic packaging and fast-food containers may seem wasteful, but they actually save resources and reduce trash. The typical household in Mexico City buys fewer packaged goods than an American household, but it produces one third more garbage, chiefly because Mexicans buy fresh foods in bulk and throw away large portions that are unused, spoiled, or stale. . . . [Fruit] protected by plastic wrap and foam [is] less likely to spoil. The lightweight plastic packaging requires much less energy to manufacture and transport than traditional alternatives like cardboard or paper. Food companies have switched to plastic packaging because they make money by using resources efficiently. A typical McDonald's discards less than two ounces of garbage for each customer served—less than what's generated by a typical meal at home."[31]

Even the widespread bottle deposit laws don't work in quite the way that recyclers had imagined. Merely collecting all those empty vessels of Coke and Pepsi and Mountain Dew costs, on average, about $500 per ton. A far cheaper solution has been found in those states, such as Texas and Washington, that have resisted the bottle-deposit craze. They simply pay people to pick up roadside trash. The states spend far less money, and the workers pick up garbage that goes far beyond soft-drink containers.

There is a species of environmentalist who is forever warning us of impending shortages of resources: wood, oil, minerals, even food. For instance, a New York City-based group called the Environmental Action Coalition—and what true lover of the outdoors could possibly live in Manhattan?—promotes recycling in part because, as one spokeswoman says, "75,000 trees are cut to make the Sunday *New York Times*."[32]

Yet the twentieth century witnessed the extraordinary phenomenon of American reforestation. More of the country is covered with forest today than was the case in the nineteenth century. In Vermont, forest covers three-quarters of the state today, compared to barely one-third of the Green Mountain State a century ago. This is unprecedented in the history of the world. The supply of timber is three times greater today than eighty years ago. As Jerry Taylor, director of natural resource studies at the Cato Institute, told John Tierney, "We're not running out of wood, so why do we worry so much about recycling paper? Paper is an agricultural product, made from trees grown specifically for paper production. Acting to conserve trees by recycling paper is like acting to conserve cornstalks by cutting back on corn consumption."[33]

Bjorn Lomborg devoted an eye-opening chapter of *The Skeptical Environmentalist* to the alleged crisis of deforestation. Despite the hysteria—for instance, *Time* magazine headlined one article "Forests: The Global Chainsaw Massacre"—Lomborg found that "Globally, forest cover has remained remarkably stable over the second half of the twentieth century,"[34] and in fact actually increased slightly. As for those wicked newspapermen of the *New York Times* who are killing all those trees, Lomborg points out that "the world's demand for paper can be permanently satisfied by the wood production of just 5 percent of the current forest cover."[35]

By the way, the Environmental Action Coalition, which sends paid propagandists into the public schools to preach the virtues of recycling, is heavily subsidized by government. According to its IRS Form 990, in 1999 the EAC received $71,960 of its total revenue of $283,034 from government grants. At least those taxpayers who are also in the recycling business are getting their money's worth.

The myths surrounding landfills and "wasteful" products are legion. Some years ago, the participants in a National Audubon Society meeting were polled on a variety of topics, including landfills. They guessed that plastic diapers, scourge of the 1980s socially conscious mother, accounted for between 25 and 45 percent of the volume of the average landfill. The real number was, at most, 1.4 percent. Odds are that the Audubonites still believe that same load of crap.

The attendees at the National Audubon Society meeting also estimated that fast food packaging—those dreaded styrofoam boxes—made up 20 to 30 percent of the average landfill's volume. The actual figure is one-third of one percent.[36]

The widespread ignorance of the true state of our nation and our world is probably due more than anything else to what grant-seeking green organizations call "education" or "outreach." When an educator comes round your street to do some outreaching, the wise and wary had best lock their doors.

Like "education," the word "environment" opens many doors. For instance, as such errantly makework projects as CETA have been tossed into the dumpster of discredited bureaucracies, believers in the virtues of public employment have cast a longing eye on the environment. What better way to pad the public payroll than by putting young people to work raking leaves, picking up roadside trash, and doing other picturesque and socially worthy jobs?

The model is the Civilian Conservation Corps (CCC), one of the most fondly remembered of President Roosevelt's New Deal jobs programs. The CCC, whose formal name was the Emergency Conservation Work, was created on March 31, 1933, just ten days after FDR had proposed "to create a civilian conservation corps to be used in simple work, not interfering with normal employment, and confining itself to forestry, the prevention of soil erosion, flood control and similar projects."[37] Over the next ten years, almost three million young men between the ages of seventeen and twenty-three would toil for the CCC in camps set up around the country.

Given the roseate hue surrounding the memory of the CCC, it was only a matter of time before calls were heard suggesting its revival. An effort in the early 1980s to establish an American Conservation Corps, modeled on the CCC, came to naught, but over the last couple of decades states and localities have created their own mini-CCCs, satisfying both environmentalists and advocates of government-as-employer.

Currently, there are 110 conservation corps operating in thirty-one states and the District of Columbia. They employ about 23,000 young men and women in tasks ranging from conservation to "infrastructure improvement." The pay is generally minimum wage, and participants also receive technical and vocational training, as well as the chance to earn a GED. (Many are high-school dropouts.) The state and local corps are joined in the National Association of Service & Conservative Corps (NASCC).

Predictably, the NASCC is an active lobbying force for higher appropriations to agencies involved in land conservation, infrastructure improvement, and the like. Ominously, it has also tried to horn in on the now-fashionable "Homeland Security" programs. Perhaps corpsmen can spy on the beasts of the fields and the birds of the sky.

The NASCC, which received $587,759 from taxpayers between 1996 and 2000,[38] was also a member of the Fair Taxes for All Coalition. Among the things our modern CCC does not wish to conserve are taxpayer dollars.

It gives one pause when organizations using words such as "environment" or "farm" have addresses in Washington, D.C. I mean, the Woman's Christian Temperance Union wasn't headquartered in Las Vegas. The Moral Majority didn't convene in the Castro district of San Francisco. Mensa doesn't meet in Orlando. Yet the American Farmland Trust (AFT), whose praiseworthy goal is to preserve rural land for farming instead of losing it to development, has its offices on Washington's notorious 18th Street, where the whores wear pinstriped suits rather than spandex pants, and charge a hell of a lot more for their services.

The American Farmland Trust urges communities to employ a variety of means, particularly the purchase of land easements, to preserve farmland in areas being overrun by suburban sprawl. Sometimes the AFT acts in the best tradition of American voluntarism, as for instance when it acts as middleman in transferring farmland from one owner to another (who is pledged to keep the land in agricultural use). At other times, however, the AFT promotes "greenspace" legislation under which localities tax residents in order to buy farmland that would otherwise be sold to developers. (Complicating matters somewhat, at least from the point of view of a free-market advocate, is that these developers often benefit from an array of subsidies themselves.)

The AFT knows something about subsidies. In 1997, the AFT received $1.32 million in government grants, with a total revenue of $9.208 million; in 1998, the most recent year for which a tax form was available, the comparable figures were $2.015 million and $8.254 million.[39] With this considerable state subvention, the AFT turns around and proposes "publicly funded farmland protection"[40]—money that would in many cases be run through the AFT. Among the AFT's grants from the Environmental Protection Agency were a trio totalling $1.137 million for "strategic pest management" (EPA Grants 825618011-13)—a sorely needed task, though one imagines that the really strategic pests went uneradicated by the AFT.

While there are many aesthetic and cultural reasons for preferring farmland to strip malls, the notion that farmland is somehow vanishing from our land of amber waves of grain is misguided. The late Julian Simon wrote, "The vanishing farmland scare is a crystal-clear example of concerted false scaremongering in which the perverse roles of the federal government, environmental organizations, and the press and television are undeniable and inarguable."[41]

Simon exposed the careful construction of this scam. It began with the National Agricultural Lands Study (NALS), a federal land-use survey. In a study released in 1979, the researchers of NALS claimed that farmland was being converted to urban uses at the rate of three million acres per year, which was triple the early 1960s rate of one million acres per year.

The NALS finding was given prominent play in the press. Readers were alarmed by such headlines as "The Peril of Vanishing Farmlands," (*New York Times*), "Vanishing Farmlands: Selling Out the Soil" (*Saturday Evening Post*), and "As World Needs Food, U.S. Keeps Losing Soil to Land Developers" (*Wall Street Journal*). Environmentalist groups issued calls for stricter land use laws in order to prevent the wholesale sell-off of the American breadbasket.

There was only one problem: the story was bunk. Several scholars, Simon among them, sensed that a con was being pulled. They plowed through the same data which undergirt the NALS study and found that the much-ballyhooed tale of vanishing farmland was hooey. Even the feds finally were led to the same conclusion. In 1984, the U.S. Soil Conservation Service published a paper by Oklahoma State University professor Linda Lee that concluded that the estimate of three million acres of farmland being lost each year was too high by 50 percent—as Simon says, "a truly amazing error for something so easy to check as the urbanized acreage of the United States."[42]

Oh, and there is an addendum to the story. After NALS settled into the dustbin of history, some ex-staffers launched an organization called the American Farmland Trust.

The Conservation Fund, based in largely un-conserved Arlington, Virginia, received a whopping $27.246 million in government grants out of total 1999 revenues of $68.331 million.[43] The Fund's worthy goal is to "protect America's legacy of land and water resources" through "land acquisition, community initiatives, and leadership training."[44] From Florida's Everglades to Nevada's Great Basin National Park, the Conservation Fund works with citizens, non-profit groups, and government agencies to set aside "open space, wildlife habitat, recreation areas, critical watersheds, historic sites, and working landscapes"[45] at the rate of about one million acres per year.

The Conservation Fund has been adept at securing the support of such "Corporate Partners" as Eastman Kodak, Firestone, and Kennecott Company. Yet it has been no less sedulous in courting "Public Partners," which is a pretty euphemism for taxpayers. The Fund works closely with the U.S. Fish and Wildlife Service and the National Park Service—which might explain why the Fund has been an energetic advocate of greater funding and power for those agencies.

In a world that made sense, those who worked for environmental organizations might have, in their private lives, at least a tenuous connection to the outdoors. They needn't be Jeremiah Johnsons, but they shouldn't all be lawyers and lobbyists who go to work in high-rise office buildings. The fact that they are, for the most part, exactly that should lead us to question the utopias they are busily devising for the rest of us. If hell, as the old joke goes, is a place where the English are in charge of cooking and the French create the pop music, then surely it is also where Washington, D.C. environmental lawyers get to design the landscape.

Those in need of a moment of levity are advised to check out the website of the Environmental Law Institute (www.eli.org). The photos of the members of the board of directors are well worth the price of admission. The 34 visages staring out from the computer monitor represent, in the aggregate, the most pasty-faced, unhealthy, ungreenish image one can find this side of an MIT math lab. Their affiliations and residences say it all: instead of "Cowboy, Oracle, Arizona," or "River Guide, Moab, Utah," we find employees of IBM, AT&T, Merck & Co., Maryland Department of the Environment, Texaco, and enough name-clotted law firms to fill the back covers of 100 phone books. These fearless guardians of rivers and meadows and glens live in New York City, Washington, and the concrete suburbs surrounding those great citadels of pure air.

And what does the ELI do? Why, it "has played a pivotal role in shaping the fields of environmental law, policy, and management, domestically and abroad"[46] for almost forty years. ELI analysts work with governments at various levels to draw up environmental laws, ELI sponsors legal education workshops, and the institute acts as a clearinghouse for information desired by "working environmentalists"[47]—by which ELI means severe men and women wearing suits and living in big cities, not working people who actually live on the land which the ELI reveres in the abstract.

Smaller, more radical green groups view ELI as a corporate front group—and they are right. The institute's corporate donors include Alcoa, AT&T, Ford, GM, Lockheed, Martin Marietta, Chevron, Texaco, Pfizer, DuPont, Intel, Coca-Cola—the list is long and lucrative. Yet the ELI is even more dependent upon government for funding. In 1999, government grants accounted for $2.120 million of ELI's $5.538 million in total revenues, or 38 percent.[48]

Empowered, to use a favorite word of ELI, by massive infusions of government and corporate cash, the institute favors the kind of rule-laden, top-down regulatory state that has usually been the dream when big business and big government come together. It calls for being "proactive in protecting the environment and public health."[49] Near the top of ELI's domestic agenda is opposition to sprawl. Now, sprawl is largely the creation of government and one of its most hallowed activities, the taxpayer-subsidized building of roads and highways. But of course the withdrawal of the very government that created the problem is seldom the policy answer of anti-sprawl advocates. Instead, ELI calls for stricter land-use laws. It also boasts of working with numerous state and local authorities to encourage "sustainable infrastructure," "biodiversity," and other buzzwords that will have readers scratching their heads twenty-five years hence. These may well be worthy goals, and ELI seems not to have the sort of knee-jerk hostility to market-oriented solutions that one finds in many environmentalist groups, but the question remains: why should taxpayers subsidize an institute (an institute that is quite capable of raising large sums of money on its own) whose purpose is to "shape" the law as its sees fit? Ought not such a task be pursued with private money?

* * *

Nothing vexes the establishment environmentalist quite as much as fossil fuel consumption. Coal, oil, natural gas: we greedy gluttonous Americans use too much of these, and besides, we're running out!

We've always been running out, and we haven't run out yet. As far back as 1914 Americans were told by the bureaucrats of the U.S. Bureau of Mines that the world had only a decade's worth of oil remaining. The Bureau's warning was updated periodically by other Chicken Littles, both public and private, so that Professor Frank Notestein of Princeton would crack, "We've been running out of oil ever since I've been a boy."[50]

In fact, we have not run out of oil, or coal, or natural gas, and probably never will. Reserves of these three resources have increased, not decreased, over the last several decades. For instance, in 1978 we were warned that the proven oil reserves of 648 billion barrels constituted a 29.2 year supply; by 2007, we could be out of oil. Unless we were vrooming around in those electric cars which, as the folklore of the day had it, the automobile companies were keeping hid from us, America faced the end of its car-based culture.

A funny thing happened: despite the continuing extraction and burning of those reserves, the supply of oil actually increased. At this writing, the proven reserves of oil are enough to last us forty-some years. Would anyone care to bet that in 2045 the world will not be on the verge of running out of oil?

There are vast untapped sources of oil, coal, and natural gas, which will be tapped, once demand is sufficient to encourage companies to extract the resources. So vast are these reserves that France Cairncross of the British journal, the *Economist*, has estimated that total reserves of fossil fuel—those already discovered and those waiting to be discovered—"could last 650 years at current rates of consumption."[51] Moreover, steady advances in technology have consistently driven the cost of production down, and we can expect this to continue. Finally, human beings are adaptable: if one resource becomes expensive or scare, we substitute another. At various times, people have opted for coal instead of wood, or oil rather than coal. We may expect fusion energy to eventually eclipse current energy sources, and Bjorn Lomborg speculates that solar energy "probably will be available at competitive prices within 50 years."[52]

Solar advocates don't want to wait that long. Organizations like the Renewable Energy Policy Project (REPP), which is funded in part by the U.S. Department of Energy and the EPA, push solar, wind, biomass, and other "alternative" energies with an almost religious fervor. Bowing to its audience on the left, the REPP assures the labor union movement that it "appreciates the goals of labor organizations," which, unfortunately for REPP, include protecting the jobs of their members who are engaged in energy-related work. Although REPP bravely suggests that wind, biomass, and solar power will fund plenty of "family-wage jobs"[53] in the twenty-first century, the unions are, as yet, not biting.

And for energy sources that are said to be as natural as the sun that shines above us, solar and the others sure need a lot of artificial, man-made boosts. The Center for Renewable Energy and Sustainable Technology, which promotes solar and other alternative energies from its base on sunless 18th Street in Washington, gets about half its annual revenues ($434,821 out of $801,553 in 1998; $155,391 out of $320,484 in 1999)[54] from the government.

Could any organization be less green than one founded by powerful members of the U.S. Senate and studded with names that virtually scream "Establishment"?

Certainly it would be hard to find a duller lobby than the Alliance to Save Energy, headquartered on 18th Street NW in Washington,

D.C. The Alliance was founded in 1977 by Senators Hubert Humphrey (D-MN) and Charles Percy (R-IL) at the height of the energy "crisis." The board of directors has included such outdoorsmen as Henry Kissinger, Senator John Heinz, and what the Alliance boastfully terms a "Who's Who of leaders in the public and private sectors in a unified effort to promote a national commitment to energy efficiency."[55]

The language should give one pause. Unified. National commitment. This sounds very much like what Jimmy Carter, borrowing from William James, called the "moral equivalent of war." And war always vastly expands the size of the federal government.

The Alliance for Energy was born in the citadels of power and has been funded therefrom. In 1998, government grants accounted for well over half (57 percent: $2.443 million out of $4.281 million) of its total revenue. In 1999, government monies made up 60 percent—$2.759 million out of $4.604 million[56]—of the Alliance's revenues. Its activities include "education" and "advocacy,"[57] and the advocacy takes predictable form: in favor of more funding for weatherization programs, tougher regulatory standards for air conditioners and heat pumps, and a higher budget for the U.S. Department of Energy. Like its founders, it has not been content to remake America: the world must be reformed. The Alliance for Energy has received funding from the U.S. Agency for International Development to bring the blessings of energy efficiency to six cities in the Ukraine. (U.S. AID and the Department of Energy are the greatest single financial supporters of the Alliance to Save Energy.) It has received numerous grants from the EPA for everything from "educational outreach"[58] (which in less euphemistic circles is known as propaganda) to "investigation[s] into public attitudes,"[59] or public-opinion polling.

The Alliance is one of the most egregious of taxpayer-funded advocacy groups: it was founded by senators to lobby the Senate to spend more money. And the damndest thing is: it works.

* * *

The late Julian Simon, who did so much to expose the specious reasoning and imaginative statistics of the Chicken Littles of our age, left us with a simple and wonderfully sanguine forecast: Things are getting better, and will continue to get better, even though the pessimists will insist otherwise. In his posthumously published book,

Hoodwinking the Nation (1999), Simon closed with three reasons why we should believe him rather than the Paul Ehrlichs, who, like the poor, will always be with us. Simon's reasons why we should believe him were:

- This "side" has been right across the board in the forecasts we have made in the past few decades, whereas the doomsayers have been wrong across the board.

- Throughout the long sweep of history, forecasts of resource scarcity have always been heard, and—just as now—the doomsayers have always claimed that the past was no guide to the future because they stood at a turning point in history. But the turning point forecasts have been wrong; there have been ups and downs, but no permanent reversals. In every period those who would have bet on improvement rather than deterioration in fundamental aspects of material life—such as the availability of natural resources—would usually have been right.

- I'll bet my reputation and my money on these forecasts (if I win, the money goes to pay for research), whereas the doomsayers back off from putting their money where their mouths are; they refuse to put either their cash or their names on the line to back what they say. Indeed, the most famous of the doomsayers was burned badly when in 1980 his group actually did wager on some of his forecasts.[60]

Allow me to add one addendum to Simon's always-prescient forecasts: governments will remain a highly prized resource among the Beltway environmentalists, who will stop at nothing to perfect new technologies of taxpayer-dollar extraction. In this, at least, let us hope devoutly for scarcity.

Notes

1. Robert Lerner and Althea Nagai, "Explorations in Nonprofits: Environmentalists Gain Ground; Education and Human Service Nonprofits Remain Dominant in '90s," *Foundation Watch* (Washington, DC: Capital Research Center, July 2002), p. 1.
2. Wilfred Beckerman, *Through Green-Colored Glasses: Environmentalism Reconsidered* (Washington, DC: Cato Institute, 1996), p. x.
3. Joseph L. Bast, Peter J. Hill, and Richard C. Rue, editors, *Eco-Sanity: A Common-Sense Guide to Environmentalism* (Lanham, MD: Madison Books, 1994), p. 203.
4. Paul Georgia, "The Environmental Movement in 2002: Post Clinton, Post September 11," *Organization Trends* (Washington, DC: Capital Research Center, July 2002), p. 2.
5. Ibid., p. 3.
6. Bennett and DiLorenzo, *Destroying Democracy*, p. 146.
7. Samples, Yablonski, and Osorio, "More Government for All," p. 6.
8. "A Proud History of Accomplishment," undated Sierra Club brochure.

9. "Take Action Main," whistler.sierraclub.org/action/?alid=24, December 20, 2001.
10. "Subject: Support Affordable Access to Family Planning," whistler.sierraclub.org/action/?alid=27, December 20, 2001.
11. Bjorn Lomborg, *The Skeptical Environmentalist* (Cambridge: Cambridge University Press, 2001), epigraph.
12. Ben Wattenberg, "Foreword," in Julian Simon, *Hoodwinking the Nation* (New Brunswick, NJ: Transaction Publishers, 2000), p. vii.
13. Simon, *Hoodwinking the Nation*, p. 8.
14. Lomborg, *The Skeptical Environmentalist*, p. 137.
15. Quoted in Peter Huber, *Hard Green: Saving the Environment from the Environmentalists* (New York: Perseus, 1999), p. 3.
16. Lomborg, *The Skeptical Environmentalist*, p. xix.
17. Ibid., p. 4.
18. "Wildlife Activists," www.worldwildlife.org/defau...id=71, June 23, 2001.
19. IRS Form 990, World Wildlife Fund, Inc., 1997, 1998.
20. "2000 Annual Report: Financial Overview," www.worldwildlife.org/defau...d=152, June 23, 2001.
21. "What is the Conservation Action Network?" http://takeaction.worldwildlife.org/about.html, June 23, 2001.
22. "News from Past 180 Days," www.worldwildlife.org/news/newsroom, June 23, 2001.
23. Bill Kauffman, "April's Forgotten Day," *American Enterprise* (April/May 2000), p. 51.
24. Michael P. Cohen, *The History of the Sierra Club, 1892-1970* (San Francisco, CA: Sierra Club Books, 1988), p. 442.
25. "The Activist's Checklist," in *Ecotactics: The Sierra Club Handbook for Environment Activists* (New York: Pocket, 1970), pp. 255-56.
26. David Helvarg, *The War Against the Greens* (San Francisco, CA: Sierra Club Books, 1997), p. 393.
27. IRS Form 990, National Recycling Coalition, Inc., 1997.
28. John Tierney, "Recycling is Garbage," *New York Times Magazine*, June 30, 1996, pp. 24–29, 44, 48, 51, 53.
29. Ibid.
30. Doug Bandow, "Our Widespread Faith in Recycling is Misplaced," Cato Institute release, August 27, 1997.
31. Tierney, "Recycling is Garbage," *New York Times Magazine*.
32. Ibid.
33. Ibid.
34. Lomborg, *The Skeptical Environmentalist*, p. 111.
35. Ibid., p. 117.
36. Simon, *Hoodwinking the Nation*, pp. 9-10.
37. Rick Praeger, "Youth Employment: A Summary History of Major Federal Programs, 1933-1976," Congressional Research Service, March 30, 1977, p. 3.
38. Samples, Yablonski, and Osorio, "More Government for All," p. 5.
39. IRS Form 990, American Farmland Trust, 1997, 1998.
40. "What's Hot at Farmland.Org," www.farmland.org, June 21, 2001.
41. Simon, *Hoodwinking the Nation*, p. 17.
42. Ibid., p. 24.
43. IRS Form 990, The Conservation Fund, 1999.
44. "Mission," www.conservationfund.org/conservation/introduction.html, April 24,

2001.
45. "Year in Review 1999," www.conservationfund.org/ conservation/annualrep/99review.html, April 24, 2001.
46. "Welcome to the new www.eli.org," April 24, 2001.
47. "President & Chairman's Statement," www.eli.org/about/ preschair.html, April 24, 2001.
48. IRS Form 990, Environmental Law Institute, 1999.
49. *1999 Environmental Law Institute Annual Report*, p. 6.
50. Lomborg, *The Skeptical Environmentalist*, p. 122.
51. Bast, Hill, and Rue, editors, *Eco-Sanity*, p. 29.
52. Lomborg, *The Skeptical Environmentalist*, p. 136.
53. "Labor and Renewables," www.repp.org/initiatives.html, February 25, 2001.
54. IRS Form 990, Center for Renewable Energy and Sustainable Technology, 1998, 1999.
55. "About the Alliance to Save Energy," www.ase.org/about/ about.html, February 25, 2001.
56. IRS Form 990, The Alliance to Save Energy, 1998, 1999.
57. "About the Alliance to Save Energy."
58. EPA Grant 825077011, awarded 9/11/97.
59. EPA Grant 824373012, awarded 9/5/97.
60. Simon, *Hoodwinking the Nation*, pp. 123-24.

5

Heart, Lungs, and the Big C: The Big Three Take Aim at Your Wallets and Your Liberty

Shakespeare got it wrong. The American Lung Association, by any other name, would not be a respected Gargantua of advocacy-group lobbying but rather just another tax-seeking gang of Washington-based busybodies who take your money with one hand and with the other write legislation under which your individual liberties go up—how else?—in smoke.

The same is true for the American Heart Association (AHA) and the American Cancer Society (ACS), which along with the ALA constitute the Big Three of health charities, as well as the whole range of American [Fill in Illness or Internal Organ] Associations that exploit the fear of sickness and death to raise money and shake down taxpayers.

Mary Lasker, a major figure in the exponential growth of the ACS in the post-World War II era, gave a revealing account of a Damascene fund-raising epiphany:

"When I asked my husband for [a personal donation] for the American Cancer Society to do research, he said, 'No, I'm not going to give you any money'—although he did. But he said, 'The place to get the money is the federal government.' And I said, 'I don't know anything about the government.' And he said, 'There are unlimited funds. I'll show you how to get them.'"[1]

Inspiring, eh? In any event, Mr. Lasker taught his wife well. From humble beginnings, the ACS eats up close to the better part of a million tax dollars annually.

Health charities need to be nimble. Sometimes life throws them a curve. For instance, when polio was cured, the March of Dimes, which had been established as the National Foundation for Infantile

Paralysis by President Franklin D. Roosevelt himself, was left without a raison d'être. It eventually hit upon birth defects, but it still looks back fondly upon its heyday in the 1940s and 1950s.

The American Lung Association has undergone four name changes, gradually dropping the word "tuberculosis" from its banner as that disease has been vanquished. (Though it seems to be making something of comeback in the new millennium.)

In recent years the ALA has emphasized, at least for public consumption, its efforts to assist those with asthma, particularly children. A grant of $204,730 in 2001–2002 from the Centers for Disease Control, to be used toward "school and community-based asthma education and management programs,"[2] is one fruit of this campaign.

The organizations sometimes display a competitiveness that borders on the ghoulish. For instance, the American Lung Association advertises that while lung disease is only "the third highest cause of death in the United States," it is "rising faster than the death rate from any other cause."[3] The Emphysema Foundation for our Right to Survive (EFFORTS) asserts that chronic obstructive pulmonary disease (COPD) is "the leading cause of death in the United States."[4] Casting a wary eye on a sympathetic and rapidly growing charitable cause, the ALA of Pennsylvania tactfully points out that "more U.S. women died of lung cancer than breast cancer."[5] Not to be outdone, the American Heart Association asserts that "Diseases of the heart are the No. 1 killer in America, and stroke is the No. 3 killer."[6] (Take that, American Lung Association!)

Astronomical costs are tacked onto each of the diseases. The ALA of Virginia claims that the "economic cost" of lung disease is $4 billion annually in the Old Dominion alone.[7] EFFORTS pegs the cost of COPD at $30.4 billion annually,[8] not to mention the hopeless confusion people feel when snowed under by an avalanche of acronyms. But acronym-dizziness is the least of our problems: the Big Three are deft as Parisian pickpockets when it comes to getting into the taxpayers' purse.

* * *

The American Lung Association's IRS Form 990s disclose government grants of $688,000 in 1998 (of a total revenue of $40.876 million) and $767,000 in 1997 (of a total revenue of $33.492 million).

The ALA's national office and its seventy-eight affiliates, known in aggregate as the National Lung Association, received $11.119 million in government grants during 2000, the last year for which figures were available. This constituted about 6.6 percent of the National Lung Association's combined total revenue of $167.897 million. One interesting footnote to this health group's financial statement is that it spent a whopping $22.558 million in fundraising.[9]

"When you can't breathe, nothing else matters," says the American Lung Association's trademarked catch phrase. Tough to argue with that. In providing services and education to asthmatic children and sufferers from chronic lung diseases, the ALA and its local affiliates do meritorious work.

Just how effective this work is remains open to question. The ALA has never been reluctant to blow its own horn. In 1919, in the ALA's previous incarnation as the National Society for the Study and Prevention of Tuberculosis, the NSSPT boasted that its efforts had led to "a drop in the country's tuberculosis mortality rate of 33 percent." Impressive, eh? The problem, as one historian has noted, is that "as every epidemiologist knows, the tuberculosis death rate had been declining for years before the establishment of the [NSSPT]."[10] So tangential were the NSSPT and ALA in the heroic conquering of TB that Frank Ryan's exhaustive history, *The Forgotten Plague: How the Battle Against Tuberculosis Was Won*, contains just a single mention of the ALA, and that is in reference to its lobbying activities in the 1980s.[11]

Although the American Lung Association's ancestry dates to 1904, it is as fad-conscious as the most nitwitted teenager at the mall. Of late, "diversity" has filled the ALA air. The entire annual report of 2000 was dedicated to its affirmative action of the lungs. With the sort of patronization of which only the most clueless upper-middle-class white liberal bureaucrats are capable, the ALA brags that its "staff has become much more diverse in the past two years."[12] In other words, this bastion of Caucasian do-goodism went out and hired it some black folk. Well, praise de Lawd. The grinning faces of the ALA's top officers are as pale as ever, but we may be assured that black faces now occupy the usual token slots in Human Resources.

We are told that asthma attacks blacks with greater ferocity than whites—or, rather, we learn that black Americans are hospitalized for asthma with more frequency than are whites, which may have a cultural instead of racial explanation. The ALA has teamed up with Head Start—once held up as the shining jewel of the Great Society, the one anti-poverty government program that unmistakably worked, but now conceded even by its erstwhile champions to be basically a wash—to produce a multicultural farrago called "Sesame Street A is for Asthma." Touching every base possible, this bilingual asthma awareness project borrows from public television, the federal government, and the daycare industry to teach a "culturally diverse population"[13] about asthma. (Middle-class white kids: you're on your own.)

The diversity beat goes on: Asians and Pacific Islanders are at greater risk for tuberculosis. Childhood asthma occurs more frequently in Puerto Ricans than in non-Hispanic whites. And always, the cure is a government grant. In Seattle, for instance, the ALA used an Environmental Justice grant from the EPA to pay childcare expenses so that poor people could take classes to "learn about indoor pollutants such as lead, biologicals, and pesticides."[14] Ethiopian immigrants learned about dust mites and efficient vacuum cleaners from speakers of the Oromo and Amharic languages.

While all good liberals profess their undying support for a separation of church and state, the ALA is ominously advancing an alliance of church and state-supported Big Charity. The organization is "developing partnerships with African-American churches to bring tobacco control programs to their congregations."[15]

In a campaign that is equal parts offensive and risible, the ALA reached out to "minority populations" with an educational video titled "Controlling Cockroaches in Your Home."[16] The video and an accompanying brochure were subsidized by the Environmental Protection Agency, i.e., your tax dollars.

Almost as ridiculous are the occasional ALA-sponsored public opinion polls, which display all the subtlety of an Internet fan poll asking if Anna Kournikova is hot. For example, in December 2000, when the ALA was lobbying Washington to clamp strict regulations on diesel trucks and buses, the organization released the results of a rigged poll in which an astounding 87 percent of those queried expressed a desire for "cleaner diesel fuel."[17] What is astounding is that 13 percent did not take the carrot, did not salivate when the bell rang, did not jump through the hoop for the cynics who devised such an obviously loaded question.

The American Lung Association also claims to "fight for environmental justice."[18] This would seem to be a rather different face than that which it presents to the public at fund-raising time, but to say that such organizations are two-faced would be taken by them as a compliment. Just what "environmental justice" means is a mystery. If it means standing with residents of a neighborhood that is threatened with destruction by an expensive, exhaust-reeking highway project built with the tyrannical assistance of eminent domain, then what a wonderful thing it is. But do we really need to say that that is emphatically not what the ALA means by environmental justice?

No, the defenders of American lungs spend their money—two-thirds of a million dollars of which comes from the public treasury—promoting stricter emissions standards for automobiles, lobbying for greater federal expenditures on Clean Air Act programs, and sucking up to Power, for instance presenting Clinton administration EPA Administrator Carol Browner with the "prestigious ALA President's Award."[19] To the ALA, "environmental justice" does not involve standing up for ordinary people and small neighborhoods; it is simply throwing in with the establishment East Coast liberals and their favorite causes.

No cause is more sacred than the holy crusade against tobacco. This is the crossroads at which the health lobbies meet: to score cheap points, to agitate for more Big Brother controls, and, most importantly, to pick the pockets of the demonized tobacco industry.

The ALA supports any and every piece of legislation, here and abroad, to regulate, harass, and, eventually ban the wicked weed. The list of measures pushed by the government-funded ALA is long enough to tax the patience of an Evelyn Wood speed-reading graduate: it favors "stronger, bolder tobacco package warning labels" (the skull and crossbones, one assumes); a ban on such "alternative" cigarettes as R.J. Reynolds' "Eclipse"; greater authority for the Food and Drug Administration to regulate tobacco products; and a "global ban on the advertising and promotion of tobacco products."

The contempt with the which the ALA views such anachronistic concepts as personal freedom and economic liberty may be gleaned from its effort to "exclude the tobacco industry from the negotiations"[20] over a global ban on tobacco advertising. This is, remember, a legal industry, yet the ALA desires it to be punished out of existence—and to not even have the right to state its case before its persecutors.

Like the rest of the Big Health-Industrial complex, the ALA was a clamant voice for squeezing every last dollar out of the tobacco industry in the various state and federal "tobacco settlements" of the late 1990s. Four states reached individual settlements with the industry, and the other forty-six states and their attorneys general squeezed "Big Tobacco" for $206 billion in payments through 2025. This money was ostensibly to be used to allay the health costs of treating those with tobacco-related illnesses, and if you believe that a Mr. Clinton would like to take your teenaged daughter to the Georgetown Hilton for a tour of hotel wall-art.

The ALA took a particular interest in the ultimate destination of the tobacco windfall. Its position may be summed up as "in our coffers." When cities or states debated or opted to use this manna from judicial heaven for purposes other than health-related—for a library in San Diego, education in Ohio, a football dome in South Dakota—the ALA screamed in outrage at the top of its. . . .well, you know.

With a $30,000 grant from the federal Centers for Disease Control, the ALA sponsored a May 1993 conference boldly called "Seize the Initiative: A National Training Conference for Increasing Tobacco Excise Taxes Through Initiated Acts." Now, "initiated acts" has a rather suggestive air about it, but there was nothing alluring about this conference: its goal was to teach busybodies from across America how to frame, finance, and promote voter initiatives to pick your pocket and the deep pockets of the tobacco industry, with the pelf being funneled to worthy organizations such as, say, let's take for example . . . the American Lung Association.

As my colleague Thomas J. DiLorenzo points out, this conference was just "one of several recent ALA seminars designed to train anti-smoking activists in how to lobby for higher tobacco taxes."[21] The ALA is a constant presence in statehouses across the land, as it lobbies for higher excise taxes on cigarettes and tobacco products, with the tax revenues designated for the ALA and similar groups. When states refuse to jack up excise taxes, it is merely evidence that "Big Tobacco continues to wield undue influence in statehouses around the country,"[22] according to ALA CEO John R. Garrison.

Given that each and every item on the ALA legislative agenda serves or would serve to enhance the power of the state, is it any wonder that the state is so generous in endowing the ALA? The association is a loud voice in favor of increased funding for the National Institutes of Health and supports sharp increases for the research, control, and just plain featherbedding in the fights against asthma and tuberculosis. He who takes the king's shilling may become the king's man, but it works in reverse, too. He who positions himself as the king's man has all that greater a claim to the king's shilling. And few organizations are better at shilling for the king and taking the king's shilling than the American Lung Association.

The list of Environmental Protection Agency grants to the American Lung Association and its affiliates—obtained by a Freedom of Information Act request—is longer than a White House Christmas card list. As of October 2001, the EPA's catalogue of recent and active grants included a whopping eighty to the various ALA affiliates around the country. There's hardly a section of the country that hasn't been visited with an EPA/ALA collaboration: Tallahassee, New York, Monterey, Los Angeles, San Diego, St. Louis, Denver, Chicago, Phoenix, Bismarck, Seattle, and even the presumably smoke-free oasis of Salt Lake City.

The names of some of these programs give a flavor of just what the federal bureaucracy is up to in these days after the unlamented President Clinton declared the era of big government to be over. Don't bother looking for constitutional authorization for any of these expenditures in your pocket copy of the U.S. Constitution: you're as like to run into the Reverend Al Sharpton at a Police Benevolent Association meeting. The ALA is being paid by taxpayers through the EPA to run such programs and administer such grants as: State Indoor Radon Grant Program Support; Brownfield Pilots Cooperative Agreements; Shallow Injection Well Initiatives; Environmental Equity Program; Tribal Lead Grants; Senior Environmental Employment Program; Underground Storage Tanks State Program Support; Assistance for Promoting Protection of Children from Environmental Threats; and the Regional Multi-Media Initiatives Program, among many others.

As the eyes glaze at page after page of grants, one starts to wonder if the American Lung Association is a charity or an office of the Environmental Protection Agency.

The relationship is mutually beneficial. For instance, the ALA urges the EPA to establish tougher guidelines for particle soot emissions. This would require the hiring of additional EPA inspectors and analysts and enhance the agency's power. Meanwhile, the EPA is feeding the ALA on a steady diet of grants. Now, this exchange of advocacy for dollars may not be quid pro quo—but to those whose brains are not numbed by wide-eyed civics book lessons, it looks an awful lot like a profitable case of mutual back scratching.

(Just so that the grant-givers of the EPA don't miss the point, the American Lung Association's June 2001 comments on the Environmental Protection Agency's particulate matter standards contain such apple-polishing lines as "The American Lung Association would like to commend EPA staff for its thorough and comprehensive review. . .," "ALA supports the approach EPA has taken . . .," "EPA has done an excellent job . . .," and "the authors of the documents have done a good job. . . ."[23] That smacking sound you hear is a small price to pay for close to a million a year in government alms.)

Does this all seems a mite cynical? After all, doesn't the ALA run the annual Christmas Seals campaign? Any wagers on how long it takes before the diversity-mad ALA quietly drops the now-offensive word "Christmas" and starts peddling "Holiday Seals"?

Don't laugh: it's happening already. Christmas Seals have been a nifty fund-raiser for the ALA, which took over the annual program in 1920. The first Christmas Seals had sold for a penny in 1907; they were a superb example of volunteerism in action, as the proceeds from their sale were used to keep open a tuberculosis sanitarium in Delaware. Before long, they became big business: in recent years, the ALA has mailed the seals to 30 million households every Christmas season. Since most Americans feel guilty at getting something for nothing, the gimmick works, and has been borrowed by dubious associations of police officers and supposedly paralyzed veterans.

The ALA has occasionally taken heat for the Christmas Seals campaign. In 1988, it put out a press release claiming, "Lung Disease Research Spurred by Christmas Seals,"[24] although just two cents of every dollar went to that worthy end. But what kind of hard-hearted Scrooge dares utter a word against Christmas Seals?

"Christmas," however, no longer cuts it in multicultural America. The ALA has introduced "Holiday Seals" as a complement to the Christmas Seals. These holiday seals celebrate Chanukkah and the bogus African-American "celebration" of Kwanzaa, the media-hyped creation of a Temple University professor in the late 1960s. Not one in a thousand black Americans observes Kwanzaa, but no matter: the ALA presses seals in its honor. If so many Americans didn't have a religious or sentimental attachment to Christmas, you can bet that the ALA would dump the C-word faster than you can say "stricter EPA regulations."

When cold hard cash is involved, the ALA drops the warm and fuzzy Christmas Seals image and plays hardball with the best of them.

Take the organization's shameful role in the campaign against cement-producing kilns. The way in which the ALA allowed itself to be used by one segment of the waste-burning industry against another provides a stark example of what happens when Big Charities, Big Business, and Big Money collide.

First, a bit of background. American industry produces about 250 million tons of hazardous waste each year in making paints, solvents, plastics, pesticides, and other products. Before the enactment of the Resource Conservation and Recovery Act (RCRA) in 1976, much of this waste was buried or dumped into waterways. The RCRA made such dumping illegal; it also required companies to treat many forms of waste before disposal. Eventually, EPA regulations mandated that many hazardous wastes be incinerated, for high-temperature incineration (above 2000 degrees Fahrenheit) destroys the hazardous properties of these wastes, reducing them to harmless ash and gases.

Private firms rushed to meet the new demand for commercial hazardous waste incinerators (HWIs). These HWIs dominated the market, at first, until the high prices they charged led some hazardous waste producers to build their own on-site noncommercial incinerators and to take steps to reduce the volume of waste produced. At the same time, a second noncommercial competitor emerged, as the cement industry began to burn hazardous wastes in its kilns.

Cement kilns had a number of advantages over the commercial HWIs. For one thing, temperatures within reach 3500 degrees Fahrenheit, far above the mandated minimum. Moreover, paints, solvents, and rubber products such as discarded tires produce amounts of energy equivalent to conventional fuels, and actually reduce cement producers' fuel costs. Burning hazardous wastes for fuel conserves nonrenewable energy sources. HWIs, by contrast, produce no salable product.

By June 1994, fourteen companies operated twenty-one HWIs, while twelve cement companies burned waste in forty-three kilns. Dozens of other "captive" incinerators had been opened by companies producing wastes. The incineration industry was experiencing excess capacity. The cement industry, using its cost advantages, captured more than two-thirds of the market for thermal treatment of hazardous wastes. The commercial HWI industry was reeling. HWIs simply could not compete with the far more efficient cement kilns. As one newspaper noted, "What really has incinerator owners hot is that cement kilns charge less to burn toxic waste. Incinerators charge an average of $284 a ton to burn liquid waste. Cement kilns charge about $100 a ton."[25]

Clearly, something must be done. So in the time-dishonored tradition of favor-seeking industries everywhere, the HWIs turned to those last refuges of scoundrels: lobbying and public relations.

On December 3, 1993, six large HWI firms announced the formation of something called the Association for Responsible Thermal Treatment (ARTT). Art may be in the eye of the beholder, but ARTT was in the pocket of the HWI industry. The press release heralding its arrival bemoaned the way in which RCRA had been interpreted to "permit the burning of hazardous waste in cement kilns."[26] Ominously, the volume of hazardous waste burned in these kilns was growing by 50 percent annually. Unless something was done—and unless that something was backed by the iron fist of the state—the HWIs were headed for obsolescence.

ARTT was nothing if not artful in the way it played the Washington game. It placed two washed-up Democratic politicians at its head: former New Jersey Governor and Congressman James J. Florio, who had chaired the House Commerce Committee's Consumer Subcommittee, and Dennis Eckart, a blow-dried nonentity who had represented an Ohio district in Congress.

With Florio and Eckart as hireling lobbyists, the ARTT opened another front in its campaign. It was obvious even to the most clueless dolt that an ARTT attack on cement kilns was a self-serving promotion of its own economic interests. What was needed was a respected organization, above reproach but greedy for money, that could give the ARTT campaign an air of legitimacy. Enter the American Lung Association.

In 1994, ARTT gave the ALA a grant of $150,000. In return, the ALA opened an offensive against cement kilns in Michigan, Florida, Ohio, and Texas. These attacks were noteworthy for their underhandedness: for instance, the ALA-Texas, which received $14,000 of the ARTT grant, screened a video for members of the press in which sick and deformed cows, calves, and horses were linked to Texas Industries' cement plants in Midlothian, Texas. The evidence was so farfetched that even the press, for once, cast a skeptical eye on the claims.

Alas for the ALA, there was no plausible connection between cement kilns and run-of-the-mill health hazards, much less bovine deformation. Had the ALA cared to investigate the matter responsibly, it would have reviewed the health records of kiln managers and employers. But it would have found nothing amiss. Labor unions have uttered not a peep about working conditions in kilns. The ALA might also have tried to find pending lawsuits claiming injury from kiln pollution. It would have looked in vain. Even the Clinton-era EPA, in its multi-volume Report to Congress on Cement Kiln Dust, concluded that neither the kilns nor the products they produce pose any significant hazard to humans or the environment.

By contrast, the commercial HWI industry has been plagued by environmental-related problems. WMX Technologies, a commercial incinerator, paid $3.1 million in fines after "an explosion, a runaway chemical reaction and other alleged violations"[27] at its Sauget, Illinois facility. It also paid penalties of $3.75 million, $2.5 million, and $3.0 million for violations at its Chicago incinerator. The ALA was conspicuously quiet about these violations. But then, no cash was changing hands.

The HWI vs. cement kiln imbroglio was nicely summed up by A. James Barnes, a former EPA official and Dean of the School of Public and Environmental Affairs at Indiana University, who complained that "operators of the nation's largest hazardous-waste incinerators have begun an intensive public relations and lobbying campaign to attack rival businesses." This was "intrabusiness warfare"[28] from which the federal government should refrain from taking sides.

The question we are left with, however, is this: why did the American Lung Association take sides? And why wasn't its reputation tarnished as darkly as a smoker's lung?[29]

One final glimpse of the American Lung Association in the full flower of its taxpayer-funded hypocrisy. Its annual fund-raising appeals tug at the heartstrings and draw upon the finest tradition of charitable giving: that of one-to-one assistance, as a benefactor aids someone in need. Fund-raising letters of the last several years have contained the following promises and asked the following questions:

- Would you spend a few dollars to help a small child overcome the effects of chronic asthma?

- By remembering the lung association in your Will, you can help us provide . . . patient care.

- If you could help save someone who was dying—would you? We're asking you to do just that.

- Your last gift to Christmas Seals helped little Amy. She's now six, and can control her tragic asthma. Thanks to your gift, Amy is able to run and play like other little girls.[30]

This last-named is an especially moving testimonial. Breathes there a soul in the land who would not send in a few bucks to help little Amy? The ALA forgets to mention just one little thing: its annual reports reveal that the national headquarters and all of the ALA's affiliates spend less than one percent—less than one percent—on "assistance to individual patients."[31] Sometimes fiction is so much to be preferred to the truth.

* * *

To the amusement of those who enjoy a good bureaucratic tussle, the Big Three (American Lung Association, American Heart Association, American Cancer Society) are fighting over possession of the valuable tobacco issue like teenaged boys clawing at a *Playboy* centerfold. Tobacco is hot, tobacco is sexy, tobacco brings in big bucks and fawning media attention. When tuberculosis resurged in the 1990s, the American Lung Association, which until 1973 was known as the National Tuberculosis and Respiratory Disease Association, barely noticed. Tuberculosis had lost its cachet; those fighting the disease hadn't the hip credentials of anti-cigarette crusaders, who are lionized on *Sixty Minutes* and impersonated by Russell Crowe in the movies. Who in hell wants to deal with a roomful of poor people hacking their lives away with tubercular coughs when there's money to be made and glory to be gained in publicizing the health risks of smoking—health risks that every American with an IQ above the mid-double digits is already well aware of.

No organization has pursued the tobacco money with as much single-minded diligence as the American Cancer Society (ACS), and what the American Cancer Society wants, the American Cancer Society usually gets. According to the Society's website, ACS headquarters in Atlanta and its state and local affiliates had a combined annual income of $824.5 million in the fiscal year ending August 31, 2001.

The ACS used to claim that "the Society accepts no money from federal, state, or local government."[32] With government grants accounting for $676,480 on the most recent available IRS Form-990 (1998), this is no longer a tenable claim. The ACS has become a favored grantee of the federal Centers for Disease Control. In 2001–2002, the Society received $1.43 million dollars from the CDC to develop and disseminate "comprehensive information on cancer prevention and early detection."[33]

Founded by a group of New York City physicians and businessmen in 1913 as the American Society for the Control of Cancer, the ACS is perhaps the best-known "disease" charity in the world. Very few of us have not lost a friend or loved one to cancer; no organization could start with a greater reservoir of public goodwill than one which seeks to conquer cancer. The ACS states as its mission "eliminating cancer as a major health problem by preventing cancer, saving lives and diminishing suffering from cancer through research, education, advocacy, and service."[34] A thoroughly noble goal.

Many of the activities undertaken by the ACS within communities are in the best tradition of American voluntarism. The society and its members drive cancer patients to their treatments; loan medical equipment; conduct rehabilitative programs; sponsor cancer-patient support groups; provide information on cancer treatment to the afflicted and their relatives; and help patients obtain temporary housing near medical centers when they need to travel in order to receive medical care. These are worthy, admirable acts, for which the American Cancer Society and its employees and volunteers deserve much praise. In no way should any criticism I might level at the ACS—or other health charities—be taken as a disparagement of the good work they do. Not all the work, however, is good.

Despite its mission and its millions, the ACS has not conquered cancer, and it has not always made the best use of its prodigious resources. For years, the American Cancer Society was best known for its widely distributed list of "Cancer's Danger Signals." In 1947, when the education program went into full swing, these numbered seven:

1. Any sore that does not heal.

2. A lump or thickening in the breast or elsewhere.

3. Unusual bleeding or discharge.

4. Any change in wart or mole.

5. Persistent indigestion or difficult swallowing.

6. Persistent hoarseness or coughing.

7. Any change in normal bowel habits.[35]

This not so magnificent seven was scrapped in the 1980s, but they had already penetrated deeply into the national consciousness. The wonder of it is that the ACS hadn't turned every last American into a raving hypochondriac. For instance, by the time the ACS quietly dumped the list, a Gallup poll was finding that "an estimated 62 million Americans in any given month have heartburn."[36] Medical journalist Lynn Payer was reporting that "an enormous percentage [of Americans] report they they've experienced some sort of ache or pain"[37] in recent weeks. More than a quarter of men and women report indigestion, more than a third of men report a troublesome cough, almost a quarter of respondents claim shortness of breath, and so on.

As early as the 1920s, an article in the *Journal of the American Medical Association* was criticizing a forerunner of the seven deadly signs list. (Then there were just four.) The researcher wrote that "to warn the public that 'moles, excrescences, fistulas, and warts are the first signs of cancer' is to erect a specter capable of shattering even a normal mentality. . . . To say that 'symptoms of indigestion' are 'signs of cancer' is so small a part of the whole truth that it is better left unsaid."[38]

There is no need today—there was no need yesteryear, either—to exaggerate the incidence of cancer. It is far too pervasive already. James Coupal, President Coolidge's personal physician, said in 1928, "Cancerphobia must be inculcated into everyone over 31."[39] The

ACS has helped to do this—but whether cancerphobia is good for anyone other than those who raise money for the ACS has never been clear.

Since 1928, the symbol of the American Cancer Society (then called the American Society for the Control of Cancer) has been the sword with twined snakes forming its hilt. The sword symbolizes "the crusading spirit of the cancer control movement,"[40] according to the ACS website. It might also symbolize the ferocity with which the society raises funds, especially when the money falls, manna-like, from the besieged tobacco companies.

One of the more unseemly tussles over how to spread the tobacco-industry booty occurred in Colorado in the summer of 2001. Governor Bill Owens proposed that part of the money be used to secure treatment for low-income women who had been diagnosed with breast or cervical cancer. Such a plan would seem to be almost politically unassailable, but where "free" money is concerned, there are no sacred cows.

"There are better funding sources," said a spokeswoman for the American Cancer Society, which understood full well that every dollar spent curing a Colorado woman of cervical or breast cancer was a dollar not headed for the ACS coffers.

An Owens flack reacted with incredulity. "It is unbelievable that someone would suggest that using tobacco settlement money to save women's lives is inappropriate," charged Owens's press secretary. "The American Cancer Society has clearly lost sight of its mission in favor of feeding its bureaucracy."[41]

Touché. That thrust cut awfully close to the bone. But it is a rare politico who has the guts to take on the Big Three or to stand between a mega-charity and funds.

Lori Fresina, advocacy director in the Boston office of the ACS, spoke with admirable bluntness when she said of efforts to divert tobacco money to uses not directly related to tobacco use, "Once the piggy bank is broken, you don't get the money back in."[42]

The American Cancer Society, American Lung Association, and American Heart Association are unquestionably, indubitably, profoundly right on one big issue: smoking is bad for one's health. But must they, and the federal government that funds them, continue to spend tens of millions of dollars annually telling Americans what all of us already know?

Does this seem a tad excessive? Surely all of us don't know that smoking is harmful. Hell, all of us don't even know that the earth goes round the sun.

Astonishingly enough, all of us really do know that smoking kills. Even the nanny par excellence, the cigar-smoking martini-drinking paternalist Dr. C. Everett Koop, President Reagan's hyperactive surgeon general, conceded in 1985 that "the smoker today is well educated about the health hazards of smoking."[43]

"Well educated" is the understatement of last century. In 1988, Gerald M. Goldhaber, chairman of the Department of Communications at the State University of New York at Buffalo, testified before the House Committee on Energy and Commerce: "When the pollsters asked whether, regardless of what they believed, people had heard that smoking was dangerous, an astonishing 99 percent responded in the affirmative." Goldhaber went on to note that only 89 percent of those polled knew that George Washington was the first president of the United States, 72 percent of those polled in 1976 had known that the U.S. declared its independence in 1776, and 38 percent of Americans can name their congressional representatives.[44] (In the last case, ignorance can be bliss.)

So the problem is not that Americans—any Americans—don't know of the health risks associated with the use of tobacco. Rather, the problem is that they consider these risks and smoke anyway.

The ACS has a two-part response to this problem. First, keep shoveling money into "education," even though there's not a single solitary American left to educate. And second, coerce. Forbid. Command.

The very first item in the American Cancer Society "Tobacco Control" agenda reads, "Fighting for laws and public programs at all levels of government, in schools and other public areas to eliminate tobacco use."[45] Yes, eliminate. This is not the language of moderation.

Like the ALA, the ACS has little patience with anachronistic arguments to the effect that whether or not one smokes is one's own business.

The mega-charities are strong supporters of vast increases in cigarette taxes. Despite combined state and federal taxes that boost the price of a pack of smokes by more than a dollar in virtually every state in the union, the ACS and ALA push for even greater hikes.

Fifty cents a pack; a dollar a pack; the sky, it seems, is the limit. And when an advocate of personal liberty such as Eric Schippers, executive director of the hopelessly un-PC-denominated National Smokers' Alliance, predicts that lower-income smokers will simply turn to the black market instead of paying astronomical prices for cigarettes, all the ACS can do is huff in indignation.[46]

Some people will continue to smoke, no matter the dangers. While the percentage of smokers has declined sharply from 45 percent in 1965, shortly after the Surgeon General of the United States issued his heralded report on the perils of smoking, to about 25 percent today, the ACS has proclaimed a goal of halving this to 12 percent by 2015. An ambitious goal, and one that is probably unachievable absent coercion on a totalitarian scale—and massive expenditures in the form of grants from the federal government to such nanny organizations as the American Cancer Society.

If "totalitarian" seems a mite strong, then let's take the ACS at its own word. In its publication, *Cancer Prevention & Early Detection: Facts & Figures 2001*, the ACS concedes, turgidly but unmistakably, "Multi-faceted efforts that focus on tobacco control at the community rather than the individual level are essential to enhance cessation and decrease uptake of smoking in the United States."[47]

In other words, rather than seek to convince individual Americans not to smoke, the ACS intends to press for broad-based legislation restricting, or banning, the freely chosen decision to smoke tobacco products. If it's any consolation to those of you who nurse old-fashioned American attitudes about overweening government and the rights of individuals, this is for your own good.

The harmfulness of "second-hand smoke" has never been established scientifically, but like alligators in sewers and maniacs prowling Lover's Lane, this urban legend refuses to die.

When a Suffolk County (NY) legislator wondered why the ACS wanted to ban smoking outside public buildings in the county— "It's outside," he noted in exasperation—the local ACS spokesman blandly replied, "It is limited, I'll give you that." But he added, "There is no safe level."[48]

No safe level. In other words, if a fellow strikes up a smoke in the great outdoors of, say, Colorado Springs, he is somehow posing a threat to me in Virginia.

The American Cancer Society enjoys an especially close—incestuous might be the better word—relationship with the National Cancer Institute, one of the federal government's National Institutes of Health. Since the birth of the NCI, its growth has been helped along by savvy ACS lobbying. Historian Walter Ross writes, "Spurred by the effective lobbying of the ACS, the NCI budget began growing rapidly. In 1950 it totaled nearly $19 million; in 1960 it had risen to $91 million; and by 1970 to $190 million."[49] In 2002, it had ballooned to $4.128 billion.

The panjandrums at the National Cancer Institute have returned the favor. To give one of the more egregious examples, the NCI has provided upwards of $100 million to anti-smoking agitators to lobby for higher tobacco taxes at the state level.

The money has been funneled through the NCI's Project ASSIST, which stands for the American Stop Smoking Intervention Study for Cancer Prevention. Yes, I know, it's ungrammatical, and withal, it should be Project ASSISCP, but acronyms must make sense, even if the programs for which they stand don't.

ASSIST was launched in 1991 with the ostensible goal of supporting grass-roots groups that organize public-education campaigns to discourage smoking. This "discouragement" was not limited to informing smokers and potential smokers of the possibly lethal consequences of the nasty habit. Why try moral suasion and appeals to self-interest when the heavy hand of government is ready and willing to have a swing?

We know more of the messy details of ASSIST as it operated in Colorado than in other states, for a lawsuit was filed against the Colorado Department of Health, the agency charged with disbursing ASSIST funds in the Rocky Mountain State. The resultant documents painted a sordid picture. Front groups were created to provide a smokescreen for lobbying. State bureaucrats used state offices to facilitate lobbying.

Colorado had been prime ground for ASSIST. The state had a noisy anti-smoking lobby which had been trying to raise tobacco taxes for years. So when the National Cancer Institute awarded the Colorado Department of Health (CDH) an ASSIST contract for $6.977 million for the period September 20, 1991, to September 29, 1998, it expected results.

Emboldened by the prospect of a federal subsidy, anti-smoking crusaders placed an initiative on the November 1994 state ballot that would have raised cigarette taxes by fifty cents per pack and boosted taxes on cigars and smokeless tobacco by 50 percent of the manufacturer's list price. The tax revenues were then to be distributed to hospitals, health charities, pliable academics, and the anti-smoking groups that drew up the initiative. After all, they were doing the hard work: didn't they deserve a cut of the pie?

The tax initiative was promoted by the Fair Share for Health Committee (FSHC), which was organized by the Colorado branches of the American Cancer Society and American Lung Association as well as other charities, hospitals, and anti-tobacco activists. The FSHC (no easy to remember acronym for them!) employed Arnold Levinson as executive director: he pulled down $50 an hour—paid for by ASSIST. In other words, the federal government was paying the director of FSHC, whose job it was to promote a statewide tax increase.

Levinson's general outlook was summed up by an article he wrote for the ASSIST newsletter with the headline "To Get Rid of Tobacco: TAX IT!" Nothing subtle about that. And in fact, the NCI knew full well what ASSIST was about. The Colorado Department of Health admitted to the NCI that ASSIST would use tax money to promote such ideas as:

- Colorado should increase economic incentives and taxation to discourage the use of tobacco products.

- The price of tobacco products needs to be greatly increased through taxes and/or sales-license fees.

- The Colorado ASSIST Alliance will work to increase public knowledge of the need to increase the cigarette tax substantially.

- Educational presentations will be made to all [areas] regarding the need and current efforts to increase tobacco taxes.

- Strategies to advocate increased tobacco taxes will be incorporated into the ASSIST media plan.

- Information will be presented . . . regarding the rationale and need for sales license fees on tobacco sales.[50]

No obfuscating there.

Yet all was for naught. Colorado voters soundly defeated the tax increase, leaving us with two questions, neither of which has yet been answered:

Is it proper for the National Institutes of Health and its divisions, including the National Cancer Institute—whose purported mission is to research the causes of and to find cures for disease—to divert millions of dollars to advocacy group politics?

And is it proper for health charities, including the American Cancer Society, to embrace politics while abandoning their most valuable role of providing assistance to victims of disease?

* * *

Rounding out the Big Three of megacharities is the American Heart Association. Founded by a sextet of cardiologists in 1924, it was refitted in 1948 as a broader-based, voluntary health agency which has expanded as exponentially as the Grinch's heart.

Calling the American Heart Association huge is like calling Drew Carey chubby. Its annual budget is a whopping $337 million annually, and it claims 22.5 million "volunteers and supporters,"[51] though these seem to be defined loosely as anyone who has ever had even a glancing relationship with the organization. (Big Three charities like to boast of their many volunteers, which deflects attention away from the robust salaries in these organizations, which year in and year out spend over one third of their income on compensation.) In the most recent year (1998) for which tax returns were available, the American Heart Association received $1.054 million in government grants.[52]

Like the other members of the Big Three, the AHA performs its share of worthy acts, such as encouraging the wide availability of automated external defibrillators, which use an electric shock to restore normal rhythm to a heart that has gone into cardiac arrest. The heart association sponsors fine programs such as "free" blood pressure checks and unobjectionable programs such as cholesterol screenings (even though the relevance of cholesterol levels to mortality has been cast into serious doubt by medical researchers). It oversees a support group, Mended Hearts, Inc., which provides counsel and assistance for the families of patients with heart disease.

It also offers advice, much of its so commonsensical that one wonders why the AHA must spend time and millions in its promulgation:

- Don't smoke.

- Have your blood pressure checked regularly.

- Eat foods low in saturated fats and cholesterol.
- Stay physically active.
- Maintain proper weight.[53]

Fine. Although the cholesterol advice is of questionable importance, no one can possibly object to these injunctions. They are time-tested, they are sensible, and if obeyed, they may add a few months or years to your life—and at least they won't hurt.

And yet, behind the good works and the good intentions, lies the inevitable Office of Public Advocacy in Washington, D.C. The lobbyists. The AHA spends over $2 million annually in lobbying—usually for more federal monies, which, once received, can be used (since such money is fungible) in lobbying for yet more monies. The circle, it seems, is unbroken.

Emboldened by the integrity of its mission, the AHA has the gall to wrap its lobbying activities in the shroud of sanctimony. This is no mere advocacy group, ever ready to support any program that might pump money back into its own coffers. No, according to the AHA, "Every time we help pass a bill, we save lives."[54]

Yeesh. Give me the naked self-interest of the oil and gas industry any day of the week.

For the bills which the AHA helps pass are not simply wooly-headed fantasies along the lines of the "Act to Abolish Heart Disease." No, the AHA is more hardheaded than that. Its top priority is increasing funding for federal agencies that oversee heart-related health matters—and, by extension, increasing funding for charities that receive money from such agencies, as for example the AHA.

Year in and year out, the top legislative priorities for the AHA are (1) supporting higher federal spending on AHA-related programs; and (2) punishing the tobacco industry and harassing smokers. As with other health charities, the American Heart Association is a stranger to the word "liberty."

When it comes to federal spending, more is never enough for the AHA. When the spendthrift Republican George W. Bush proposed a record-breaking 13.8 percent increase for the National Institutes of Health in his fiscal year 2002 budget, the AHA applauded—but its President, Rose Marie Robertson, called this only an "opening step." She wanted an extra $600 million dropped into the package.[55]

More money for stroke prevention was also a "top priority," as were expanding the Centers for Disease Control's Cardiovascular Health Program and its stroke and heart disease screening program, which is known as WISEWOMAN. (A great acronym, at least: it stands for Well-Integrated Screening and Evaluation for Women Across the Nation.)

The AHA presents a classic case of a taxpayer-funded lobby that turns around and lobbies for more dollars. Take its American Heart Association Grassroots Network. This is the grandiose name given to the AHA's effort to get people to write their congresshuman demanding higher expenditures on AHA-related causes. Its "Networker Guide" provides a sample letter to one's solon urging support for "H.R. 4506, the 'Teaching Children to Save Lives Act.'"

Now, what sort of moral monster could oppose "teaching children to save lives"? The fine print explains that this "vital legislation" would provide grants to school districts, which would then "work in conjunction with . . . the American Heart Association"[56] to teach children the basics of cardiopulmonary resuscitation.

This is an eminently worthy activity, though one wonders why, even in the absence of the passage of the vital H.R. 4506, the AHA can't send its staffers or volunteers into the schools to teach CPR without a federal grant. Besides being a boon for the mannequin industry, H.R. 4506 is, in effect, a $10 million subsidy to the AHA.

The AHA is nothing if not shrewd. Understanding that lawmakers like to attach their names to causes of impeccable purity, it established a Congressional Heart and Stroke Coalition, which is not a support group for ailing members of Congress but a self-described "resource center on heart and stroke issues,"[57] including, front and center, the necessity for spending more tax dollars. The Coalition spans the spectrum, from the most liberal Democrats to the most conservative Republicans, and it even includes the heroic libertarian Republican Ron Paul (R-TX), who votes against all spending and programs that are not explicitly authorized by the U.S. Constitution. Congressman Paul—a physician—keeps the Congressional Heart and Stroke Coalition from being a monolithic force for greater expenditures.

Taxing, badgering, and someday, perhaps, outlawing smokers is never far from the AHA's heart. It advocates greater scrutiny of tobacco by the Food and Drug Administration, which would be a large step toward restricting the distribution of tobacco, much as the FDA restricts the sale and use of the various drugs within its bailiwick. As American Heart Association CEO M. Cass Wheeler explained the group's position, placing tobacco under the FDA "would provide another positive step toward improving public health, and also protect the nation's young people from the often predatory marketing and advertising tactics of the tobacco industry."[58]

The locution is revelatory: giving the FDA authority to regulate tobacco would be just a "step." The pathway along which this step would be taken is not mentioned, but it would look, smell, and feel an awful lot like prohibition—though the AHA, as a marketing-savvy big (charitable) business, would never use the P-word, which still carries about it a bad odor.

The AHA has also ventured into legislative territory seemingly far removed from matters of the heart. The heart association formally joined in support of the McCain-Feingold campaign-finance reform proposal, because, said AHA Chairman of the Board William J. Bryant, the draconian bill would "finally curb the heavy-handed influence of . . . the tobacco industry."[59] If you can't best them in the court of public opinion, or in the elected legislature, then ban 'em.

The purity of the American Heart Association was cast into serious doubt in 1988, when it launched its ill-advised HeartGuide Seal of Approval program. Prior to that point, the AHA charter had banned the endorsement of products. But money is the lifeblood of charities as well as politics, so in July 1988 the AHA's House of Delegates ratified a plan to award seals of approval to healthy foods—provided that the producers or marketers of those foods coughed up fees of as much as $640,000 per brand per year.

The resultant howls of outrage daunted the faint hearts of the AHA. Government nannies pointed out, correctly, that a healthy diet depends upon the totality of the foods consumed, not the individual elements of a diet. In any event, the AHA insisted on keeping its guidelines secret—a curious practice for an organization that purports to educate consumers about nutrition. Stranger yet, some of the first products to receive the AHA HeartGuide Seal were crackers, margarines, and cooking oils, which are not exactly part of the breakfast (or dinner) of champions. As the *New York Times* observed, "many of the products that . . . received the heart association's endorsement were products that are 100 percent fat, such as cooking oils, or nearly 100 percent fat, such as margarines."[60] It was as if the AHA had suddenly developed a subversive sense of humor, and was permitting John Candy to award its HeartGuide Seals.

Under intense pressure, the American Heart Association scrapped its HeartGuide Seal on April 2, 1990.

On the prowl for new sources of income, the AHA hit upon . . . need I say it? . . . the tobacco settlement billions. Even in California, which has outpaced the other states in propagandizing against tobacco usage, American Heart Association spokesman Marc Burgat complained that "no new dollars whatsoever are being put into the state's tobacco prevention program."[61]

The AHA was every bit as exercised as its Big Three sisters when, for instance, San Diegoans debated using part of the tobacco windfall to build a new downtown library.

"We don't feel a downtown library is an appropriate use of these funds," sniffed the AHA director of advocacy, Molly Bowman. "This money did not fall out of the sky. People paid for it with their lives."[62] Therefore it should enrich the AHA. QED. Such is the tenor of the times that one is surprised to find that library advocates did not argue that had smokers only read the available books about the dangers of smoking, they would yet be alive, so therefore a library filled with books warning of the health hazards of the demon weed is an entirely appropriate use of the tobacco money.

* * *

So zealous are the Big Three to protect their favored status among health charities that they have testified at congressional hearings urging that other charities targeting the same illnesses be subject to federal sanction. Then-chairman Keith A. Greiner of the American Cancer Society told the House Subcommittee on Transportation and Hazardous Materials (the jurisdictional quirks of the Congress never cease to amaze) that "fund-raising by the look-alike organizations . . . ought to be stopped." Greiner declaimed, "The best interests of the public are not being served by what look-alikes do, and therefore, some legislation ought to be in order."[63]

Greiner was incensed that other charities were using the word "cancer" to raise monies. One gets the impression that were the c-word copyrightable, the ACS would stake ownership.

The American Lung Association is similarly peeved about organizations that use the word "lung" to solicit funds, and while "heart" is hardly the exclusive property of the American Heart Association, then-chairman William Van't Hof envisioned a "national solution"[64] to the scourge of competing charities.

Van't Hof's outrage was particularly amusing. He condemned look-alike heart charities for "seeking profit."[65] What a bizarre criticism to emanate from the American Heart Association, whose much-maligned HeartGuide Seals were to be sold, if you will recall, for up to $640,000 per product per year—even to producers of foods that were 100 percent fat!

Of course, other health charities want in on the action, and are not loath to take government funds to do the government's bidding. I have already mentioned the thriving AIDS industry, which performs praiseworthy acts of mercy one minute and hectors Uncle Sam for money and privileges the next.

As much as AIDS-related organizations like to pretend that they are countercultural, hip dissidents in the grey world of public health, in fact they are often about as anti-establishment as the Department of Commerce.

Take the National Association of People with AIDS, or NAPWA, an acronym suggesting Elmer Fudd at an auto-parts store. NAPWA, which is based in downtown Washington, D.C., "advocates on behalf of all people living with HIV and AIDS in order to end the pandemic and the human suffering caused by HIV/AIDS."[66] The hubris is as characteristic of such groups as it is puzzling: did "all" people living with HIV and AIDS ask NAPWA to act as their advocate? Isn't it a breathtaking denial of their personhood, their individuality, to act as if every single person with this disease can be spoken for in one voice? With one monolithic program?

The activity in which NAPWA seems to take the most institutional pride is its sponsorship of AIDSWatch. This has an unpleasantly voyeuristic ring, as if it were in a league with the Whale Watches on which so many East Coast schoolchildren go as part of their field trips. But no, on an AIDSWatch, the only folks who should be doing any watching are the taxpayers, who are advised to keep an eye on their wallets. AIDSWatch, according to NAPWA, is "the largest annual constituent-based federal HIV/AIDS lobbying" event in the United States. Hundreds of lobbyists descend upon the Capitol, buttonholing congressmen and urging support of the primary item on the AIDSWatch legislative wish list: "a strong federal commitment of funding"[67] on HIV/AIDS programs.

This is all perfectly legal, of course. Defense contractors, travel agents, corporate farmers, schoolteachers: all have their own DC lobbyists, so why shouldn't people afflicted with a devastating illness have their own, too?

The problem is that NAPWA is a virtual subsidiary of the government. In the most recent available IRS Form 990 (1998), the National Association of People with AIDS reported government grants totaling $1.038 million out of a total revenue of $2.366 million—or 44 percent. For all intents and purposes, NAPWA is a government dependent.

A hefty chunk of the group's budget—$158,272—was spent on a "lobbying contract" for the Sheridan Group, a Washington, D.C. lobbying firm.[68] So it goes round and round: Uncle Sam subsidizes NAPWA, which uses the subsidy to pay lobbyists who secure even more money for NAPWA. Where it stops—if it stops—nobody knows.

Before leaving the health field, in the spirit of federalism we should acknowledge that state advocacy groups are also becoming adept at using tax dollars to promote higher state spending.

Their umbrella organization, the Cleveland-based Universal Health Care Action Network (UHCAN!—get it?), was created in 1992 to serve as a "national resource and strategic center"[69] for those far-flung groups seeking a government-sponsored system of national health care. (Just why such groups insist on using the phrase "universal" health care instead of "national" is unclear—surely they don't advocate the U.S. taxpayer shelling out for health insurance for the population of Latvia—not to mention the residents of Neptune, Alpha Centauri, Betelgeuse. . . .)

UHCAN! is allied with the left-most elements of the Democratic Party. It has assisted advocates of "universal single-payer health care" in Maine and "health care for all"[70] in Maryland. Its propaganda asserts that since the unfortunate defeat of Hillary Clinton's Rube Goldbergish health scheme in 1994, "UHCAN! members have continued to advocate for comprehensive, universal health care as the only solution to the health crisis in the U.S."[71] ("Crisis"? one asks.)

In 1999, UHCAN! joined with the Gray Panthers and the National Council of Churches to launch Universal Health Care 2000, out of which came the Congressional Universal Health Care Task Force, which is the congressional caucus whose mission it is to foist a socialized health insurance system on the citizens of the United States.

Again, the actions of UHCAN! are perfectly legal and legitimate—except for the single fly that always seems to be splashing around in the ointment. You see, just as UHCAN! supports socialized health care, it also supports socialized lobbying. In its Year 2000 Financial Summary, UHCAN! noted that $141,938 of its total revenue of $442,017 came from the Ohio Developmental Disability Council—an agency subsidized by the taxpayers of Ohio.[72]

Tennesseans have the same dubious pleasure. The Tennessee Health Care Campaign (THCC), a member of the Fair Taxes for All Coalition, is a minor recipient of public funds ($4,200 in years 1996–2000)[73] and a major advocate of extending its state's TennCare program, which provides health-care coverage to 1.35 million Tennesseans (800,000 of whom are eligible for Medicaid, and 550,000 of whom are "uninsured and uninsurable"[74]).

THCC—no catchy acronym for them, though the phoneticized spelling might be "Thick"—issues the usual hysterical denunciations of any proposal by the governor or legislators that would do anything but bloat TennCare into a Medicaid-like obesity. That it receives money from the Tennessee Disabilities Council ought to perhaps cast the THCC in the role of government-subsidized lobbyist for more government. But the press can be counted on to portray the valiant agitators of THCC as tireless champions of the little guy—if not little government.

But then little government has never been the desideratum of health-care lobbies. From the Big Three on down through the Want-to-be-Big Three Thousand, the self-appointed tribunes of Americans' health have seldom bothered to count the cost of their crusades: a cost heavy in both liberties and taxpayer dollars.

Notes

1. James T. Bennett and Thomas J. DiLorenzo, *Unhealthy Charities: Hazardous to Your Health and Wealth* (New York: Basic Books, 1994), p. 34.
2. Centers for Disease Control, Grant #220205, 8/15/2001-8/14/2002.
3. American Lung Association of Virginia, undated brochure.

4. "Lung Association Testifies at Senate Judiciary Hearing on Stalled Federal Tobacco Lawsuit," ALA press release, September 5, 2001.
5. Nathan G. Mains, "Curb Tobacco Industry," *Pittsburgh Post-Gazette*, April 23, 2001, p. A12.
6. "Research Facts 2001," American Heart Association.
7. American Lung Association of Virginia, undated brochure.
8. "Lung Association Testifies at Senate Judiciary Hearing on Stalled Federal Tobacco Lawsuit."
9. *American Lung Association Annual Report 2000*, p. 16.
10. Carl Bakal, *Charity, U.S.A.* (New York: Times Books, 1979), pp. 130–31.
11. Frank Ryan, *The Forgotten Plague: How the Battle Against Tuberculosis Was Won—and Lost* (Boston: Little, Brown, 1993), p. 390.
12. *American Lung Association Annual Report 2000*, p. 1.
13. Ibid., p. 6.
14. Ibid., p. 3.
15. Ibid., p. 1.
16. Ibid., p. 8.
17. "Voters Overwhelmingly Support Clean Trucks, Clean Diesel Fuel," ALA press release, December 5, 2000.
18. *American Lung Association Annual Report 2000*, p. 1.
19. Ibid., p. 10.
20. Ibid.
21. Thomas J. DiLorenzo, "Tax-Funded Politics: The Centers for Disease Control and the American Lung Association," Alternatives in Philanthropy (Washington, D.C.: Capital Research Center, February 1996), p. 1.
22. Brian Carlson, "Missouri, 5 Other States Have Yet to Allocate Tobacco Money," *St. Louis Post-Dispatch*, February 10, 2001, p. 5.
23. Deborah Shprentz, "Comments on U.S. EPA's Air Quality Criteria for Particulate Matter; Second External Review Draft," March 2001.
24. Bennett and DiLorenzo, *Unhealthy Charities*, p. 45.
25. Monte Paulsen, "Profit Fuels Waste Battle," *The State* (Columbia, SC), September 5, 1994.
26. ARTT, "Dismantling of Nation's Hazardous Waste Law Drives Formation of New Association," press release, December 3, 1993.
27. Jeff Bailey, "Incinerators Take on Kilns in Hazardous-Waste Battle," *Wall Street Journal*, December 22, 1993.
28. A. James Barnes, "EPA Smothered by Rival Lobbyists," *St. Louis Post-Dispatch*, March 31, 1994.
29. For an overview of the kiln controversy, see James T. Bennett, "Selling its Reputation: The American Lung Association," *Alternatives in Philanthropy* (Washington, D.C.: Capital Research Center, January 1995), pp. 1-6.
30. Bennett and DiLorenzo, *Unhealthy Charities*, p. 194.
31. Ibid.
32. Walter S. Ross, *Crusade: The Official History of the American Cancer Society* (New York: Arbor House, 1987), pp. 4-5.
33. Letter to the author from Lynn Armstrong, Centers for Disease Control, October 4, 2001.
34. "Cancer Prevention and Early Detection: Facts and Figures 2001," American Cancer Society, p. 2.
35. "ACS History," www2.cancer.org/about_acs/index, June 23, 2001.
36. Sandy Rovner, "Heartburn—'Tis the Season," *Washington Post*, December 26, 1989.

37. Lynn Payer, *Disease-Mongers: How Doctors, Drug Companies, and Insurers Are Making You Feel Sick* (New York: Wiley, 1992), pp. 105–106.
38. Richard Carter, *The Gentle Legions* (Garden City, NY: Doubleday, 1961), p. 146.
39. Payer, *Disease-Mongers*, p. 219.
40. "ACS History," June 23, 2001.
41. Michele Ames, *Rocky Mountain News*, July 20, 2001, p. 7A.
42. Rick Klein, "Tobacco Windfall Use in Question," *Boston Globe*, February 4, 2001, p. A1.
43. "Interview of Surgeon General C. Everett Koop," *New York Times*, December 13, 1985.
44. U.S. House of Representatives, Cigarettes: Advertising, Testing, and Liability: Hearings Before the Subcommittee on Transportation, Tourism, and Hazardous Materials, 100th Congress, 2nd session, 1988, pp. 441-42.
45. "Tobacco Control," www2. cancer.org/advocacy/index, June 23, 2001.
46. Jennifer Heldt Powell, "Smokes with Richer Flavor," *Boston Herald*, January 22, 2001, p. 25.
47. "Cancer Prevention and Early Detection: Facts and Figures 2001," p. 7.
48. Emi Endo and Michael Rothfield, Newsday, August 29, 2001, p. A8.
49. Ross, *Crusade*, p. 214.
50. James T. Bennett, "The National Cancer Institute and Colorado's Project ASSIST," *Alternatives in Philanthropy* (Washington, D.C.: Capital Research Center, February 1996), p. 4.
51. American Heart Association, undated form letter.
52. IRS Form 990, American Heart Association, 1998.
53. Bennett and DiLorenzo, *Unhealthy Charities*, pp. 109-110.
54. *American Heart Association 2000 Annual Report*, p. 9.
55. "American Heart Association applauds President Bush's proposed increase for NIH," press release, February 28, 2001.
56. "The American Heart Association Grassroots Networker Guide," undated brochure.
57. "The Congressional Heart and Stroke Coalition," www.americanheart.org/Support/Advocacy/Coalitions/CHSC.html, June 23, 2001.
58. "American Heart Association commends Reps. Greg Ganske, John Dingell and Henry Waxman's legislation to grant the Food and Drug Administration full regulatory authority over tobacco," press release, March 15, 2001.
59. "Statement of William J. Bryant, Chairman of the Board, American Heart Association on support for campaign finance reform legislation," press release, January 31, 2001.
60. Marian Burros, "Heart Group Begins Food Labeling amid Outcry," *New York Times*, February 1, 1990.
61. Lynda Gledhill, "Heart Association Criticizes Gov. Davis on Tobacco Funds," *San Francisco Chronicle*, July 13, 2000, p. A2.
62. Ray Huard, "San Diego Urged to Battle Smoking with Tobacco Funds," *San Diego Union-Tribune*, May 15, 2001, p. B4.
63. U.S. House of Representatives, Subcommittee on Transportation and Hazardous Materials, Committee on Energy and Commerce, Deceptive Fund-Raising by Charities, Hearings before the Subcommittee on Transportation and Hazardous Materials, 101st Congress, 1st session, 1989, p. 105.
64. Ibid., p. 158.
65. Ibid., p. 155.

66. "Welcome to NAPWA," www.napwa.org, December 14, 2001.
67. "AIDSWatch," www.napwa.org/aidswatch.html, December 14, 2001.
68. IRS Form 990, Nat'l Association of People With AIDS, 1998.
69. "Universal Health Care Action Network," www.uhcan.org, December 14, 2001.
70. "Progress Continues on Campaigns for Health Care for All in Maine and Maryland," Action for Universal Health Care (Sept./Oct. 2001., p. 2.
71. "Strategies for Universal Health Care," undated brochure.
72. *UHCAN Annual Report 2000*, p. 4.
73. Samples, Yablonski, and Osorio, "More Government for All," p. 6.
74. Tennessee Health Care Campaign, Inc., Public Welfare Foundation Interim Report, Grant # 00-136, March 12, 2001, p. 2.

6

The Black, the Brown, and the Old

Robert Woodson, president of the National Center for Neighborhood Enterprise and a skeptic of forced busing, recalls a televised debate with the then-head of the NAACP Legal Defense Fund. Woodson asked him, "If black children were excelling in an all-black school, would you support a demand that those children be bused to a white school, even if the white school offered a lower caliber of education?"

The NAACP official replied with an emphatic "yes."[1]

Well, at least he was honest.

Hard as it may be to believe, in its early years, the National Association for the Advancement of Colored People was committed to "the abolition of color-hyphenation and the substitution of straight Americanism."[2] Its founders, men and women of principle, demanded that black Americans receive their full rights as citizens of a United States of America whose founding, growth, and flowering were in no small part due to the hard work of African-Americans, both free and slave.

The NAACP established a Washington bureau in 1941 and within several years became a significant lobbying force. If its program in its early years on Capitol Hill concentrated on extending federal civil rights protections to black citizens of Southern states, today it simply wishes to extend federal powers everywhere, for any reason, and at all times. Perhaps this is not surprising, given that from 1996–2000, this member of the Fair Taxes for All Coalition received $1.281 million in government monies.[3]

The NAACP's legislative report card for the 107th Congress (2001) graded senators and members of the House on such votes as spending more to hire teachers, spending more on technology in schools, spending more on bilingual education (a curious concern for an organization putatively representing millions of the most deeply rooted native Americans), spending more for the repair of ostensibly "local" schools, spending more on Head Start, spending more on relief for the Sudan, and of course opposing tax cuts. Of twenty-two votes, the NAACP took the pro-liberty side just twice: in opposing federal funding for school vouchers and in opposing federally mandated reading and math tests in the states.[4]

The NAACP also supports a minimum wage hike, which most economists agree would harm unskilled minority workers by pricing them out of the necessary entry-level jobs.

In certain of its projects, the NAACP is simply an appendage of the state. For instance, the NAACP Nevada Housing Development Corporation, an Anaheim, California-based (where else?) outfit which "provided low-cost housing to 115 families," reported total revenues of $842,812 in 1999—and government grants of $842,812.[5] You don't get any more subsidized than that. Yet NAACP leaders insist on posing as "outsiders," as perpetually aggrieved protesters lobbing Molotov cocktails from far beyond the palace gates—when in fact they are sipping potable cocktails inside the palace.

The NAACP's leading competitor as spokespeople for black Americans has been the National Urban League.

The National Urban League was founded in 1910, as the Southern black diaspora from the rural South was creating sizeable black ghettoes in Northern cities. Although it claims to have been the child of "an historical alliance of white and black,"[6] the Urban League, or the Committee on Urban Conditions Among Negroes, as it was known in 1910, was paid for (if not bought) by a rich white widow of a railroad baron, Ruth Standish Baldwin.

While the NAACP has focused on enlarging the political rights of African-Americans, the Urban League has focused on economics. As might be expected of an organization born of the generosity of a wealthy capitalist, it has a cozy relationship with Wall Street and the Fortune 500. The Urban League's list of major donors includes Morgan Stanley, PepsiCo, United Parcel Service, American Express, Anheuser-Busch, Xerox—the list goes on and on. Thumbing through the pages of the Urban League's "Equal Opportunity Journal"—one of those titles that fairly begs the reader, "Put me aside for another day"—one is struck by the number of corporate advertisements proclaiming "Diversity is our Strength" and other such Orwellian slogans. Each company blazons the faces of its black executives in the ads; one never knew that there were so many vice presidents for affirmative action compliance.[7]

Major corporations not only lend financial support to the Urban League, they also work with the Urban League to provide scholarships for black students. The League's Black Executive Exchange Program sponsors lectures by executives at historically black colleges and universities.

These seem like laudable programs, and when one opens the National Urban League's 2000 annual report, the phraseology of the introduction suggests that we are not in NAACP-land any more. The League hails the "21st-century current of ideas and free-market opportunity, as undiscriminating as the wind . . . waiting to capture us and sweep us along, amplifying the force of our own individual enterprise."[8] Elsewhere the term "free enterprise" is used not to mean an invidious and mysterious power that keeps African-Americans down but rather as a liberating force: a potent combination of freedom and enterprise.

The devil, alas, is in the details. The National Urban League, for all its refreshing rhetoric, seeks "empowerment" in ways not always consistent with free enterprise. In 2000, it oversaw a $600,000 grant from the U.S. Department of Transportation to six of its local affiliates. The purpose of the grant was to "prepare welfare recipients and low-income individuals for employment in highway construction and transportation technology sectors."[9] In other words, it took more than half a million dollars from the government to teach people how to be government employees. This is called doing Caesar's work for him.

Similarly, the National Urban League has run a U.S. Department of Labor-funded program called "Seniors in Community Service," a title in which three of four words are euphemisms—not exactly an auspicious start.

The extent of the Urban League's subsidy by the state is mind-boggling. According to its own report, in 2000, "government grants and contracts" made up $18.704 million of the Urban League's total revenue of $44.332 million.[10] Over the period 1996–2000, the National Urban League was gifted with $123.856 million in taxpayer support, which ranked it second only to the National Council of Senior Citizens on the list of publicly subsidized members of the Fair Taxes for All Coalition.[11]

This incredible infusion of government money permits the League to advocate with powerful voice a number of policies, the general tone of which seem indistinguishable from those supported by the NAACP. In its "Special Legislative Report" on the 107th Congress, the League's Institute for Opportunity and Education laid out a political program that can charitably be called old school welfare-state liberal. As a general rule, if it costs taxpayers money, the Urban League is for it. We should "invest" in government summer jobs programs for young people, in federal scholarships for college students, in federal programs to pay public school teachers and repair public school buildings and subsidize Internet access and provide health insurance for all and expand federal school lunch payments and child-care and Head Start and after-school programs and summer programs and family planning clinics and substance abuse treatment programs and HIV/AIDS prevention and put the Small Business Administration on the bureaucratic equivalent of steroids and . . . so on. The mind fogs, the fingers twitch, the wallet lightens as one types in the government actions of which the National Urban League approves. It also opposes the privatization of Social Security, repeal of the minimum wage, and supports hate-crimes legislation.

By the time one reaches the end of the National Urban League wish list, those poetic evocations of "free-market opportunity" and "individual enterprise" are gone with the wind.

* * *

The premier "black" think tank is the Joint Center for Political and Economic Studies, which was founded in 1970 with a two-year $820,000 grant from the Ford Foundation. The parentage spoke volumes. No organization born from the benefactions of white limousine liberals is likely to challenge the assumptions of those sugar daddies, and the Joint Center has been careful not to bite the hand that feeds it. Problem is, as the years have gone by the Joint Center has come to rely on government subsidies to such an extent that it is a virtual arm of the central state.

The Joint Center's original mission was to train newly elected black political leaders in the political arts. (New Left cynics might say that its real purpose was to co-opt potential critics of the system.) John E. Saunders III, executive director of the National Forum for Black Public Administrators, praises the Joint Center for its advocacy role over the years. "It gave ammunition to the advocates of those causes we cared about,"[12] he says, and those causes did not include the preservation of American liberties or a strict construction of the Constitution. Instead, they entailed the expansion of a centralized welfare state administered by Washington, D.C.

Today, the Joint Center's mission is to conduct "research on public policy issues of special concern to black Americans and other minorities."[13] Fed by grants from the U.S. Department of Commerce's Minority Business Development Agency and AT&T, the Joint Center has also created a Minority Business RoundTable, whose ostensible purpose is to promote "effective public policies that impact minority owned businesses." The language is not promising; but then the idea of encouraging entrepreneurship with money from the U.S. Department of Commerce is something of a nonstarter, too. The Minority Business RoundTable has lobbied for "federal efforts to raise student achievement,"[14] which in Washington means expanding the reach and realm of the federal government in what was once—back in the days when the American educational system was among the best in the world—a local affair. But then, should it really surprise us that the U.S. Department of Commerce would lavish money upon an organization that, in turn, calls for a bigger government?

Led by its quotable president Eddie Williams, the Joint Center stays in the news today with its opinion surveys and research studies. It has found, for instance, that minority parents are more supportive of school-voucher plans than are generic Democratic liberals, and it has also found broad support among blacks for the Social Security system. It is exceedingly unlikely to find any groundswell of support for limited government, at least not as long as it pulls in substantially more than $1 million a year ($1.560 million in 1999) in government contributions.[15]

Also topping the $1 million mark is the Chicago-based Leadership Council for Metropolitan Open Communities, which in 1998 pocketed $1.845 million in government grants out of a total revenue of $2.527 million.[16]

The Leadership Council, which was founded in 1966, calls itself "the nation's largest and most comprehensive fair housing organization."[17] Now, given that the Federal Fair Housing Act was enacted in 1968, one might think that this is one group that has outlived its purpose. But as long as the Sea of Grants provides nourishment, no nonprofit ever crawls off to die.

The Leadership Council uses tax dollars to file "fair housing" complaints, link minority apartment and home seekers with suitable housing (most Americans manage to do this on their own), and train realtors in the arcana of fair-housing laws.

Yet the council goes even further, taking positions on housing legislation and promoting its frankly interventionist belief that "non-discrimination is not sufficient." The council advocates that "government agencies" encourage "affirmative action" in housing. Residential housing patterns must not be left to the market, personal preferences, and anti-discrimination laws: the state must take steps to ensure "racial and economic diversity"[18] in all housing markets. Thus, in the name of "diversity," every town, every neighborhood, every street must be forced to conform to a planner's pattern. If this seems like tyranny to you, take heart: its promotion is paid for by your tax dollars.

The complex relationship between race and crime in America is perhaps best left to researchers who are terminally ill. Unless, that is, one reaches the conclusion that high rates of crime among African-Americans are caused by racism and unemployment, in which case the grant spigot will be turned on full blast.

The National Council on Crime and Delinquency (NCCD), founded in 1907 by progressives of the juvenile court movement, claims to promote "effective, humane, fair and economically sound solutions to family, community, and justice problems."[19] The "economically sound" qualifier is a nice touch, though the council's commitment to economic soundness goes only so far. In 1998, for example, government contributions constituted $6.302 million of the council's total revenue of $7.25 million.[20] Someone is telling the U.S. Department of Justice exactly what it wishes to hear.

The NCCD had once relied on such heavyweight philanthropic organizations as the Ford Foundation and the Rockefeller Brothers Fund to finance its impeccably upper-middle-class white liberal solutions to the problem of crime. (With publications bearing loaded titles like, "Educate or Incarcerate?" it's not hard to see where the NCCD is heading.) It has since become almost entirely a creature of government grants, feasting especially well in times of liberal Democratic governance.

The NCCD supports a moratorium on the death penalty. Now, people of good faith may be found on both sides of the death penalty debate. But ought taxpayers be forced to subsidize a vigorous voice on the anti-death penalty side?

In 1998, the National Council on Crime and Delinquency created the Institute on Race and Justice, which took as its mission "eliminating racial biases and rebuilding [the criminal justice system's] legitimacy in communities of color." (This phrase is meant to exclude the pale majority—as if Sicilians, Greeks, Bavarians, and even pasty Swedes were colorless.)

The Institute pronounced itself exercised over "the over-representation of minorities in the justice system,"[21] which it seeks to "address." One might bet a year's worth of government grants that it will not find the "root cause" of this admittedly tragic over-representation in the fragility of the African-American family or the perverse incentives of the welfare system. For instance, among the most widely publicized studies released by the NCCD in recent years was "And Justice for Some," which made headlines with its revelation that while young blacks are but 15 percent of the national population, they represent 60 percent of young people being sent to prison. The reason: racism, natch. That same year, the NCCD lined up against California's Proposition 21, which would have required certain juvenile offenders to be tried in adult courts and sent to adult jails. Whatever the wisdom of this measure, surely the presence of NCCD president Barry Krisberg at a San Francisco press conference attacking the Proposition was an illegitimate use of tax money.[22]

In any event, we can expect more of the same. Echoing the language of the late unlamented Soviet Union, the NCCD's National Institute on Race and Justice is "operated as a centralized secretariat."[23] It may be expected to produce reports every bit as honest and liberty-minded as those which issued from previous secretariats.

* * *

Hispanics are the nation's fastest-growing minority. In the 2000 census, they accounted for 12 percent of Americans, which put them just behind African-Americans as the nation's second-largest minority. By all demographic indicators, they will surpass blacks the next time heads are counted.

Establishment African-American organizations such as the NAACP have a big jump on the Hispanic groups, but the latter are closing fast, in whine-power if not political influence. And like the NAACP, these groups are not averse to living on the public dole while very publicly denouncing the party of the Doles.

Take the National Council of La Raza, which bills itself as "America's premier Hispanic think tank."[24] Based in Washington, which removes it by thousands of miles from the country's Hispanic population base, La Raza may be translated as "The Race": and wouldn't that be a charming name for, say, a lobby of white supremacists? Wanna guess how much federal pork "The White Race" would get from Washington?

The name has bedeviled La Raza, so much so that in its list of "Twenty of The Questions Most Frequently Asked About the Latino Community," number one is "What does the term 'La Raza' mean?"

As you can imagine, the answer is a model of sophistry. The organization claims that La Raza means "the people," or, in the term coined by Mexican writer Jose Vasconcelos, "La Raza Cosmica," or "the cosmic people." Given that "cosmic" has unalterable associations with the recreations of hippies and other gentle people of the recent past, La Raza is probably right to drop the word.

"Inclusiveness" is the password that buzzes nonprofits into the treasury departments of grant-making foundations and governments, so La Raza does its best to argue that The Race—excuse me, The People—"is clearly an inclusive concept, meaning that Hispanics share with all other peoples of the world a common heritage and destiny, and that Latinos provide an example of a world in which traditional concepts of race can be transcended."[25]

Thus, by sleight of hand, does a clearly racist moniker become a name signifying anti-racism. This is an admirable example of chutzpah, but in the world of Washington lobbies, all is fair in love and the war for federal boodle.

La Raza was founded in 1968. Its mission, and that of its 250 affiliates, is to act as a "nonpartisan" advocate for the reduction of "poverty and discrimination, and improve life opportunities, for Hispanic Americans." It seeks to infuse a "Hispanic perspective"[26] into a wide range of political and social issues. This "Hispanic perspective" would come as a surprise to the millions of Hispanic-Americans who believe in such unhyphenated American values as hard work, self-reliance, national pride, and a government of limited powers. La Raza is a down-the-line supporter of a profligate welfare state, though it does serve up this stagnant brew with a twist: in La Raza's view, people who live in this country illegally should also be eligible to suckle at the bounteous teat of our Holy Mother the State.

Though entrepreneurship and mutual aid are hallmarks of Hispanic-American culture, La Raza prefers the language of victimization. "Help stop the discrimination that affects Hispanic Americans every day,"[27] whines its website, which would have you believe that every American of Spanish origin is a trod-upon peasant living in a filthy shanty and screwed out of rightful earnings by a heartless Republican (or is that a redundancy?) boss and landlord.

La Raza claims—accurately, of course—that "Latinos want what most Americans want: excellent schools; the opportunity to work, earn a decent living, and save; access to health care; fair and respectful treatment; and a chance at homeownership and the 'American Dream.'"[28] Alas, in the world of La Raza, that dream is unattainable absent a regulatory apparatus that Teddy Kennedy might find excessive. For starters, it urges "major, sustained increases"[29] in the budgets of such civil-rights-related agencies as the Equal Employment Opportunity Commission and divisions within the U.S. Departments of Justice, Health and Human Services, and Housing and Urban Development.

La Raza's newsletter "Agenda" is filled with warnings that, for example, "Federal Efforts to Ensure Against Discrimination Toward Individuals on the Basis of Limited English Proficiency Under Attack."[30] After all, nothing must be allowed to come between "individuals"—note the nonuse of the term "citizens"—and their federal benefits. La Raza supports a full range of welfare benefits to "lawfully present immigrants," which is not another way of saying "American citizens."

La Raza takes forthright stands on a variety of political issues. It supports federally funded bilingual education. It would use federal power to abolish the practice of "racial profiling," so that airport screeners can spend as much time harassing eighty-seven-year-old Baptist spinsters from Shreveport as they do sullen twenty-four-year-old Saudi nationals traveling without luggage. It supports federal hate-crimes legislation, though presumably making reference to "The Race" will not fall under the inevitable hate-thought statutes to follow. Responding to the 2000 presidential election, which sent to the White House the wrong man, it would bring state and local election procedures under greater federal control. (Eviscerating the remaining rights of states and localities and other entities independent of the national leviathan is a consistent theme among racial pressure groups.)

There are occasional exceptions to La Raza's worshipful attitude toward state power. For instance, it views the Immigration and Naturalization Service the way the libertarians view the Drug Enforcement Administration: as a basically illegitimate entity that does its job very badly. But La Raza takes its complaints about law enforcement to a level not often scaled in the nonprofit world. In the words of its Public Policy Briefing Book: The "'get-tough' approach to law enforcement tends to harm Latinos and other minority groups disproportionately."[31] The sharp reductions in crime experienced throughout urban America in the 1990s—in significant part due to the "get-tough" approaches of popular mayors—count for nothing. Never mind that the greatest beneficiaries of this reduction in crime live in the barrios and ghettos. La Raza stands with the thugs, at least as long as they are Hispanic. The race, baby.

Social security reform is of particular worry to La Raza, whose publications argue that "the Social Security system, in its present form, tends to benefit Latinos." Sure, it is on the verge of implosion, but that's not our problem. With its typical scrupulously partisan nonpartisanship, La Raza insists that "preserving the system with guaranteed benefits is crucial for Latinos."[32] Any form of privatization is abhorrent, and perhaps racist to boot. Certainly organizations and individuals must be free to make these and any other arguments about the Social Security system, but ought the rest of us be compelled to subsidize this drivel? For subsidize it we do, to the tune of $8.597 million from 1996–2000.[33]

La Raza also opposed the Bush administration's 2001 tax cut. Your tax dollars just keep on working.

National Council of La Raza president Raul Yzaguirre has made "The Case for Affirmative Action," and why not? He's done well by it, most recently by being named to the board of directors of Sears, Roebuck, and Co. Yzaguirre draws the usual distinction without a difference when he says, "The fact of the matter is that no one is advocating for preferential treatment of minority students. What we are recognizing when we support affirmative action is that there is still ongoing discrimination that needs to be compensated for." (Given his prolix speeches, one suspects that Yzaguirre is paid by the word.)

Yzaguirre goes on to call for just such preferential treatment of minority students. His speech making the case for affirmative action—why don't we just cut the verbiage and call them quotas?—is a classic in self-pitying victimology. Devoid of humor or the slightest evidence of self-deprecation, he tells us that as a high-school sophomore, he led a debate team that was far superior to that captained by a senior Anglo—but of course the Anglo received a national merit scholarship, while counselors suggested that Yzaguirre learn mechanics. He then petulantly declares, "To this day, I refuse to know anything about fixing a car," a classist knock at automobile repairmen, who do more good in a single workday than a New Class scam artist like Yzaguirre does in ten years. He then claims that every single intern working at the National Council of La Raza was told by his or her high-school counselor not to apply to an elite university. Yet they all did, and are doing fabulously well. This is obviously—let us be charitable—a fable. Finally, Yzaguirre asserts that tests are riddled with "extreme cultural bias," though the only example he gives is an anecdotal story of a test that used the phrase "soup to nuts," which is apparently so Eurocentric a trope that anyone who uses it is just begging for a stint in the hate-crime jail. All in all, a pathetic performance. Which would not concern us did not Raul Yzaguirre sit atop one of the most efficient collectors of tax dollars in all of victimhood.[34]

He obviously revels in his role as token Hispanic on countless boards. His biography on the La Raza website calls him a "key player," "one of the most widely recognized leaders," and the "spearhead" of "the most influential and respected Hispanic organization in the country."[35] One expects that when Mr. Yzaguirre enters a room, there is never room for another ego.

And then there is immigration. Reasonable people may differ on the proper immigration policy, but the self-interest of La Raza is obvious: the more Hispanic immigrants, legal and otherwise, the greater is La Raza's purported constituency and political strength. La Raza's position may be represented, without much caricature, as: Come one, come all. And those who are already here, whether legally or not, stay. Whether this is wise or not is not the point: the point is, La Raza gets oodles of federal boodle to promote an immigration policy that would be of great organizational benefit. To borrow a word which La Raza is not loath to use, is this fair?

La Raza senior vice president Charles Kamaski has warned the Bush administration that anything shy of a full-scale amnesty for the several million illegal immigrants currently in the United States would be "extraordinarily damaging"[36]—whether to Bush's political prospects or the country he did not say.

And while La Raza stakes its increasing claim to the U.S. Treasury—a whopping $2.87 million in 1998 out of a total revenue of $15.334 million[37]—it begrudges the rest of us the right to keep our own money. "The Race" opposed the very modest 2001 Bush tax cut because Latinos "need targeted investments in health, nutrition, and education programs."[38] In other words, they need the money which you have earned to be spent on welfare state programs of dubious value. Perhaps instead of being called La Raza, the lobby can rename itself Los Bandidos.

Uncle Sam also subsidizes the advocacy of the other major association of Americans of Spanish origin, the League of United Latin American Citizens, or LULAC.

On paper, LULAC lacks the 1960s welfarist orientation of La Raza. Its Code is downright inspiring, encouraging Latin American citizens to embrace their country while honoring the land of their ancestors. The LULAC Code begins:

> Respect your Citizenship and preserve it; honor your country, maintain its tradition in the spirit of its citizens and embody yourself into its culture and civilization.
>
> Be proud of your origin and maintain it immaculate, respect your glorious past and help to defend the rights of all the people.

The Code also enjoins belief in God, self-reliance, and being "sociable, upright, judicious, and . . . sober." The related LULAC Philosophy professes a belief in "individual political and religious freedom,"[39] libertarian phraseology not often found in the gimme gimme language of ethnic lobbies.

Actuated by its Code and Philosophy, LULAC, in its Aims and Purposes, pledges, among other things, to "exert our united efforts to uphold the rights guaranteed to every individual by our state and national laws," to "combat with every means at our command all un-American tendencies and actions that deprive American citizens of their rights," to foster "an understanding and recognition of and an appreciation for the dignity, worth and potential of the individual," and even to encourage the "fluent use of the English language that we may thereby equip ourselves and our families for the fullest enjoyment of our rights and privileges and the efficient discharge of our duties and responsibilities to our country."[40]

Where do I sign up?

Alas, there is a fly in the ointment. There is always a fly in the ointment. The LULAC Legislative Platform, which translates the pretty words into concrete proposals and lobbying efforts, seems to have been written by someone who has not read the LULAC Creed, Philosophy, or Aims and Purposes. It reads, if I may be forgiven a joke—always a dangerous offering in discussing ethnic politics—as if it were written by a student who did not take the LULAC injunction to learn English to heart. For the LULAC Legislative Platform is as drearily and sclerotically statist-liberal as any refried platform dished up by La Raza.

LULAC endorses affirmative action. LULAC urges "stronger sentencing and more aggressive prosecution for hate crimes," and offers the incredible proposal that "words" offensive to Latinos should be criminalized. In the realm of "Economic Opportunity," wherein so many Hispanic citizens have already succeeded fabulously, thanks to cultures based on thrift, family ties, and hard work, all LULAC can do is burble about "diversity." LULAC wants higher federal spending on Head Start, WIC, and public education; it opposes school vouchers. It demands more money for the U.S. Department of Housing and Urban Development, which has done so much to make life paradisiacal for Hispanic renters. It "strongly advocate[s] that the next justice appointed to the Supreme Court be Hispanic." (But heaven help the Hispanic nominee who dissents from the tripe offered up by LULAC lobbyists.) LULAC supports expanded Medicare, subsidized prescription drugs, and the other beams and joists of a medicine that is socialized in all but name. LULAC is against privatizing Social Security and for giving higher benefits to Social Security recipients. It does not say that Hispanic workers should be exempted from the inevitable hefty increase in payroll taxes, but then it doesn't have to; we can read between the lines.

And oh, yes: all those grand statements about achieving fluency in English are so much speechwriter's guff. LULAC endorses government-funded bilingual education, though it has the political savvy to call bilingualism "English Plus." A rose by any other name. . . . (This is not to say that LULAC doesn't occasionally stumble into a constitutionally sound position now and then. For instance, it opposes federal "English First" or English immersion mandates on local school districts: a position entirely compatible with traditional American federalism. But would anyone care to wager what LULAC's position would be on legislation to impose pro-bilingual federal mandates on local school districts?)[41]

Okay, so LULAC is Washington-based hypocrisy with a Spanish accent. Big deal. Is it a crime to profess noble ideals which are contradicted by one's actions?

No, but it ought to be a crime to act as a political advocacy group while taking government money. And in LULAC's case, the amount of the subsidy is staggering. Its LULAC National Educational Service Centers, based in Washington and "advancing the education of youth," received $2.962 million in government grants out of a total revenue of $4.352 million in the latest year for which figures were available.[42]

But these alms were used for advancing the education of youth, you protest, not for lobbying for a fatter welfare state. I repeat: this money is fungible. The almost $3 million transferred from taxpayers to LULAC's educational arm frees up $3 million for LULAC to use in lobbying, propagandizing, or blitzing Capitol Hill.

If LULAC really valued respecting its members' citizenship, honoring their country, or embodying its culture and civilization, it would return its millions of dollars in handouts. Don't hold your breath waiting for that to happen, amigos.

* * *

In recent years, lobbies for the elderly—so patronizingly known as "senior citizens"—have horned in on the civil rights game. You might think of old people as wise elders, blue hairs, and gray beards whose years and experience have given them a grandfatherly (or grandmotherly) solicitude for their country. Just as the grandmother at the dinner table would not dream of taking the last piece of pie if her grandchildren were still hungry, so would the elderly citizen of our ideal refuse special favors and stipends from a government whose tax burden is carried by his or her grandchildren.

Somewhere in this favored land such old people really may exist. Just not in Washington. For the self-styled advocates of "senior citizens" are among the most voracious and greedy tax hogs in the whole menagerie along the Potomac. They are fierce promoters of Social Security, Medicare, and other programs which constitute massive transfers of wealth from the young (grandchildren) to the old (the shameless grandparents).

The poster boys for greedy geezerhood are the National Committee to Preserve Social Security and Medicare. This Washington-based lobby was born in 1982, in the wake of the demagoguery whipped up when the National Commission on Social Security Reform, chaired by Alan Greenspan, tinkered with the system to supposedly guarantee its soundness for the next generation.

The panderers to fear were in high gear. No one exploited the moment with as much unscrupulous skill as James Roosevelt, the black-sheep eldest son of former President Franklin D. Roosevelt. Cashing in on his father's name and reputation, Roosevelt created one of the sleaziest fund-raising machines in all of Washington—and that is high praise, in a way, akin to being the most promiscuous gal at the Mustang Ranch.

The National Committee to Preserve Social Security and Medicare became a fearsome lobby by virtue of scare tactics. In Committee mass mailings, dark forces were always conspiring to erase the welfare state in the dead of night, leaving a nation of feeble and helpless old people to fend for themselves or, God forbid, move in with the children. (Interesting, isn't it, the extent to which the comforting arms of the national state have replaced the bosom of family?)

The National Committee to Preserve Social Security and Medicare was widely regarded as the sleaziest lobby of the 1980s. In 1988, the group was even threatened with legislation—cosponsored by Senate leaders of both parties—that would require it to state in large letters that it was not an agency of government. It seems that committee envelopes bore a deceptive resemblance to official mailings. But then, given that the committee lobbies day and night for a greater government presence in our lives, perhaps those faux-official envelopes were a case of wishful thinking.

In 2000, the committee raised a whopping $27.6 million from donors, mostly through direct-mail scare packages. Frightening widows and retirees into sending checks in order to keep those Social Security and Medicare checks coming is a disgraceful business, but some sleazebag has to do it. The group also made $1.3 million by renting out its mailing list to other groups that prey upon the elderly.[43] All told, the National Committee to Preserve Social Security and Medicare claims to have 5.5 million members—an absurd claim, if no more ridiculous than the membership estimates of most D.C.-based fund-raising groups, who often conflate mailing lists with membership. The committee asserts that it is the second-largest advocacy group for the elderly, after the mammoth American Association for Retired Persons, though it lacks the AARP's marketing genius and its (*Modern*) *Maturity*.

The committee likes to claim that it has cleaned up its act since the death of James Roosevelt in 1991, but a recent mailing is typical. In huge type on the outside of the envelope the reader is warned, "THE PUSH TO PRIVATIZE SOCIAL SECURITY IS UNDERWAY." (Perhaps the committee justifies the use of the giant font by the failing eyesight of the letter's recipients.) A six-page letter is enclosed; it threatens, "Privatization would put retirement security at real risk." The only way to save Social Security from the wolves at the door is to send ten bucks or more to a campaign "to counter all those who would tear down Social Security."[44]

The group's position may be stated simply: Social Security is a wondrous gift bequeathed us by President Franklin D. Roosevelt, and any modification to it—unless that modification increases the scope and benefit package of the program—is a blasphemy to be fought at as shrill a pitch as possible. As for Medicare, which after all was a legacy of LBJ rather than the sainted FDR, President Martha McSteen concedes that the "National Committee recognizes the need to shore up Medicare's finances."[45] This is to be done by adding prescription drug coverage, mental health coverage, physical therapy coverage, and a variety of other services that are to be paid for by the overburdened grandchildren of those suckers who send in their checks to the National Committee to Preserve Social Security and Medicare. As Martha McSteen demanded in remarks to the White House in November 2000, "This is a time to celebrate those in government."[46] Those in government have amply exhibited their gratitude.

The National Committee's legislative agenda is notable for its hostility toward those who are not old. While conceding that there is a need to "balance Social Security financing and spending over the next 75 years," the committee suggests "modest increases in payroll taxes"[47] as a possible remedy. The payroll taxes are harshly regressive; they hurt young families of modest means most of all. As if the ravenous oldsters even care. The committee even opposes any form of means-testing for Medicare benefits: a Rockefeller or Gates has "earned access" to Medicare. In 1997, it led the hysterical opposition to a proposal to increase Medicare fees for single retirees with annual incomes above $50,000 and retired couples with incomes over $75,000. The committee dispenses with even the illusion that Medicare is designed to help poor or needy old people: it is for all old people, who must be nestled in the welfare safety net just because they are old.

As for young people who view Social Security and Medicare with a certain degree of skepticism, National Committee spokesman Richard Renault has an answer: "I think that they don't realize what the program is about. Do you know, you're buying yourself the best insurance in the world. . . . You can't buy a better insurance policy."[48] In the strictest sense, he is correct: you can't buy a better insurance policy with that money, because the government won't let you.

The committee is frankly partisan. Executive vice president Max Richtman injected himself into the 2000 Nebraska U.S. Senate race between Democrat Ben Nelson and Republican Don Stenberg. After Stenberg endorsed the idea of permitting workers to privately invest a small part of their payroll taxes, Richtman appeared at an Omaha press conference with Nelson to say that "The Stenberg plan takes the security out of Social Security." (How many consultants did he have to pay to come up with that witticism?) Stenberg protested that this was part of "Democrat attempts to frighten seniors."[49] Stenberg lost, in a close race. Senator Nelson was last seen fitting snugly into the National Committee's pocket.

In 2000, the National Committee to Preserve Social Security and Medicare was also thrust—or barged—into the hot Missouri U.S. Senate race between incumbent Republican John Ashcroft and Democratic Governor Mel Carnahan. The Missouri Democratic Party ran ads with "ominous music in the background" and an announcer intoning, "According to the National Committee to Preserve Social Security and Medicare, John Ashcroft has one of the worst records in the entire U.S. Senate."[50]

Another ad featured Max Richtman himself, who said, "At the National Committee to Preserve Social Security and Medicare, we judge senators by what they do, not what they say. And Senator John Ashcroft's record on seniors' issues is one of the worst. Ashcroft supports spending Social Security funds on tax cuts mainly for the rich. He voted to raise the eligibility age for Medicare, and voted repeatedly against providing affordable prescription drug coverage for all seniors. Call John Ashcroft. Tell him to stop voting against Social Security and Medicare."[51]

The Ashcroft forces struck back, labeling the National Committee to Preserve Social Security and Medicare as "the worst interest group in Washington," and a practiced hand at "shaking down the elderly."[52] An Ashcroft spokesman said, "This sleazy outfit has a sickening record of tricking the most vulnerable Americans out of money they need for the necessities of life."[53] Right he was. But Carnahan died in a plane crash, won anyway on the strength of a sympathy vote, and his wife Jean took his seat. Ashcroft went on to become the Bush administration's Attorney General, from which position he attacked civil liberties with all the zeal of Max Richtman attacking fiscal responsibility.

No matter. However menacing Ashcroft may be as Attorney General, he ought not to have been vilified with government money—for incredibly enough, the National Committee to Preserve Social Security and Medicare has its hand in the federal till. Not way into the till—its take from 1996 to 2000 was $21,000[54]—but the principle remains constant. Taxpayers ought not to have to subsidize this kind (or any kind) of partisanship.

Evincing the same dinosaurish liberalism as the National Committee to Preserve Social Security and Medicare is the Center for Medicare Advocacy, which between 1996 and 2000 consumed $133,000 in taxpayers' dollars.[55]

The Center for Medicare Advocacy, based in Connecticut, claims to provide "education, advocacy, and legal assistance to help elders and people with disabilities obtain necessary healthcare." That "necessary healthcare" is government-subsidized healthcare; the Center files appeals for those denied Medicare benefits and trains people who are interested in "learning about healthcare rights."[56]

There is nothing illegal in acting as a kind of broker for the welfare state, but the Center for Medicare Advocacy is another objectionable recipient of government monies. It agitates for a more expensive Medicare system, and is rewarded with state subsidy to agitate for a more expensive Medicare system. . . . The daisy chain goes round and round.

The Center's political position on Medicare may be explained in a single word: More. It supports more spending on prescription drug coverage. More people eligible for that coverage. More of everything except cost-consciousness.

The Center opposed the 2001 Bush tax cut as a "raid of the Medicare Trust Fund." Every dollar earned by an American rightly belongs to Medicare recipients, after all; the Bush plan meant that "Medicare beneficiaries lose out to tax cuts."[57]

Is it any wonder that the Center for Medicare Advocacy is a government grantee? He who does the king's shilling earns the king's shilling.

The National Senior Citizens Law Center (NSCLC), based in Washington, naturally, was into the government for grants of $580,000 from 1996–2000,[58] which did not prevent it from joining the Fair Taxes for All Coalition.

The NSCLC advertises itself as a "unique resource" that assists elderly persons with "litigation support services in cases involving Medicare, Medicaid, health insurance, age discrimination, Social Security,"[59] and on and on down the roster of welfare-state agencies. It premise is that "you"—hey you, old man!—are entitled to a range of taxpayer-supplied benefits with as little hassle or red tape as possible. The NSCLC, in turn, is entitled to taxpayer dough, too—and anyone who complains is probably a misanthropic right-wing fanatic.

Finally, we arrive at the granddaddy (if you will forgive the expression) of all the tax-consuming political advocacy groups for the elderly, the National Council on the Aging.

The Washington, D.C.-based National Council on the Aging might as well be given its own government building on Constitution (or Great Society) Avenue. In the last year for which an IRS Form 990 was available (1998), an incredible $45.152 million of the NCOA's total revenues of $50.013 million came from government grants. That's 90.3 percent. The National Council on the Aging makes the Department of Health and Human Services look like a private club.

The NCOA asserts that two of its prime goals are "increasing funding for Older Americans Act programs" and "enacting a new Medicare prescription drug benefit that provides affordable, meaningful coverage." It frankly admits to being a "powerful advocate for public policies,"[60] which is within its rights, though it fails to mention in its literature that this advocacy is paid for almost entirely by taxpayer dollars—many of them funneled through the same programs (such as the Older Americans Act) which the NCOA supports so vociferously!

"Politics is not a dirty word,"[61] declares the NCOA in defending its activities on Capitol Hill. Maybe not. But the NCOA is hardly proof of that proposition. Come to think of it, very few of the organizations mentioned in this book could serve as advertisements for the cleanliness and wholesomeness of American politics.

Notes

1. Joseph H. Brown, "Black Schools Don't Have to be Unequal," *Tampa Tribune*, June 25, 2000, p. 6.
2. Clint Bolick, *The Affirmative Action Fraud* (Washington, DC: Cato Institute, 1996), p. 34.
3. Samples, Yablonski, and Osorio, "More Government for All," p. 5.
4. NAACP Legislative Report Card for the 107th Congress, July 2001.
5. IRS Form 990, NAACP Nevada Housing Development Corporation, 1999.
6. *National Urban League 2000 Annual Report*, p. 5.
7. *Equal Opportunity Journal* (July 2001).
8. *National Urban League 2000 Annual Report*, p. 1.
9. Ibid., p. 10.
10. Ibid., p. 22.
11. Samples, Yablonski, and Osorio, "More Government for All," p. 5.
12. Terence Samuel, "A Washington Think Tank Has Helped Fuel Three Decades of Black Political Success," *St. Louis Post-Dispatch*, May 7, 2000, p. A12.
13. "Joint Center for Political and Economic Studies," www.jointcenter.org, June 14, 2001.
14. "Minority Business RoundTable," www.jointcenter.org/mbrt/ policy.html, June 14, 2001.
15. IRS Form 990, Joint Center for Political and Economic Studies, 1999.
16. IRS Form 990, Leadership Council for Metropolitan Open Communities, 1998.
17. "History and Mission," www.lcmoc.org/history.html, June 21, 2001.
18. "Policy Statement," www.lcmoc.org/pstatemene.html, June 21, 2001.
19. "The NCCD Mission," www.nccd-crc.org/who.html, December 14, 2001.
20. IRS Form 990, National Council on Crime and Delinquency, 1998.
21. "The National Institute on Race and Justice," www.nccd-crc.org/race.html, December 14, 2001.
22. Peter Y. Hong, "Law Enforcement Officers Oppose Initiative on Crime," *Los Angeles Times*, February 18, 2000, p. B1.

23. "The Criminal Justice System and Racial Equality," www.nccd-crc.org/policy/crimjust.html, December 14, 2001.
24. NCLR folder, undated.
25. "Twenty of The Questions Most Frequently Asked About The Latino Community," NCLR, May 1999.
26. "The National Council of La Raza," www.nclr.org/about, June 23, 2001.
27. "Civil Rights," www.nclr.org/policy/civil.html, June 23, 2001.
28. NCLR 2001 Public Policy Briefing Book, p. 1.
29. Ibid., p. 3.
30. Marcela Urrutia, "Federal Efforts to Ensure Against Discrimination Toward Individuals on the Basis of Limited English Proficiency Under Attack," *Agenda* (Summer 2001), p. 12.
31. *NCLR 2001 Public Policy Briefing Book*, p. 4.
32. "Social Security," www.nclr.org/policy/socialsecurity/social_ security.html, June 23, 2001.
33. Samples, Yablonski, and Osorio, "More Government for All," p. 5.
34. "Remarks of Raul Yzaguirre," National Conference on Race & Ethnicity in American Higher Education, June 3, 2001.
35. "Raul Yzaguirre, President NCLR," www.nclr.org/president/rybio. html, June 23, 2001.
36. Julia Malone, "Immigration: Mass Amnesty high on Hispanic agenda," *Atlanta Journal and Constitution*, August 18, 2001, p. 7A.
37. IRS Form 990, National Council of La Raza, 1998.
38. "Tax Cuts," *Agenda* (Summer 2001), p. 18.
39. "Creeds," www.lulac.org/About/Creeds.html, June 14, 2001.
40. Ibid.
41. "The 2001 LULAC Legislative Platform," www.lulac.org/Issues/ Platform.html, June 14, 2001.
42. IRS Form 990, LULAC Nat'l Educational Svc. Centers Inc., 1998.
43. "Senior Groups Make Money," AP, *Newsday*, July 27, 2001, p. A26.
44. Ibid.
45. "About the NCPSSM," www.ncpssm.org/about/index.html, September 10, 2001.
46. Martha McSteen, "National Committee's White House Comments on the Older Americans Act," November 21, 2000.
47. NCPSSM 107th Congress Legislative Agenda, p. 3.
48. Diana Block, "Clinton Linkup a Near Dud at Carnegie Mellon," *Pittsburgh Post-Gazette*, February 18, 1999, p. A12.
49. C. David Kotok, "Senate Rivals At Odds Over Social Security," *Omaha World-Herald*, September 9, 2000, p. 49.
50. Jo Mannies, "Post-Dispatch Ad Check," *St. Louis Post-Dispatch*, July 13, 2000, p. A7.
51. Jo Mannies, "Post-Dispatch Ad Check, *St. Louis Post-Dispatch*, July 6, 2000, p. A10.
52. Jo Mannies, "Post-Dispatch Ad Check," *St. Louis Post-Dispatch*, July 14, 2000, p. A7.
53. Jo Mannies, "Democratic Ads Charge that Ashcroft Is an Enemy of Social Security, Medicare," *St. Louis Post-Dispatch*, July 6, 2000, p. A10.
54. Samples, Yablonski, and Osorio, "More Government for All," p. 6.
55. Ibid.
56. "About the Center for Medicare Advocacy," www.medicareadvocacy.org, September 10, 2001.

57. "Tax Cuts May Cost Medicare Beneficiaries Their Health Benefits," www.medicareadvocacy.org/bush, September 13, 2001.
58. Samples, Yablonski, and Osorio, "More Government for All," p. 5.
59. "NSCLC's Services for Advocates," www.nsclc.org/advocates.html, December 14, 2001.
60. "Public Policy & Advocacy," www.ncoa.org/advocacy.html, June 23, 2001.
61. "Advocacy," www.ncoa.org/membership/join_05.html, June 23, 2001.

7

Gravy Train Conservatives

Once upon a time, before the dawn of what *Weekly Standard* editor Fred Barnes proudly dubbed "Big Government Conservatives," activists on the political right received relatively few grants from the federal government.[1] Although certain Reaganites were more than willing to put aside small-government principles when it came time to channel tax dollars to their friends, the ideological imbalance remains, at least to an extent. Those with a philosophical commitment to constitutional government are less likely to ask for, and thus to receive, government dollars.

For instance, in her exposé, *The Right to Lifers*, investigative reporter Connie Paige boasted that she would document "who they are, how they operate, and where they get their money."[2] Whether she succeeded or not is best left up to the reader, but one thing is clear: the right-to-lifers do not get their money from the government. Paige did not list a single government grant to a pro-life organization.

But just as there are many lefts, so too are there a variety of "rights." The libertarian right takes almost no government money; to paraphrase the crusty ex-Arizona Senator Barry Goldwater, any libertarian who takes federal funds deserves a swift kick in the ass. The traditionalist conservatives also receive little if any funding from the central state, in part because they have been so effectively demonized by the mass media. Establishment conservatives in Washington, on the other hand, have learned to play the grant game with oily skill, and as for the "neoconservatives," those urban ex-socialists who joined the right primarily as a means to promote U.S. military intervention abroad . . . well, they could give lessons in grant-grubbing to the most seasoned con artist.

The array of neoconservative, hawkish, and pro-intervention think tanks that propagandize for U.S. military involvement abroad is heavily subsidized by the very government whose reach they seek to extend. The National Endowment for Democracy has often been called a slush fund for neoconservatives, but the appellation applies also to Freedom House, the Center for Strategic and International Studies, and other interventionist organizations that take the king's shilling and then praise the deployment of all the king's men.

But the hypocrisy of such armchair warriors is almost too much to bear. They take the king's shilling, they defame the king's opponents, and they flack for the king's wars—though, signally, the corps of senior analysts and research associates never seem to get around to signing up to fight these wars. Belligerent eggheads are so much more useful on the home front instead of in the trenches.

Freedom House, the oldest of the pro-war lobbies, was created with a very simple goal: to "destroy isolationism forever,"[3] as it declared in a January 1943 newspaper ad. By "isolationism," Freedom House meant the innate preference of most Americans to refrain from fighting foreign wars unless the territory of the United States has been attacked or is credibly threatened with attack. In the postwar world, this preference for peace would not do: benighted Americans from places like Iowa and Montana and Alabama must be made to understand that not a leaf could drop in Vietnam, or a bird fall from the sky in East Timor, without the "vital interests" of the U.S. being at stake.

If this bloated and expansive definition of vital interests seemed preposterous to most people, well, then they must be re-educated. (As the Communist playwright Bertolt Brecht said of an abortive revolt of East Germans against their Stalinist government in 1953, it was time for the government to elect a new people.) So successful has Freedom House been in creating an innocuous image for itself—despite its origins in the interventionist socialist left—that the *Washington Post*, typically, refers to it as "an American pro-democracy group."[4] How sweetly unobjectionable!

Freedom House was founded during the Second World War. Its parents included Eleanor Roosevelt and the great fraud Wendell Wilkie, the liberal utilities executive whose Republican nomination in 1940 was Henry Luce's greatest production.

This gang of socialists turned neo-conservatives has become, more or less, a government agency. In 1998, government grants totaled $2.902 million, or 65 percent of its total revenue of $4.465 million.[5] Paraphrasing Janis Joplin, it seems that freedom's just another word for cashing Uncle Sam's checks. And with this government subvention, Freedom House agitates for . . . a more active government. By its own admission, Freedom House promotes an agenda that includes "U.S. engagement in international affairs,"[6] a euphemism for a hyper-interventionism. Should it surprise us that that same government lavishly funds its ardent cheerleader?

Freedom House sponsors conferences, funds the work of scholars and publicists who toe the party line, and ships money abroad to like-minded organizations. It is perhaps most famous for its annual assessment of freedom around the globe, a brilliant p.r. move that since 1972 has identified this band of welfare-warfare state liberals with free speech and free markets. The nations of the globe are categorized as "Free," "Partly Free," or "Not Free," and while few would dispute the placement of such a Stalinist hellhole as North Korea in the "Not Free" column, Freedom House bases its ratings more on "political rights" than on the equally important "economic rights." Being free to own property and to buy and sell at a local bazaar or trading post would seem to be of far more significance to most people than having the right to cast a single ballot in an election in which millions will also cast ballots—but then the employees of Freedom House tend to be people with little or no experience in the private sector.

Today, Freedom House has seized upon the threat of terrorism to call for vast new interventions by the U.S. government in the affairs of other nations. Citing a "democracy gap"[7] in the Muslim world, Freedom House advisory board chairman Bill Richardson, whose once-promising political career bottomed out when the Energy Department he led in the Clinton administration turned out to be a sieve for atomic secrets, has called for the U.S. to alter the form of government in the Arab nations of the Middle East. By what authority the U.S. would undertake such a mission is unclear, as is the extent of the military entanglement that such a crusade would entail, but then these mundane details seldom concern global busybodies like Richardson, who always seem to have avoided military service when they had the chance to don a uniform. (Richardson has gone on to conduct foreign policy from the governorship of New Mexico.)

As the federal government expands, Freedom House—if not freedom—seems certain to expand apace.

* * *

The National Endowment for Democracy was born in a June 1982 speech by President Reagan to the British Parliament. Reagan read from the teleprompter: "The objective I propose is quite simple to state: to foster the infrastructure of democracy—the system of a free press, unions, political parties, universities—which allows a people to choose their own way, to develop their own culture, to reconcile their own differences through peaceful means."[8]

Put that way, the NED seems unobjectionable, and in fact the legislation creating this boondoggle passed easily the next year. Colorado Republican Congressman Hank Brown, an early and persistent critic of the NED, saw it differently: "To institute an international political action committee that interferes with existing democracies makes a sham out of our efforts to advance self-government. For those who have forgotten, America's holding high the torch of freedom means something far different than NED's efforts to manipulate foreign democracies or waste taxpayers' dollars."[9]

The NED combines two of the worst features of American democracy: moralistic busybodyism and patronage politics.

To gain bipartisan support for its spending, the NED launders its grants through four satellites: the American Center for International Labor Solidarity, a front for the U.S. AFL-CIO; the Center for International Private Enterprise, a front for the U.S. Chamber of Commerce (note the delicious irony that this center for "private enterprise" is fed by government monies); the International Republican Institute, a front for the Republican Party; and the National Democratic Institute for International Affairs, a front for the Democratic Party. Thus big labor, big business, and the Democratic and Republican parties have been paid off. In the world in which NED types circulate, who else is there to please?

The NED's board is studded with useful politicos of what has been rightly termed the "dead center." The long-time chairman, recently retired, was John Brademas, an arrogant liberal congressman from Indiana who was finally swept away in the Reagan landslide of 1980. His comrades included the eternal Indiana Senator Richard G. Lugar, forever known as "Richard Nixon's favorite mayor" from his years as chief executive of Indianapolis, and perhaps the only man ever to run for the Republican presidential nomination (in 1996) on a platform that we need to spend more on foreign aid; and the former New York Democratic Congressman Stephen Solarz, who was bounced from the House in 1992 in the wake of the great House of Representatives' check-bouncing scandal.

The Endowment's first president was Carl Gershman, whose roots were in the socialist movement and whose previous job was as a resident fellow at Freedom House, that war-born propaganda mill whose idea of "freedom" is not exactly consonant with that of, say, Thomas Jefferson. Twenty-plus years later, Gershman is still at the helm: when a socialist policy geek finds a cushy government-paid sinecure, he guards it with his life.

Michael Kinsley, then of the *New Republic*, provided the most succinct explanation of the National Endowment for Democracy: "What we have here is a pork barrel for intellectuals. Money for study grants, for conferences, and especially for layers of administration, as the government gives money to the Endowment, which gives it to a Foundation to give it to an Institute to fund a fellowship program. Money for the boys, as Mayor Daley used to say."[10]

This money for the boys has grown to an annual subsidy of $33 million, and as the "war on terror" seems to have opened the treasury wide for any opportunist or money-grubber with an eye for the main chance, odds are that the NED's budget is about to swell.

The list of foreign political parties and movements that have been subsidized by the U.S. taxpayer through the NED is staggeringly long: from the Civic Forum in Czechoslovakia to feminist groups in the Congo to the Mongolian Social Democrat Party. From 2000–2002, the anti-Milosevic Serb opposition received $77 million, a subsidy that backfired when the unpopular Serb president scored political points by claiming that his democratic foes were American puppets. Some of the above-mentioned are undoubtedly good causes; others are dubious. But just where in the U.S. Constitution is the federal government authorized to tax citizens of this country and send the revenues to political parties overseas? (Of course, referring to the Constitution as anything but a quaint dead letter locked away in the National Archives is enough to make NED-types suspect critics of a dangerous "radicalism." Anyone who actually believes in the ideas of the American Founders would be exceedingly unlikely to walk away with gobs of NED cash. Then again, he or she would never apply for NED money.)

In its infancy, the NED blundered into friendly countries like Bill Clinton groping through a room full of comely Capitol Hill interns. The tart-tongued Senator Ernest Hollings (D-SC) remarked, "This thing is not the National Endowment for Democracy but the National Endowment for Embarrassment."[11] For instance, it intervened in that notorious dungeon of totalitarian dankness, France, by funneling money to a labor union known as the Force Ouvriére. The French were both amused and outraged; as the influential newspaper *Liberation* mockingly put it under the headline "The Secret Funds of Reagan in France,"[12] the land of De Gaulle and Bridget Bardot is "a country where democracy does not seem fragile."[13] Congressman Hank Brown asked how Americans would feel if "they learned that the French Government was giving millions of dollars to the AFL-CIO to oppose the policies of Ronald Reagan."[14]

The endowment was the obvious sugar daddy behind an abortive springtime 2002 coup in Venezuela, wherein the elected president, Hugo Chavez, was briefly deposed before reassuming office. It didn't take Sherlock Holmes to discover the source of the coup: the NED had hurriedly quadrupled its budget for interference in Venezuelan affairs, to $877,000, as it smelled Chavez's blood.

George A. Folsom, president of the International Republican Institute, the Venezuela-based mouthpiece of the endowment, burbled in the early hours of the attempted overthrow, "The Venezuelan people rose up to defend democracy in their country. Venezuelans were provoked into action as a result of systematic repression by the government of Hugo Chavez."

The hapless Folsom spoke too soon. Chavez turned the tables on the U.S. puppets who sought to oust him. The National Endowment for Embarrassment had struck out again.

In the wake of the Venezuela debacle, Richard Cummings, a former intelligence officer, wrote with disgust, "[W]e have a Congress and a federal bureaucracy tossing around our money so some jerks can play at being power brokers around the world. The National Endowment for Democracy is a hoax. Now everyone in Latin America knows we were up to our ears in trying to get rid of Chavez. The whole thing backfired. The politicians walk away and we pick up the bill. Some democracy. But what I really want to know is, is there a Ritz in Caracas, so the hacks on the gravy train can meet to overturn a democratically elected government at our expense? And this stuff happens because we let it happen. If we choose to be a nation of sheep, we have only ourselves to blame."[15]

If the National Endowment for Democracy is a state agency in fact, other ostensibly "private" foreign-policy organizations are state agencies in all but name.

Take the Center for Strategic and International Studies, which for forty years has served as the tax-exempt Washington-based headquarters for both architects and mere publicists of the national security state. (In a nice symbolic linkage, CSIS has co-hosted with the NED such events as "Securing the Balkans: The Unfinished Agenda." You can bet that the theme of this conference was not that the Balkans could be secured by anything other than an expensive and extensive U.S. involvement.)

The Center acts as a kind of shadow national security council filled with men who would be Kissingers. It advertises its "bipartisan outreach to Congress"[16] via frequent congressional testimony. In its own bureaucratese, the Center claims that it "generates strategic insights," "convenes strategic networks," "develops today's and tomorrow's leaders," and, most ominously, "crafts policy solutions."[17]

In 1997, CSIS took in $152,662 in government grants; the next year, it banked $264,919 from taxpayers out of a total revenue of $12.951 million. By 2000, the pump was primed so as to be the envy of any Keynesian. Government contributions totaled $1.007 million, or a whopping 37.5 percent of the total revenue of $2.688 million.[18] CSIS was close to becoming an arm of the state—and so it is no surprise that its policy recommendations consistently advocate a larger role for that very same state.

The CSIS President is John J. Hamre, a former deputy secretary of defense under President Clinton. He succeeded Robert Zoellick, whose role as an advisor to the 2000 campaign of George W. Bush brought the CSIS the kind of explicitly partisan profile that it would prefer to shun. Zoellick went on to serve as Bush's U.S. trade representative, sliding easily from the world of the subsidized think tank into the world of government.

The CSIS congressional advisory board reads like a roll call of Capitol Hill statists: it includes Senators Bob Graham (D-FL), John Warner (R-VA), Jay Rockefeller (D-WV), and John McCain (R-AZ) as well as Representatives John Murtha (D-PA), Jim Leach (R-IA), and David Dreier (R-CA). Various CSIS working and study groups involve the most interventionist members of Congress, including the dynamic duo of an activist U.S. government: Senators Joe Lieberman (D-CT) and Richard Lugar (R-IN). If the word "liberty" ever passes between the lips of such men, it is in praise of an abstract liberty across the seas—never at home.

The CSIS Board of Trustees is studded with three-star names from the insular world of the military-industrial-diplomatic complex: Brent Scowcroft, James Schlesinger, Felix G. Rohatyn, Zbigniew Brzezinski, William E. Brock, and even the graying eminence of Cold War diplomacy, Henry Kissinger.

Washington Times editor Arnaud de Borchgrave made $119,423 as a "senior advisor,"[19] which provides an easy avenue of access to Washington's "conservative" paper, which is often mocked by liberals but read by Republicans in the nation's capital.

The center understands perfectly well how the game is played in Washington. In April 2002, it bestowed the Admiral Arleigh Burke Leadership Award on Rep. John Murtha (D-PA), citing his "character and principled approach to public service."[20]

The content of Murtha's character has been revealed many times since his election to the House in 1974. He represents Johnstown, Pennsylvania, site of the infamous 1889 flood which killed 2,200 people. His district's favorite son is Jimmy Stewart, born in nearby Indiana, PA, though we may think of Murtha as the precise opposite of Stewart's naive and idealistic Mr. Smith who went to Washington. John Murtha would have had Jimmy Stewart for breakfast, and still had room in his stomach for a big helping of pork.

Murtha's only moment in the national political sun was when he was named as a figure in the early 1980s' Abscam scandal (an FBI sting operation using phony Arab sheiks with briefcases full of money). He was never indicted, and the abortive scandal seems not to have hurt him. He'll be in Congress for as long as he likes.

And if the military-industrial complex against which President Eisenhower warned us has anything to say about it, John Murtha will be in Congress till the end of time. His approach to public service has been to support whatever the Pentagon and the defense establishment wants. He was the man most responsible for blocking the bipartisan Penny-Kasich cuts in defense spending in 1993; the supposed rebate which taxpayers were to receive upon the termination of the Cold War never appeared in our mailboxes. Instead, the military spent the 1990s going hither and yon—to Bosnia, Haiti, Serbia, the Sudan, and other places whose relationship to the national interest was obscure at best.

It was John Murtha who kept the pipeline of military spending flowing, and for this the rent-a-scholars of CSIS thanked him profusely.

Typically, a CSIS report in January 2001 bemoaned the "antiquated equipment and dilapidated and insecure facilities"[21] which the State Department was forced to endure. The figurehead of the panel that produced the report, Frank Carlucci, had been a Secretary of Defense in the Reagan administration. The State Department, of course, welcomed the report, as it always welcomes "nonpartisan" recommendations that the State Department get more swag.

One month later, a February 2001 CSIS report warned of an impending "train wreck"[22] because military spending was dangerously low—though as it turned out, the primary deficiency of the U.S. defense establishment was in low-tech intelligence gathering. Nevertheless, CSIS has used the September 11, 2001 attack as talking point #1 for what it always supported: a larger, more intrusive military presence, at home and around the world.

Even before 9/11, CSIS had taken what might charitably be described as a proactive stance on Middle Eastern affairs. In November 2000, the *Independent* of London reported that a draft CSIS paper by Anthony Cordesman, a former advisor to the presidential campaign of Mad John McCain, urged the Palestinian Authority to use "interrogation methods that border on psychological and/or physical torture" in an effort to "ruthlessly"[23] suppress its opponents. Even Yassir Arafat, who has never evinced what might be called a Jeffersonian concern for individual rights, was appalled.

After 9/11, Cordesman, now billed as a "terrorism specialist"— the guy knows a growth industry when he sees one—urged unprecedented powers upon the Orwellian-named Office of Homeland Security.

CSIS scholars cheered President Bush's speechwriters as he identified Iran, Iraq, and North Korea as an "axis of evil," neatly linking nations theretofore as dissimilar as rotten apples, rotten oranges, and rotten kiwi fruit. Expect the CSIS to profit handsomely from the war on terrorism. Alas, what's good for CSIS is not necessarily good for America.

* * *

The National Committee on U.S.-China Relations, a New York-based nonprofit founded in 1966 to engage in "dialogue with Chinese citizens,"[24] is heavily funded by the U.S. Departments of State and Education. In 1998, government grants accounted for $676,616 of the organization's total revenue of $3.112 million;[25] the remainder came largely from corporate interests seeking closer ties between the U.S. and China.

The advisability of such ties is not at issue; rather, the question is should taxpayers be subsidizing a committee that pushes a very definite political program of engagement and trade with China.

Although the National Committee on U.S.-China Relations is perhaps most famous for its sponsorship of the 1972 table tennis games between teams from the two nations—and don't you dare call it ping-pong!—it has also sponsored numerous trips, speeches, and seminars featuring such eminently unathletic personages as Henry Kissinger, Premier Zhu Rhongji, and countless ambassadors, Chinese and American functionaries, and Sinologists whose views are roughly compatible with those of the committee. The National Committee also publishes a newsletter and booklets that make the case for stronger U.S.-China relations.

The committee has enjoyed an ever-increasing slice of the federal budget since the mid-1970s, after President Nixon's normalization of relations with what was once so quaintly known as "Red China." Almost the only bump in its road to the disbursement office of the U.S. Treasury came in 2000, when that bogeyman of good liberals everywhere, Senator Jesse Helms (R-NC), chairman of the Senate Foreign Relations Committee, temporarily held up the State Department's fiscal year 2000 grant of $355,000 to the National Committee.

Helms's complaint was a perfect example of what ails the Beltway Right. He sent a letter to National Committee on U.S.-China Relations President John L. Holden requesting that the committee begin holding human rights and religious freedom seminars within China. He also chided the committee for escorting its Chinese visitors to the offices of the usual liberal warhorses (the American Civil Liberties

Union, Planned Parenthood) and ignoring the National Right to Life Committee and the Ronald Reagan Presidential Library.

A Helms spokesman explained that "this organization runs programs heavily tilted toward the Communist Chinese and . . . directly engaging the regime. If they want federal funding, they should have a more balanced program that supports civil society and bringing freedom to China."[26] In other words, if you take the king's shilling, you play the king's tune. Apparently it never occurred to Senator Helms or his mouthpiece that private organizations promoting any policy toward China—from intimate friendship to belligerent warmongering—should receive zero federal monies.

Eggheads who sit in the dead center of our stagnant political waters have the best chance of feeding on government monies. The Brookings Institution, long the gray eminence of establishment liberal think tanks, is being nothing if not consistent with its statist orientation when it takes government contributions ($844,926 in 1997)[27] to fund its work.

And what policy recommendations do the Brookings scholars come up with? "Strengthening" the Orwellian Office of Homeland Security. "Promot[ing] National Service,"[28] the smiley-face name for conscription. Supporting national missile defense. Encouraging school vouchers. "Resurrecting the Estate Tax." "The Case Against Tax Cuts."[29] Supporting NAFTA. The list goes on. Some may be good ideas, some bad, but Mr. Jefferson's question hovers over the whole affair: Why should American citizens be compelled to fund Brookings?

Brookings employees also seized on the events of September 11, 2001, to argue that the modest 2001 Bush tax cuts should be rescinded so that more money could be pumped into the war on terrorism. But the real augury of Brookings's future direction came when in January 2002 Strobe Talbott, former *Time* magazine bloviator and Clinton's Deputy Secretary of State, was elected its president.

Talbott expressed his vision of a post-American paradise in an infamous 1992 essay in *Time*: "All countries are basically social arrangements. . . . No matter how permanent and even sacred they may seem at any one time, in fact they are all artificial and temporary. . . . Within the next hundred years . . . nationhood as we know it will be obsolete; all states will recognize a single, global authority. A phrase briefly fashionable in the mid-20th-century—'citizen of the world'—will have assumed real meaning by the end of the 21st."[30]

Isn't that a cheery thought? All of us, whether Bulgarian or Bolivian or French or Thai or American, bowing to a "single, global authority." Whose reports will be written by the flacks at the Brookings Institution, no doubt.

Brookings's counterpart on the centrist right, the American Enterprise Institute, is similarly unaverse to taking the king's shilling while producing policy reports, though AEI, to its credit, is far less hoggish than Brookings. In 2000, AEI received $37,500 in government contributions out of a very healthy total revenue of $24.490 million.[31] This is less than the proverbial drop in the bucket, which raises the question: Why not forswear government grants altogether, so as to keep a praiseworthy independence from the state (and to please Mr. Jefferson withal)?

* * *

The second President Bush's emphasis on "compassionate conservatism" highlighted the good works often done by church and nonprofit organizations in ministering to the needs of the poor. Such private efforts are demonstrably superior to government provision of social welfare, but again we run into that nettlesome question that the Beltway Right prefers to run away from: If we are to "de-fund the left," as the cry went up from New Right partisans twenty years ago, must we then "fund the right"?

Perhaps the favorite nonprofit of the "compassionate conservative" Republicans is the National Center for Neighborhood Enterprise (NCNE), which was founded in 1981 by an engaging and charismatic activist named Robert L. Woodson, Sr.

Woodson is an impressive man. The NCNE website calls him "the godfather of the movement to empower neighborhood-based organizations."[32] Active in community development projects since the 1960s, Woodson was the director of the National Urban League's Administration of Justice division before joining the American Enterprise Institute. In 1981, he started the National Center for Neighborhood Enterprise with a $300,000 grant from the conservative Sarah Scaife Foundation. He quickly became a leading figure in the nascent African-American right, along with Clarence Thomas, Thomas Sowell, Walter Williams, and Jay Parker.

Woodson's message was a refreshing alternative to the stagnant welfarism of the black establishment. "I say give money directly to poor people," he told a gathering in Reagan-era Washington. "Let them make choices."[33] If this was not exactly a prescription to get the government out of our wallets, at least it would chop away at the regulatory forest on the Potomac.

The National Center's exact purpose is—like many community-activist groups—a bit murky. According to its publicity material, the Center "provides effective community and faith-based organizations with training and technical assistance, links them to sources of support, and evaluates their experience for public policy. Societal problems addressed by NCNE's grassroots network include youth violence, substance abuse, teen pregnancy, homelessness, joblessness, poor education and deteriorating neighborhoods."[34] In something of a mixed metaphor, Center publicists describe it as a "'Geiger counter' that canvasses low-income communities, finds out what's working, and then applies 'miracle-grow' in the form of training, technical assistance, and linkages to support."[35]

Rather than impose solutions upon the inner city from without—solutions designed by middle-class white bureaucrats whose hoods were stamped "Land's End"—the NCNE sought out indigenous leadership. By assisting these modern "Josephs," as Woodson biblically labels community leaders, the National Center helps promote healing and restoration from within the afflicted areas. Among the NCNE's more innovative programs was an inner-city peace initiative which recruited ex-inmates to steer young black males away from gangs.

The NCNE became a favorite of Jack Kemp, the Republican congressman and later Secretary of Housing and Urban Development in the first Bush administration. When Newt Gingrich and his purported GOP revolutionaries stormed Washington after the 1994 congressional elections, Woodson's stock rose even higher. So eager were the Gingrichites to lavish money upon the National Center that in 1997, House Judiciary Committee Chairman Henry Hyde (R-IL) tried to steer $25 million over five years to the NCNE through the National Youth Crime Prevention Demonstration Act.

This is the kind of windfall that enchants the dreams of nonprofit officers. There was just one problem: although the NCNE had been receiving about $200,000 from the Justice Department since 1991, department subalterns expressed "very strong reservations" about whether or not the National Center was capable of administering such an enormous amount. The bureaucratic rebellion scuttled Hyde's demonstration program, though the NCNE walked away with a grant for youth programs worth $2.5 million.

As the NCNE's star was waxing brightest, the *Washington Post* undertook an investigation into its finances. This is just the sort of muckraking that is never done to liberal nonprofits, but nevertheless, the *Post* uncovered some unsettling facts.

For instance, in 1999, only 14 percent of the NCNE's $2.2 million in private and government funding was sent to the neighborhood groups whose mission it is to help. About half of that $2.2 million was spent on salaries ($600,000) and consultants ($464,000). While in 1996 the NCNE handed out $62,000 to neighborhood groups, it spent almost twice that amount ($120,000) on a promotional video for a dinner.[36]

Though Woodson is not a conventional conservative, he has taken "Republican" positions on a variety of issues: for instance, he has written in favor of school choice and Social Security reform.

President George W. Bush has publicly praised Woodson as a "social entrepreneur."[37] Bush has spoken under NCNE auspices, a symbolic act of immense importance in encouraging conservative foundations to direct their money National Center-ward. Woodson has returned the favor, praising the White House Office on Faith-Based and Community Initiatives and offering withering criticism of its critics.

"Many of the religious leaders who say they 'won't touch government money with a 10-foot pole' probably wouldn't touch some of the people who need these services with a 10-foot pole either,"[38] writes Woodson, seeming to impute racism and bad motives to religious people who refuse to accept government money. This is rich: in the age of Bush II, Republicans denounce Americans for refusing to take welfare.

To be fair, Woodson denies that "compassionate conservatism" means turning on the federal tap. He wrote the *Washington Post*, "The point of the 'faith-based initiative' is not to put faith-based groups on the federal payroll. Many do not want government funds, and they need not apply. The purpose of . . . the president's initiative is to give individuals in need of help a choice among secular and faith-based providers. Empowering that choice also means looking at larger issues such as regulatory barriers and letting individuals direct funding choices through charitable tax credits and vouchers for services."[39]

Nevertheless, as the *Post* reported, the NCNE has come a long way from its origins as a privately supported organization. In 2001, the majority ($1.8 million, or 58 percent) of its funding came from the federal government. With a Republican White House, it seems, the NCNE is going to get while the gettin's good.

Like Woodson's National Center for Neighborhood Enterprise, the National Fatherhood Initiative (NFI) has the best intentions in the world. But perhaps the "National" in its title should be the tipoff: organizations with "national" ambitions usually have their eyes set on "national" money. And few have succeeded in tapping the federal treasury with as much success in as short a time as has the National Fatherhood Initiative.

The NFI was founded in 1994. Its praiseworthy aim was to "lead a society-wide movement to confront the problem of father absence." It sought to do so not by increasing welfare payments to single mothers—thus substituting the cold embrace of the state for that of a husband—but rather "by increasing the proportion of children growing up with involved, responsible, and committed fathers."[40]

The absence of fathers is perhaps the most insidious and crippling pathology afflicting American families, particularly African-American families. By emphasizing the vital role that fathers and husbands play in healthy families, and by seeking ways to restore fatherhood as both an obligation and an honor, the NFI has its heart in the right place. Alas, it has its hand in your wallet.

By 2000, government contributions to NFI amounted to $497,189, or 29.3 percent of its total revenue of $1.697 million.[41] And now the National Fatherhood Initiative looks to have hit the jackpot in the Bush administration. As governor of Texas, George W. Bush steered a $416,000 state grant to NFI in 1999 to create a Texas Fatherhood Initiative, a state facsimile of the national initiative. President Bush appointed Wade Horn, the energetic ex-president of the NFI, to a position as Assistant Secretary of Health and Human Services. Responding to his feminist critics, Horn honked, in a language livelier than that of the typical zestless nominee, "I don't want to trap women in a troubled marriage or an abusive relationship. I'm not suggesting we outlaw divorce or bring back shotgun marriages. And I have no interest in running a dating service for unwed fathers. But I do want to help couples develop the skills needed to sustain a healthy marriage."[42]

Much of NFI's agenda is uncontroversial: few outside the most Amazonian circles would disagree with NFI President Roland Warren that the fact that one in three children is not living with his or her father is a profoundly disturbing social trend. The National Fatherhood Initiative sponsors summits, honors meritorious fathers, and promotes a favorable view of fathers in the mass media (in which Dad is usually a dolt). But it also pursues a political program—while carefully noting that as a nonprofit organization, the NFI "does not take an advocacy position on any legislation before Congress." This disclaimer is made by every politically charged nonprofit in America, left, right, and center, and should be taken with a large grain of salt.

For instance, President Roland Warren publicly praised the Bush administration's 2002 effort to expend $100 million on programs to support healthy marriages.[43] Is it being cynical to ask what NFI's cut of that $100 mill might be?

One "family-values" group that would probably love to get a seat on the Bush gravy train—but hasn't a chance in Hades of coming anywhere near it—is the Traditional Values Coalition, headed by the Reverend Lou Sheldon, a Presbyterian minister and former aide to Pat Robertson. Sheldon has been a *bête noire* to gay activists since the 1970s. In 1978, he directed the campaign for an unsuccessful initiative in California that would have barred publicly acknowledged homosexuals from teaching in public schools. Like many on the religious right, Sheldon is seemingly of two minds about liberty. On the one hand, he has taken forthright stands against those Orwellian monsters known as "hate-crimes" laws, which would place us on a very slippery slope toward "hate-thought laws." Moreover, these laws have bizarre consequences. If Joe bashes Fred over the head and takes his wallet, he is guilty of one crime. If Joe bashes Fred over the head and takes his wallet while calling him a "faggot," he is guilty of a much more serious crime. This is of dubious consolation to Fred, and would seem to set the stage for the criminalization of the slur "faggot." And if you don't think that outlawing speech is on the agenda of the gay rights movement, you haven't read its propaganda. Then again, you may simply be a homophobe in need of a stint in a re-education camp.

The Traditional Values Coalition is headquartered in Anaheim, California, but has an office in Washington, D.C. Like its ancestors in the New Right of the late 1970s and early 1980s, it is more frenetic than anything else, supplying a steady barrage of electronic petitions to the president, your congressman, and even the director of the Office of Management and Budget. These petitions are viewed by their recipients as being as worthless as the cyberpaper on which they're printed, but all that action at least gives the illusion that the TVC is doing something.

The petitions range from the obscure ("RE: Bachus Amendment in the Sudan Peace Act") to the voracious ("Support increased funding for abstinence programs!") to the obviously partisan ("Just Say No to Richard Riordan").[44] This last-named petition was aimed at the former Los Angeles mayor as he sought—unsuccessfully—the GOP nomination for Governor in 2002. Coincidentally, Riordan's opponent, Bill Simon, had hired Lou Sheldon's son Phil as a campaign consultant. This nepotism went unmentioned in the TVC petition, which savaged Riordan for hiring liberals on his own staff.

The hiring of Phil Sheldon elicited the usual howls from the corporate media, for which the Traditional Values Coalition is a reliable demon. In the *Sacramento Bee*, Peter Schrag called the TVC "virulently antigay [and] antichoice,"[45] the latter phrase a tipoff to a journalist who makes no bones about his position on abortion.

Phil Sheldon pocketed $30,000 and was then unceremoniously dumped by the Simon campaign. His familial links to the TVC, it seems, made him a liability in the Golden State. Doing the usual damage control, Simon minimized Sheldon's role in the campaign. "We retained Phil Sheldon on a one-time basis as a consultant, basically to rent an address list from him,"[46] said the candidate, standing by his man in the manner of George McGovern jettisoning Senator Thomas Eagleton as his 1972 running mate after it was revealed that Eagleton had undergone electroshock therapy.

The Sheldons blamed the gay-rights lobby, or "radical homosexuals," as the TVC line goes, for the younger Sheldon's ouster. They were partly right. But then, they had dished out dirt of their own in a previous fight. When Bill Clinton appointed the openly gay James Hormel as ambassador to Luxembourg, the TVC had been among the most vociferous opponents of the nomination.

The TVC is as interventionist on foreign affairs as any establishment Beltway think tank. It takes a special interest in the Sudan, which has brutally persecuted Christians. One TVC petition bore a headline of almost comically absurd tendentiousness: "TO: PRESI-

DENT BUSH: American youth cry out—peace in Sudan."[47] Change a word or two and you've got the typical placard of a Communist front "youth group" of days gone by.

The TVC is as fervently pro-Israel a pressure group as exists anywhere; it sharply attacked the conservative Rep. Steve Largent (R-OK), chairman of the 1999 Congressional Prayer Breakfast, when he invited Palestine Liberation Organization leader Yassir Arafat to the breakfast.

The Traditional Values Coalition's position on abstinence funding reveals its basically worshipful attitude toward state power. Some organizations seek to take the government out of the bedroom; the TVC wishes to use government money to remove unmarried men and women from the bedroom. Its complaint isn't so much that federal monies go for sex education and the promotion of contraceptives as it is that promoters of abstinence aren't getting a cut of the loot, too. In a petition drawn up in 2002, TVC members were encouraged to demand that the Bush administration "increase funding for abstinence programs" to at least "the current amount allotted to contraception based programs."[48] The possibility of getting government out of sexual relations altogether and leaving "abstinence" and "contraception" to the good judgment of parents, churches, and families seems not to have crossed the TVC's collective mind.

Scrambling for government cash has, though. In 1999, the Traditional Values Coalition received $46,000 in government grants, or 14.6 percent of its total revenue of $315,036.[49] Chicken feed, to the heavy-duty lobbies. But for the TVC, it's a start. It may counsel abstinence for teenagers with raging hormones, but don't expect the Traditional Values Coalition to abstain from the group grope for government cash.

* * *

Twenty years ago, when my colleague, Tom DiLorenzo, and I started studying government-subsidized political activism, we saw a well-organized, generously funded network of left-wing special-interest groups that were receiving regular infusions of taxpayer support. They were, in the main, anti-free market and anti-capitalist, anti-private property, and sometimes explicitly Marxist. They favored a government-directed redistribution of wealth, domestically and even internationally.[50]

These groups ranged from the Institute for Policy Studies (IPS), the Washington, D.C.-based left-wing think tank that is still humming after forty years, to such now-forgotten relics of the past as the California-based Campaign for Economic Democracy (CED), the vehicle of Tom Hayden, the ex-radical turned husband of Jane Fonda.

A common joke within the New Left was that Tom Hayden gave opportunism a bad name. One measure of his opportunism was the very name of the CED, whose platform was essentially socialistic but wisely eschewed the S-word. As Hayden associate Derek Shearer said at the time, "activists should avoid using the word socialism. We have found in the greatest tradition of American advertising that the word 'economic democracy' sells. You can take it door to door like Fuller Brushes and the door will not be slammed in your face."[51] The Shearers of the left may decry the culture of advertising, and demand tighter regulation of misleading claims by corporations, but when the dissemblers have their hearts in the left place . . . no problem.

Our emphasis in this chapter on the funding of the Right should not be taken as a sign that the Left has been defunded. It has not. It has simply been joined at the trough by the establishment Right, which once upon a time, long ago and in a galaxy far away, claimed that it wanted to downsize the federal government. Having tasted of the fruits of power in Washington, it found that it liked the flavor; the Right was co-opted, tamed, bought off, made fat and happy by its participation in the Washington merry-go-round. But the Left is still there, not much worse for the wear, and resigned to sharing the booty with its erstwhile foes.

A glance down the list of the Fair Taxes for All Coalition members reveals that the paid-off Left is alive if not always well. Some of its healthiest members are in the "community development" sector.

The Rural Development & Finance Corporation (RDFC), which took in $500,000 in government grants from 1996–2000,[52] is a "private nonprofit community development financial institution."[53] The RDFC was created in 1977 to assist small businessmen and entrepreneurs in rural areas to build their businesses. It provides loans, technical assistance, and consulting advice.

Though born in Washington, it relocated to San Antonio in 1984; in recent years, it has shifted its emphasis away toward the Texas-

Mexico border, pouring money into such programs as providing computer access to Mexican-Americans in El Paso, Texas. Now, the last time I checked, the population of El Paso was 563,662. That doesn't even fit a Manhattanite's definition of "rural." But computers are all the rage, and the RDFC has evidently tired of trying to help the dying towns of predominantly white rural Mid-America. One expects that a name change—"rural" is so 19th century—is in the offing.

That El Paso computer-access project, which the RDFC has dubbed a CTC (Community Technology Center), was funded in part with monies from the U.S. Department of Housing and Urban Development.[54]

Another federally subsidized community development organization, REACH, has set the standard in reaching for government handouts. REACH was founded in the early 1980s by neighborhood activists in southeastern Portland, Oregon. Their neighborhood was declining, and they wished to "avoi[d] gentrification" while at the same time creating "livable, affordable neighborhoods."[55]

In the years since, REACH has become a major property manager in Portland, with an annual budget of over $3 million dollars; two-thirds of its income is generated by property management. REACH has spent over $30 million in real estate development: its projects have ranged from renovating single-family homes to building huge apartment complexes (which are no one's idea of livable, human-scale development).

What sets REACH apart from most other real-estate developers is that it unabashedly asks for government monies each year. One-quarter of its annual income comes from government grants. Indeed, on the Cato Institute's list of the taxpayer-supported members of the Fair Taxes for All Coalition, REACH ranks a very impressive 17th (with $1.617 million from 1996–2000),[56] ahead of such veteran almoners as the NAACP, the American Federation of Teachers, the National PTA, and the Communications Workers of America. Not bad for a bunch of neighborhood guys and gals from Portland. No wonder they oppose reducing the taxes that other people pay.

Portland is not the only city whose neighborhood organizations are willing to shill for bigger government while taking government money. The Oregon Hill Home Improvement Council, which is not another Oregon-based group but rather one centered in the Oregon Hill section of Richmond, Virginia, was another member of the Fair Taxes for All Coalition. Its taxpayer take from 1996–2000 was $263,784.[57]

The Philadelphia Association of Community Development Corporations, an association of over 75 community-development groups in the city of Brotherly Love—also a coalition member—raked in $116,001 over the same period.[58] Its "advocacy" projects include so-called Smart Growth, under which state and local governments restrict land usage; increased government subsidy of childcare and out-of-the-home after-school activities; and that old will-o'-the-wisp called "job training," which has been all but demolished as an effective strategy for matching workers with jobs. (The welfare mother to end all welfare mothers in the community development game, the Washington, D.C.-based National Congress for Community Economic Development, also a member of the Fair Taxes for All Coalition, received $5.16 million in taxpayers' money from 1996–2000.[59])

Placing the word "community" prominently in one's name is always a good strategy—even if the policies an organization promotes are destructive to real community.

The Institute for Community Economics (ICE), based in Springfield, Massachusetts, is essentially an arm of the state. Of its total revenues of $2.629 million in the last year for which an IRS Form 990 was available (1998), about 43 percent, or $1.125 million, came from government grants. In 1999, the organization received a $405,000 federal grant from the Community Development Financial Institutions Fund in order to underwrite a long-term mortgage subsidy. ICE, it seems, has melted the door to the treasury.

No doubt ICE, like most such organizations, does some noble work. It offers technical assistance in the creation of community land trusts (CLT), which are nonprofit organizations that "hold land for the benefit of a community and individuals within a community."[60] Typically, the CLT builds or renovates homes, which it then sells or rents to people of modest incomes. Unlike most land trusts, which prevent wilderness areas from being developed, the community land trust is generally in urban areas or small cities. ICE has a revolving loan fund of $2.6 million, from which it disburses monies to local CLTs.

Alas, ICE, which is heavily subsidized by the U.S. Department of Housing and Urban Development, lists among its functions "advocacy." To its credit, ICE seems not to roam far afield, advocating policies on matters of state greatly removed from its area of expertise. But it does promote greater public spending on CLTs—a classic example of government-funded advocacy, even if in a "good cause."

Other subsidized advocacy groups have causes that are less obviously "good." For instance, ACORN, or the Association of Community Organizations for Reform Now, a member in good standing of the Fair Taxes for All Coalition, raked in $1.004 million in taxpayer monies between 1996 and 2000.[61] Not bad for an organization which is about as hard left as grant-seekers come.

ACORN was born in 1970 as the Arkansas Community Organizations for Reform Now. Its founder, Wade Rathke, had been an activist with the National Welfare Rights Organization (NWRO). Hard as it to recall now, in these days when "welfare as we know it" has been ended by Clintonian reform—or so it is said—but in the late 1960s and early 1970s, the bizarre "welfare rights" movement organized people on the dole to lobby for . . . a greater dole! Handouts, Not Jobs! might have been their plea. ACORN, which rapidly moved beyond its Arkansas cradle, was at the forefront of the movement of mendicants.

But don't get the idea that ACORN grew naturally out of an Arkansas seedbed. Rathke was no Arkansan: he was sent to Little Rock by NWRO head George Wiley to build a "constituency for economic justice."[62]

ACORN's growth was greatly facilitated by a series of government grants from agencies ranging from the National Endowment for the Humanities to the Community Services Administration. VISTA, the domestic version of the Peace Corps, became an ACORN patron: in 1977, it supplied eighty workers to ACORN affiliates in seven states.

ACORN agitates for a cluster of policies that can be called, if one is in a charitable mood, big-government liberalism. (Others might prefer to call it dinosaur socialism.) ACORN lobbies for more low-income housing complexes, which are breeding grounds for crime. It supports "living wage" ordinances, which would double the minimum wage in affected municipalities (and pretty much price unskilled workers out of the job market, sending them onto the welfare rolls, which perhaps is the point after all).

"Under attack from the right, ignored by the center and many progressives, the poor grow in numbers every day,"[63] declares the ACORN website. The solution? Government.

Not for ACORN are the weasel words, the dissembling, the pretenses to nonpartisanship of most subsidized advocacy groups. In the organization's house history, written by Professor Dan Russell of Springfield College, we learn that the "goal of the Reagan Administration was to redistribute wealth upward." But ACORN was undaunted. It decided to "back the Rainbow Coalition and Jesse Jackson" and through alliances with other leftist groups, *enhance its power, the bottom line in all its efforts.*" (Emphasis added: at least ACORN is candid.) The Clinton years were fruitful; after all, "Democratic control of the federal government meant that ACORN had increased access to top officials with more sympathetic ears."[64] The Republican resurgence was unwelcome, but ACORN remains committed to its bottom line: power.

The Center for Community Change (CCC), a Washington, D.C.-based clearinghouse for "community-based" organizations, is a more buttoned-down version of ACORN. In the last year for which figures were available (1998), the CCC received government grants totaling $1.279 million out of total revenue of $10.807 million.[65]

The CCC boasts that it teaches community activists "Advocacy 101." An organization publication concedes that many granting institutions "shy away" from giving money for the purpose of advocacy, but there's no need to respect their wishes. After all, "it is not illegal to use foundation money for advocacy." (It may be immoral to use money for purposes other than those for which it was expressly granted, but hey, CCC is in the business of politics, not ethics.)

During the years of the abortive "Gingrich Revolution" in Congress, when Republicans took control of the House and for a time looked ready to make real and lasting reforms, the CCC offered such nonpartisan advice to community groups as "why not build a shanty town and call it 'Newtville' (a la Hooverville during the Depression)"?[66]

It is a measure of the meagerness of Newt's Revolution that the Center for Community Change is still on the public dole, long after Gingrich has removed to the private sector.

Numerous advocates of "housing"—and what kind of wretch could oppose housing?—are also government-funded lobbyists. Fair Taxes for All Coalition member the Minnesota Housing Partnership, whose bill for supping at the public trough in 1996–2000 cost taxpayers $857,940,[67] is an advocacy group that tries to "impact public policy on affordable housing issues at the state and federal levels."[68] (What it lacks in prose style it makes up for in aggressiveness in soliciting funds.) The MHP believes the building of homes and subsidizing of rents to be essentially a state responsibility, which would be news to the sturdy Scandinavian pioneers who peopled Minnesota back in the dark ages, before HUD came to the rescue.

The Minnesotans are mere pikers when compared to the nuns who run the Mercy Housing System out of Denver, Colorado. Mercy Housing, a corporate project founded by the Sisters of Mercy in 1981, received a whopping $9.549 million in government monies from 1996–2000.[69] The Sisters use this money—a gift from Heaven, or at least from the Great White Father on the Potomac—to assist in the construction of housing projects around the country. Most of these seem to be low-income apartments: horrible news for those homeowners who live in the affected areas, but as the Sisters live blissfully far away, unaffected by the crime and degradation that subsidized apartments bring to a neighborhood, they can feel justified, satisfied, and holy.

Mercy Housing, Inc., was among those organizations that lobbied against the 2001 tax cuts. The Sisters, it appears, display their mercy with other people's money.

Far less subsidized than the Sisters but even more desirous of shaking the tax tree is the National Low-Income Housing Coalition, a hard-left welfare rights organization that somehow pocketed $21,259 in tax dollars from 1996–2000.[70] Not that this violates any principle of the coalition, whose president, Sheila Crowley, calls those who resist additional federal spending on low-income apartments advocates of "regressing back to an earlier stage of life."[71]

To the NLIHC, founded in 1974 and based, of course, in Washington, D.C., America is in the grips of a "housing crisis" which promises to stretch out until, it seems, all employees of the NLIHC are old and gray and living in socialized housing.

The coalition ventures farther afield than the world of housing. It calls for greater federal economic intervention across the board, from a higher minimum wage to more confiscatory tax rates.

The Baltimore-based Public Justice Center (PJC), founded in 1985, a stalwart of the Fair Taxes for All Coalition, accepted $287,961 in taxpayers' money between 1996 and 2000.[72]

The PJC claims to be "dedicated to expanding the rights of the underrepresented." The phraseology is significant. Note that it does not seek to "protect," "preserve," or "defend," the rights of the "underrepresented." No, its mission is to "expand" these rights.

The PJC's definition of an "expanding" right seems to require the concomitant expansion of the state. Its actions include defending the "right" of tenants not to pay their rent, making it easier for immigrants to receive government benefits, and involving the state of Maryland in every manner of putatively private transactions, from wills to employment contracts.

Ominously, the Public Justice Center boasts that "policy advocacy"[73] is among its activities. This is a fairly bald admission for a taxpayer-subsidized organization, but even the most obtuse legal mind can see that the evidence is overwhelming that policy advocacy is no barrier to public funding. Indeed, it might even be a help.

For instance, the Center received a grant from the U.S. Department of Housing and Urban Development to pursue a study that found—predictably—that black applicants for mortgages are rejected at a greater rate (40 percent) than are white applicants (24 percent). The fault, according to study author Calvin Bradford, is with the "regulatory agencies," that "aren't monitoring"[74] lenders as strictly as they might. The conclusion: more government oversight, which of course would mean higher budgets for those charged with the oversight. The possibility that the greater rejection rate for blacks had anything to do with well-known racial disparities in economic resources seems never to have occurred to the PJC.

An ever better moniker than the Public Justice Center is the Neighborhood Justice Center. After all, "public" sounds bureaucratic, buttoned-down, while "neighborhood" is vital, healthy, homey. And the St. Paul, Minnesota-based NJC has cashed in: more than 80 percent of its annual budget, which was $363,329 in the last year for which an IRS Form 990 was available (1998), came from government sources, primarily the state of Minnesota. The NJC seems less inclined to pursue issue advocacy than does the PJC, concentrating on offering legal defense to the "vulnerable" (one would think that their victims were somewhat more vulnerable). The NJC's literature is sprinkled with such classic p.c. locutions as "juveniles of color,"[75] and the organization steers clients toward the vast array of public services in the modern welfare state.

Even better than the catchwords "justice" and "community" is "family." The Right has known this for years. Now the Left is catching on.

For instance, the left wing of the New York state Democratic Party, fed up with the patronage obsessions of the Liberal Party, created a Working Families Party in the 1990s in order to provide a second line for liberal Democrats. The name is choice: the ideal family, it would seem from watching the Working Families Party in action, consists of mother the government employee, father the government employee, and a child or two in government-subsidized daycare. Welcome to the Brave New World.

Families USA, a Washington, D.C.-based liberal Democratic interest group, is every bit as misnamed as the Working Families Party. Families USA bills itself as "The Voice for Health Care Consumers."[76] Given that each of us is, now and then, a "health care consumer," this is a pretty impressive exercise in hubris, but the phrasing suggests even more the twisted view that these people have of families. Apparently families are, first and foremost, "consumers": they produce nothing, they are incapable of looking after each other, they are simply units of consumption whose well-being may be measured by how much "health care" they receive. Again, we are in a Brave New World.

Even mainstream newspapers refer to Families USA as a "liberal advocacy group."[77] Its issues are predictable: federally subsidized prescriptions for the elderly, an expansion of the Medicare and Medicaid entitlements, and the socialization of American healthcare through incessant use of the words "children," "seniors," and "vulnerable." Tax cuts are to be resisted like the pestilence they are: Families USA joined the Fair Taxes for All Coalition.

The executive director of Families USA, Ron Pollack, got into the advocacy racket by starting "an anti-hunger organization."[78] No, it wasn't a cafeteria, nor was it a farm: it was a lobby. And if it didn't feed a single hungry person, it sure kept Mr. Pollack off the breadlines.

Fittingly, Families USA holds "Grassroots" meetings in its grassless and rootless abode: Washington, D.C. Its idea of involving the rubes in the hinterlands is to issue a single command: Vote! Vote, that is, for those candidates who support federal subsidy of uninsured families. (I'd guess that Families USA is also for subsidies to single people, but once you're wedded to the word "family," it's hard to let go.)

Astonishingly, even so glaringly partisan a lobby as Families USA is on the dole, to the tune of $175,000 between 1996 and 2000.[79]

"Children" is an even warmer and cuddlier word than "families," so it should not surprise us that over that same five-year period, the Child Welfare League of America (CWLA) brought in a cool $2.351 million in taxpayer dollars.[80] As a member of the Fair Taxes for All Coalition, the CWLA publicly opposes any lessening of the flow of money from citizens to Washington.

Born in the Progressive Era, when upper-middle-class Lady Bountifuls and male bureaucrats combined to begin transferring authority over children from families—a shocking number of which lacked graduate degrees and progressive views—to the wiser and more loving Uncle Sam, the CWLA is now an association consisting of over 1,100 public and private agencies concerned with children and family-related matters.

While the word "welfare" has acquired a bad odor in recent years, and most lobbies avoid it as they would a Milton Friedman book, the CWLA proudly asserts its belief in welfare. Its agenda is almost purely welfarist: support for increased funding for everything from the "Younger Americans Act" to daycare, teen pregnancy, anti-alcohol, and child-abuse prevention programs.

The word "welfare" also remains sacred to the National Council of Churches (NCC), which never bothered to thank taxpayers for its Herodian hoarding of $18.424 million in government subsidies from 1996–2000.[81]

The NCC, long a bugbear to conservatives, styles itself "the nation's leading organization in the movement for Christian ecumenical cooperation,"[82] consisting of thirty-six mostly Protestant denominations. In recent years, the NCC has hit hard times, as churches and members have fled as the council's real purpose has become apparent: to construct a house of worship in which to pay homage to the failed god of socialism.

The basic belief of the Manhattan-based NCC, which was founded in 1950 at the height of postwar liberalism, is that "there is a basic contradiction between capitalism and the Biblical values of justice, mercy, stewardship, service, community and self-giving love."[83] The council finds no such contradiction in socialism, though it favors the euphemism "economic justice."

The National Council of Churches advocates government-paid healthcare for all Americans (and even non-Americans living in the country), confiscatory gun control, "hunger relief"[84] (which is to say more spending on food stamps and other failed aspects of LBJ's Great Society), a higher minimum wage, and greatly increased spending on public schools (vouchers are disparaged as "experiments" that must not get in the way of the government-school juggernaut).

What galls this observer about the NCC is the way it cloaks its standard-issue liberal advocacy in the language of faith. For instance, a 1998 NCC Policy Statement on "The Churches and The Public Schools at the Close of the Twentieth Century" justifies its support of liberal-statist positions on education with the Gospel passage from Mark 9:36–42: "As Christians," declares the NCC, "we are mindful of both Jesus' extraordinary care and concern for children, and of his admonition that those who put stumbling blocks in the path of children would be better off if they were thrown into the sea with a millstone tied around their necks. In our society, to fail to provide a child with the best kind of education available is to put an almost insurmountable stumbling block in the path of that child."[85]

Charming: those of us who question the wisdom of pouring more billions of dollars into an obviously defective public-education system are to be tossed into the sea with millstones around our necks. This sounds . . . intolerant, shall we say?

Of course, the NCC wants to have it both ways. It uses the Gospel to promote a typical liberal policy agenda. When former Pennsylvania liberal Democratic Congressman Bob Edgar became general secretary of the NCC in 2000, he said, "God is calling us to this moment in history."[86] God, it seems, wanted His People to be taxed at higher rates.

On the other hand, when conservatives wish to use the Bible to promote their political views, the NCC has a hissy fit. Conservatives mustn't "impose their views" on others. The NCC has denounced student-led prayers at football games on the grounds that "these prayers might not be voluntary for all students."[87] In fact, that is the whole point of having students rather than teachers or administrators lead the prayers: to emphasize their voluntary nature. The problem, perhaps, is that the petition in the Lord's Prayer is directed to God rather than Washington. One doubts that the National Council of Churches would object to asking Congress to "give us this day our daily bread."

It is a role to which Congress does not seem averse.

Notes

1. David Frum, *Dead Right* (New York: Basic Books, 1994), p. 13.
2. Quoted in ibid., p. 360.
3. Justin Raimondo, "Tale of a 'Seditionist': The Story of Lawrence Dennis," *Chronicles* (May 2000), p. 21.
4. Karen DeYoung, "More U.S. Aid Sought for Cuban Dissidents," *Washington Post*, March 8, 2001, p. A16.
5. IRS Form 990, Freedom House, Inc., 1998.
6. "Mission Statement & History," www.freedomhouse.org.
7. Edward Epstein, "U.S. Urged to Back Muslim Democracy," *San Francisco Chronicle*, December 20, 2001, p. A13.
8. *National Endowment for Democracy Annual Report '96*, cover.
9. *ressional Record*, December 18, 1985, p. H12563.
10. Quoted in David Boaz, "Money for the Boys," *Libertarian Outlook* (August 1985), p. 4.
11. Norman Kempster, "Democracy-Export Stirs Controversy," *Los Angeles Times*, February 6, 1986, p. A1.
12. Stanley Meisler, "Allocation of Funds in France Embarrassing," *Los Angeles Times*, February 6, 1986, p. A25.
13. Richard Bernstein, "Union in France Confirms It Receives Funds From U.S.," *New York Times*, December 28, 1985, p. A5.
14. Ben A. Franklin, "Democracy Project Facing New Criticisms," *New York Times*, December 4, 1985.
15. Richard Cummings, "I Met Her in Venezuela," www.lewrockwell.com, April 27, 2002.
16. "CSIS on the Hill," www.csis.org, May 7, 2002.
17. "CSIS at a Glance," www.csis.org/about/index.html, March 7, 2002.
18. IRS Form 990, Center for Strategic and International Studies, 1997, 1998, and 2000.
19. Ibid., 1998.
20. "CSIS Presents Representative John Murtha Leadership Award," www.csis.org, May 7, 2002.
21. Robin Wright, "State Dept. Mismanaged, Report Says," *Los Angeles Times*, January 30, 2001, p. A10.
22. Jack Kelly, "Smarter Spending," *Pittsburgh Post-Gazette*, February 18, 2001, p. B3.
23. Robert Fisk, "US Report Urges Arafat to Use Torture for Peace," *Independent*, November 6, 2000, p. 11.
24. "The National Committee on United States-China Relations," ncuscr.org, February 23, 2002.
25. IRS Form 990, National Committee on U.S.-China Relations, 1998.
26. Steve Mufson, "China Relations Group Feels Helms's Pull," *Washington Post*, October 19, 2000, p. A29.

27. IRS Form 990, The Brookings Institution, 1997.
28. "Chronological News Release Index," www.brook.edu, May 8, 2002.
29. "Brookings Policy Briefs," www.brook.edu, May 8, 2002.
30. Quoted in Patrick J. Buchanan, *A Republic, Not an Empire* (Washington, DC: Regnery, 1999), p. 357.
31. IRS Form 990, American Enterprise Institute for Public Policy Research, 2000.
32. "Bob Woodson," www.ncne.com/teampublish/main, March 21, 2002.
33. David B. Ottaway, "Private Social Welfare Initiative Draws Scrutiny," *Washington Post*, May 7, 2001, p. A1.
34. "National Center for Neighborhood Enterprise," www.ncne.org, March 21, 2002.
35. "About NCNE," www.ncne.com/teampublish/main, March 21, 2002.
36. Ottaway, "Private Social Welfare Initiative Draws Scrutiny," *Washington Post*, May 7, 2001.
37. "President Bush Launches Welfare Reform Initiative at NCNE Event," www.ncne.com/teampublish/main, March 21, 2002.
38. Robert L. Woodson, Sr., "What's Wrong with the Debate About Faith-Based Initiatives," www.ncne.com/teampublish/main, March 21, 2002.
39. Robert L. Woodson, Sr., "The Reality of Faith-Based Programs," *Washington Post*, July 7, 2001, p. A22.
40. "Faces of Fathers," www.fatherhood.org, March 7, 2002.
41. IRS Form 990, National Fatherhood Initiative, 2000.
42. Robert Pear, "Human Services Nominee's Focus on Married Fatherhood Draws Both Praise and Fire," *New York Times*, June 7, 2001, p. A24.
43. "$100 Million Proposal for Marriage Support Good for Families, Good for Welfare Program, Says National Fatherhood Initiative," www.fatherhood.org/articles, March 21, 2002.
44. "Current Petitions," http://64.55.184.74/tvcl, March 7, 2002.
45. Peter Schrag, "Abortion in the Governor's Race," *San Diego Union-Tribune*, March 22, 2002, p. B13.
46. John Wildermuth, "Simon Drops Anti-Gay Activist After Criticism," *San Francisco Chronicle*, March 21, 2002, p. A3.
47. "Current Petitions," http://64.55.184.74/tvcl, March 7, 2002.
48. "Your Help is Needed to Voice Support for Abstinence Funding!" www.conservativepetitions.com, March 7, 2002.
49. IRS Form 990, Traditional Values Coalition Education, 1999.
50. Bennett and DiLorenzo, *Destroying Democracy*, p. 9.
51. John H. Bunzel, *New Force on the Left: Tom Hayden and the Campaign Against Corporate America* (Stanford, CA: Hoover Institution Press, 1983), p. 46.
52. Samples, Yablonski, and Osorio, "More Government for All," p. 5.
53. RDFC undated brochure.
54. "Community Technology Centers Project Initiated," Points of View (Spring 2001), p. 5.
55. "Reach Founder Dies," *Within Reach* (Summer 2001), p. 1.
56. Samples, Yablonski, and Osorio, "More Government for All," p. 5.
57. Ibid.
58. Ibid.
59. Ibid.
60. *Institute for Community Economics Annual Report '99*, unpaginated.
61. Samples, Yablonski, and Osorio, "More Government for All," p. 5.
62. "Roots of a Social Justice Movement (1970–75), www.acorn.org/history-content.html, June 21, 2001.

63. "Who is ACORN?" www.acorn.org/who_are_we.html, June 21, 2001.
64. "Roots of a Social Justice Movement (1970–75)," June 21, 2001.
65. "Center for Community Change Financial Data," www.guidestar.org/search, March 26, 2001.
66. "How to be Heard," www.communitychange.org/howheard.html, June 21, 2001.
67. Samples, Yablonski, and Osorio, "More Government for All," p. 5.
68. "Advocacy and Community Support," www.mhponline.org/advocacy/advocacy.html, December 14, 2001.
69. Samples, Yablonski, and Osorio, "More Government for All," p. 5.
70. Ibid., p. 6.
71. "New & Special Features, Week of 9/10/2001," www.nlihc.org, September 10, 2001.
72. Samples, Yablonski, and Osorio, "More Government for All," p. 5.
73. "Public Justice Center," undated mimeograph, pp. 1–2.
74. Robert Nusgart, "Study Finds Huge Disparity in Loans to Blacks, Whites," Baltimore Sun, May 17, 2000, p. 2C.
75. *Neighborhood Justice Center Annual Report: 2000*, p. 4.
76. "Managed Care," www.familiesusa.org/htlm/managedcare/mngedcare.html, October 24, 2001.
77. Jonathan Riskind, "Insurance at Center of Negotiations," *Columbus Dispatch*, December 5, 2001, p. E1.
78. Maureen West, "They Make the Case on Capitol Hill," *New York Times*, March 21, 2001, p. H8.
79. Samples, Yablonski, and Osorio, "More Government for All, " p. 5.
80. Ibid.
81. Ibid.
82. "NCC at a Glance: Who Belongs, How it Works, What it Does," www.nccusa.org/about/about_ncc.html, December 14, 2001.
83. Quoted in Rael Isaac and Erich Isaac, *The Coercive Utopians: Social Deception by America's Power Players* (Chicago: Regnery Gateway, 1983), p. 26.
84. "Hunger Relief Act (S. 1805/H.R. 3192)," www.nccusa.org/publicwitness/hunger.html, February 2, 2001.
85. "Philadelphia Superintendent of Schools Calls for NCC to Provide Moral Leadership in Public Education," NCC press release, November 11, 1998.
86. "Faith & Values," *Minneapolis Star-Tribune*, July 8, 2000, p. 7B.
87. "Islamic, Christian Groups Decry Student Prayer Ruling," *Chicago Sun-Times*, June 23, 2000, p. 34.

8

Conclusion: As I Told the Subcommittee...

The colorful New York governor, Al Smith, used to say that nothing un-American can stand the sunlight. With a Smith-like faith, I once cherished the naive hope that perhaps the act of exposing lobbying with federal dollars might put into motion a series of events that would lead to its abolition.

For a decade, not much happened. Conservatives were aware that the problem existed, but they had bigger fish to fry, and besides, many were finding that the pool of federal money is large enough to supply the Right as well as the Left.

Then came the Republican Revolution of 1994. A cadre of bright, eager, principled, committed young Republicans came to a Congress that was in desperate need of a thorough cleansing. Under the desultory leadership of Newt Gingrich, they reformed the institution and set out to reform the polity. A few of the braver souls decided to take on the tax-funded lobbies of the nonprofit sector. David McIntosh, Ernest Istook, J.D. Hayworth, and others fought a good fight against a savvy, mediagenic, and wealthy bloc of nonprofits with a finely tuned public-relations sense. "Let America Speak!" these taxpayer-subsidized lobbies demanded, and though the idealistic young Republicans had Thomas Jefferson on their side, the author of the Declaration of Independence was no match for our modern-day declarers of eternal dependence.

I was pleased to testify before Rep. McIntosh's subcommittee in that heady summer of 1995, when real reform seemed at our fingertips.

The experience of testifying before a congressional committee or subcommittee is not to be recommended to those who have excessive self-esteem. Members of the committee are always coming and going, leaving to cast votes or visit in the committee backroom with lobbyists. If the witness is lucky, half the subcommittee will be up at on the dais, and if he is really lucky, half of them will actually listen to what he has to say.

I had prepared a statement: a strong statement, pulling no punches, but nevertheless temperate, at least for me. But after watching such liberal Democrats as Henry Waxman and Cardiss Collins showboat and demagogue and shamelessly suck up to the single most rancid specimen of tax-funded lobbying, the National Council of Senior Citizens, I had had enough. Temperateness, moderation, and the usual bland smile of the congressional witness be damned: I wanted to give them unshirted hell. So I did.

I complimented Congressman McIntosh, giving him kudos that after ten years, "Congress has caught up with a couple of college professors who wrote the book." I singled out for fulmination the National Endowment for Democracy, that slush fund for conservative foreign-policy analysts, and assured the Democrats on the panel that "I'm an equal opportunity basher."

"This isn't a partisan issue," I insisted. "Left, right, center . . . senior citizens, environmentalists, the so-called consumer activist groups. . . . I tell my wife sometimes, it's one thing after another. And she says, no, it's the same damn thing over and over again. And that's what we've got here."

I was just getting wound up by the time I had to wind it up, so I gave the subcommittee members a peroration to remember:

> [T]he whining of these groups that if we make any change whatsoever, that this will be the end of civilization as we know it should be dismissed as the total bilge that it is. It's time to get lobbyist leeches off the taxpayer's tit. Now that is putting it right down front and center.
>
> And we've been talking a lot about sinful and tyrannical. Well, we've had enough sin and tyranny here, inside and outside the Beltway. And if you're looking for somebody that's been sinned and tyrannized, it's me, because I pay my taxes. And basically, to get right down to it, what you're going to have to do . . . is simply ban lobbying, political advocacy, whatever you want to call it, by anybody who gets Federal tax dollars.
>
> Anything else invites and encourages continuing abuse. And I happen to be one taxpayer that's just had it to the gills. With that, I'll close.[1]

And with that, I'll close once again.

Note

1. "Abuse of Taxpayer Funds to Subsidize Lobbying and Political Activity," Subcommittee on National Economic Growth, Natural Resources, and Regulatory Affairs, pp. 141-42.

Index

Abbey, Edward
Abortion issues, 27-28, 31, 35, 42, 60, 161
Adams, Ansel, 94
Adams, Bob, 18
Advocacy Institute, 7
Affirmative action, 43
Agency for International Development, U.S., 105
Aging, 36
Aguirre-Sacasa, Francisco, 77
AIDS Coalition to Unleash Power (ACT UP), 48
AIDS/HIV, 42, 45-47, 60, 133-134, 142
AIDSWatch, 133-134
Air Line Pilots Union, 70-71
Alcoa, 102
Alliance for Displaced Homemakers, 38
Alliance for Energy, 105
Alliance for Responsible Trade, 78
Alliance of Retired Americans (ARA), 56-57, 82
Alliance to Save Energy, 104-105
Amalgamated Clothing and Textile Workers Union (ACTWU), 78
Amendment, Equal Rights, 18-19
Amendment, First, 18, 67
Amendment, Second, 28
Amendment, Nineteenth, 14, 19
Amendment, Prohibition, 15
American Anorexia and Bulimia Association, 22
American Association for Retired People (AARP), 54-55, 57, 154
American Cancer Society (ACS), 8, 109, 120-128, 132
American Center for International Labor Solidarity, 164
American Civil Liberties Union (ACLU), 95, 170-171
American Conservation Corps, 99

American Enterprise Institute, 172
American Express, 21, 140-141
American Farmland Trust (AFT), 99-100
American Federation of Labor–Congress of Industrial Organizations (AFL-CIO), 2, 20, 53, 56, 70-71, 78, 164, 166
American Federation of State, County, and Municipal Employees (AFSCME), 72
American Federation of Teachers (AFT), 60-61, 70
American Heart Association (AHA), 109-110, 120, 123, 128-133
American Heart Association Grassroots Network, 130
American Lung Association (ALA), 109-120, 123-124, 127, 133
American Society for the Control of Cancer, 121
American Stop Smoking Intervention Study for Cancer Prevention (Project ASSIST), 126-128
Americans for Democratic Action, 56
Amoco, 21
Anheuser-Busch, 140-141
Arafat, Yassir, 169, 178
Arkansas Community Organizations for Reform Now, 182
Ashcroft, John, 27, 155-156
Association for Responsible Thermal Treatment (ARTT), 118-119
Association of Community Organizations for Reform Now (ACORN), 182
AT&T, 102, 143

Babbitt, Bruce, 93
Bahr, Morton, 74
Baldwin, Ruth Standish, 140
Bandow, Doug, 96

198   Tax-Funded Politics

Barnes, A. James, 119
Barnes, Fred, 161
Baumgardner, Jennifer, 25
Beckerman, Wilfred
Birney, Alice McLelland, 62
Birth control, 34-35, 89, 142
Blanchard, Janice, 36
Black Executive Exchange Program, 141
Blackwelder, Brent, 87
Block grants, 66
Borchgrave, Arnaud de, 168
Bowman, Molly, 132
Boy Scouts, 8
Boys Club, 49
Brademas, John, 164-164
Bradford, Calvin, 185
Bradley, Sen. Bill (D-NJ), 87
Brandeis, Justice Louis D., 9
Brazil, 78
Brecht, Bertolt, 162
Broaddrick, Juanita, 25
Brock, William E., 168
Brookings Institution, 46, 171-172
Brown, Rep. Hank Brown (R-CO), 164, 166
Browner, Carol, 113
Bruce, Tammy, 21, 28-30, 33-34
Brumberg, Joan, 22
Bryant, William J., 131
Brzezinski, Zbigniew, 168
Buchanan, Pat, 10
Bureau of Mines, U.S., 103
Burford, Anne, 88
Bush administration, 88, 93, 148, 150, 176-178
Bush, Pres. George H.W., 80
Bush, Pres. George W., 2, 10, 32, 59, 74-75, 81, 129, 167, 172, 174-175

Cairncross, France, 104
Campaign finance reform, 19, 37
Campaign for Economic Democracy, 179
Campaign to Stop Gender Apartheid in Afghanistan, 32
Capital Research Center, 53, 78, 85
Capitalism, 85-86
Cardoso, Fernando Henrique, 78
Carlson, Allan, 15, 37
Carlucci, Frank, 169
Carnahan, Governor Mel (MO), 155-156
Carnahan, Governor Jean (MO), 156
Carson, Rachel, 85

Carter, Pres. Jimmy, 57, 105
Carter administration, 36, 53
Catholic Church, 48
Cato Institute, 2, 77-78, 96-97, 180
Catt, Carrie Chapman, 14-16, 19
Center for Community Change, 183
Center for International Private Enterprise, 164
Center for Medicare Advocacy, 156-157
Center for Renewable Energy and Sustainable Technology, 104
Center for Strategic and International Studies (CSIS), 162, 167-170
Center for Trade Policy Studies, Cato Institute, 77-78
Center for Women, Union Institute of Cincinnati, 44
Center for Women Policy Studies, 42-43
Centers for Disease Control (CDC), 29, 110, 114, 121, 130
Centers for Disease Control, Cardiovascular Health Program, 130
Chaiken, Sol "Chick," 73
Chamber of Commerce, U.S., 164
Charter schools, 66
Chase, Bob, 58
Chase Manhattan Bank, 39
Chavez, Hugo, 16
Chavez-Thompson, Linda, 56
Chevron, 102
Child labor, 70, 77
Child Nutrition Act of 1966, 62
Child Welfare League of America (CWLA), 187
Children's Bureau, 15
China, 72, 74, 170-171
Chodorov, Frank, 5
Christmas Seals, 116-117
Citizens Action, 56
Civilian Conservation Corps (CCC), 98-99
Clean Air Act, 89, 113
Clean Water Act, 89
Clinton administration, 26, 30, 33, 37, 40-42, 76, 81, 87, 93, 113, 115, 119, 163, 167, 182-183
Clinton, Pres. Bill, 25, 29, 32, 38
Clinton, Sen. Hillary (D-NY), 18, 134
Coalition of Labor Union Women, 56
Coalition on Women and Training, 40
Coca-Cola, 102
Cohen, David, 8

Index 199

Collective bargaining, 77
Collins, Cardiss (D-IL), 4, 194
Colorado Department of Health, 126-127
Commission on the Emergency in Education, 57
Commission on the Skills of the American Workforce, 82
Committee on Urban Conditions Among Negroes, 140
Communications Workers of America (CWA), 74-75, 180
Community Development Financial Institutions Fund, 181
Community land trusts (CLT), 181-182
Community Services Administration, 182
Communists, 14, 17, 21
Comprehensive Employment and Training Administration (CETA), 79-80, 98
Comstock Laws, 34
Congressional Heart and Stroke Coalition, 130
Congressional Prayer Breakfast, 178
Congressional Universal Health Care Task Force, 135
Conservation Action Network, 92-93
Conservation Fund, 101
Contextual Learning Demonstration Project, 82
Coolidge, Pres. Calvin, 122-123
Cordesman, Anthony, 169
Coupal, Dr. James, 122-123
Crowley, Sheila, 184
Cummings, Richard, 166-167

Danzinger, Gigi Guggenheim, 33
Department of Commerce, U.S., 133, 143
Department of Education, U.S., 57, 62-63, 170
Department of Energy, U.S., 94-95, 104-105, 163
Department of Health and Human Services, U.S., 29-30, 147, 151, 157
Department of Housing and Urban Development, U.S., 147, 180-182, 185
Department of Justice, U.S., 144, 147
Department of Labor, U.S., 39-40, 54-55, 81, 141
Department of State, U.S., 170
Department of Transportation, U.S., 141
Department of the Interior, U.S., 94
Dewey, John, 60-61

DiLorenzo, Thomas J., 114, 178
Distance education, 44
Drier, Rep. David (R-CA), 168
Drug Enforcement Administration, U.S., 148
Dupont, 102
Durbin, Eden Fisher, 7-8

"Earth Day," 67, 93-95
Eckart, Rep. Dennis (D-OH), 118
Edgar, Rep. Bob (D-PA), 188
Education, 57-63, 142, 151
Ehrlich, Paul, 91, 106
Eisenhower, Pres. Dwight D., 168-169
El Salvador, 76-77
Elementary and Secondary Education Act of 1965, 57
Elovich, Richard, 46
Emergency Conservation Work, 98
Emerson, Rep. Bill (R-MO), 10
Emphysema Foundation for our Right to Survive (EFFORTS), 110
Employment, 56
Endangered Species Act, 89
"English Plus," 151-152
Environmental Action Coalition, 96, 98
Environmental Law Institute (ELI), 102-103
Environmental Protection Agency (EPA), 88-89, 100, 104, 112-113, 115-117, 119
Equal Employment Opportunity Commission (EEOC), 42, 147
Equal Rights Amendment, 18-19, 59
Exxon, 21

Fair Share for Health Committee (FSFHC), 127
Fair Taxes for All Coalition, 2, 20, 36, 61-62, 71, 99, 135, 139, 141, 157, 179-187
Families USA, 186-187
Family violence, 28, 41-42
Family Violence Prevention Fund (FVPF), 27-28
Federal Bureau of Investigation, 33, 42
Federal Elections Commission, 55
Federal Fair Housing Act, 143-144
Feminist Majority Foundation, 20, 30-334
Feminists, 18-30, 33-34, 40, 44, 49
Firestone, 101

200 Tax-Funded Politics

Fischer, George, 59
Fish and Wildlife Service, U.S., 101
501(c)(3), 47, 55
501(c)(4), 55
Florio, Rep. James J. (D-NJ), 118
Folsom, George A., 166
Food and Drug Administration, U.S., 113, 130-131
Ford Foundation, 143-144
Ford Motor Co., 102
Force Ouviére, 166
Fox-Genovese, Elizabeth, 26
France, 166
Freedom of Information Act, 55, 115
Free speech, 34
Freedom House, 162-165
Fresina, Lori, 123
Friedan, Betty, 21, 28
Friends of the Earth (FOE), 87

Garrison, John R., 114
Gay Men's Health Crisis (GMHC), 20, 45-48
Gershman, Carl, 165
Gifford, Kathie Lee, 78-79
Gingrich, Newt, 20, 173, 183, 193
Goldhaber, Gerald M., 124
Goldwater, Sen. Barry (R-AZ), 161
Gore, Albert, 1, 37, 41, 71, 74, 87
Gore, Tipper, 41
Graham, Sen. Bob (D-FL), 167-168
Grants Management Office, Department of Health and Human Services, 29
Gray Panthers, 9, 135
Great Society, 54, 57, 112, 188
Greenpeace, 90
Green Thumb, 54-55
Greenspan, Alan, 153
Greiner, Keith A., 132
Griswold, Daniel T., 77
Gun control, 28, 59
Guttman, Robert, 80

Hamre, John J., 167
Harding, Warren G., 15
Hayden, Tom 179
Hayworth, J.D., 193
Hazardous waste incinerator (HWI), 117-118
Head Start, 112, 142, 151
Health care issues, 47, 56, 63, 71, 142, 156-157, 186, 188

Hearst, Phoebe Apperson, 62
HeartGuide Seal of Approval, 131
Heinz, Sen. John (R-PA), 105
Helms, Jesse, 91, 170
HIV/AIDS, 42, 45-47, 60
Hill, Anita, 25, 42
Holden, John L., 170-171
Hollings, Sen. Ernest (D-SC), 166
Homeland security, 99
Homosexuality, 44-49, 60, 68
hooks, bell, 26
Horn, Wade, 175
Horowitz, Michael, 6
Housing issues, 140, 182, 184
Humphrey, Sen. Hubert H. (D-MN), 105
Hyde, Rep. Henry (R-IL), 173

Igo, Shirley, 65
Illinois Department of Employment Security, 41
Immigration, 72-73, 76, 148-150
Immigration and Naturalization Service, U.S. 148
Independent Sector, 5-8
Industrial Union Department, AFL-CIO, 53
Industrial Workers of the World, 75
Information Agency, U.S., 20
Institute for Community Economics (ICE), 181
Institute for Policy Studies (IPS), 179
Institute on Race and Justice, 145
Intel, 102
International Association of Machinists, 56
International Ladies' Garment Workers Union (ILGW), 73, 78
International Republican Institute, 164, 166
Interstate Highway System, 86, 94
Iran, 169-170
Iraq, 169-170
Istook, Rep. Ernest (R-OK), 3, 5-6, 193

Jackson, Jesse, 9
James, William, 105
J.C. Penney, 64
Jefferson, Thomas, 1, 21, 26, 34, 165, 171-172, 193
Jefferson-Jenkins, Carolyn, 13, 19
Job training, 39-40, 79-82, 181
Job Training Partnership Act, 79-82

Johnson, Pres. Lyndon B., 54, 57-58, 154, 188
Joint Center for Political and Economic Studies, 142-143
Jones, Paula, 25, 29-30, 42

Kamaski, Charles, 150
Kayal, Philip M., 45
Kayden, Xandra, 18
Kemp, Jack, 173
Kennecott Co., 101
Kennedy, Sen. Ted (D-MA), 18, 91, 93, 147
Kinsley, Michael, 165
Kissinger, Henry, 105, 168, 170
Koop, Dr. Everett, 124
Koss, Mary, 23-24
Kourpias, George, 56
Kramer, Larry, 45-46, 48
Ku Klux Klan, 65

Labor unions, 53-79
Ladky, Ann, 42
Lafer, Gordon, 80
Lambert, Sam, 58
Landfills, 96, 98
Largent, Rep. Steve (R-OK), 178
Lasker, Mary, 109
Leach, Rep. Jim (R-IA), 168
Leadership Council for Metropolitan Open Communities, 143-144
League of Nations, 15
League of United Latin American Citizens (LULAC), 150-152
League of Women Voters (LWV), 2, 13-20, 62
League of Women Voters Department of Government and International Operations, 17
League of Women Voters Education Fund, 13, 19
Lee, Linda, 101
Leno, Jay, 30
Leno, Mavis, 30, 32
Let America Speak!, 5
Lewinsky, Monica, 25, 32
Lieberman, Sen. Joe (D-CT), 168
Lieberman, Myron, 58, 62
Lipsman, Dr. Joshua, 48
Lobbying Disclosure Act of 1995, 55
Lockheed, 102
Lomborg, Bjorn, 90-92, 97, 104
Lopez-Baffo, Minnie, 18

Lott, John, 17
Luce, Henry, 162
Lugar, Sen. Richard G. (R-IN), 164-165, 168
LULAC National Educational Service Centers, 152

Malaysia, 76-77
March of Dimes, 109-110
Markell, Ginny, 63, 65
Martin Marietta, 102
McCain, Sen. John (R-AZ), 19-20, 167-169
McGurn, William, 58
McIntosh, Rep. David, 3-5, 193-194
Meany, George, 76
Medicaid, 135, 157, 186
Medicare, 37, 54, 56, 151, 153-158, 186
MENSA, 99
Mental health issues, 73, 154
Mercy Housing System, 184
Merlino, Nell, 24-25
Mickley, Dr. Diane, 22
Millet, Kate, 44
"Million4ROE," 30
Minnesota Housing Partnership (MHP), 184
Minority Business Development Agency, 143
Minority Business RoundTable, 143
Minimum wage, 41-42, 71, 75, 182
Mink, Patsy, 43
Mondale, Walter, 24, 53
Mongolian Social Democrat Party, 165
Moral Majority, 99
Morgan Stanley, 140-141
Mott Foundation, 64
Ms. Foundation for Women, 20-27
Ms. Magazine, 21-25, 27, 29
Muir, John, 88
Murtha, Rep. John (D-PA), 168-169

NAACP Legal Defense Fund, 139
NAACP Nevada Housing Development Corporation, 140
Nader, Ralph, 94
National Agricultural Lands Study (NALS), 100-101
National American Woman Suffrage Association (NAWSA), 14
National Association for the Advancement of Colored People (NAACP), 2, 20, 33, 139-140, 142, 146, 180

National Association of People with AIDS (NAPWA), 133-134
National Association of Service and Conservation Corps (NASCC), 99
National Association of Social Workers (NASW), 73
National Audubon Society, 98
National Cancer Institute, 126, 128
National Center for Neighborhood Enterprise (NCNE), 139, 172-175
National Commission on Social Security Reform, 153
National Committee on U.S.–China Relations, 170
National Committee to Preserve Social Security and Medicare, 153-154
National Congress for Community Economic Development, 181
National Congress of Mothers, 62
National Congress of Parents and Teachers (PTA), 61-69
National Council of Churches, 2, 20, 135, 187-189
National Council of La Raza, 20, 146-150
National Council of Senior Citizens (NCSC), 53-56, 82, 141, 194
National Council on Crime and Delinquency (NCDD), 144-146
National Council on the Aging, 54-55, 157-158
National Democratic Institute for International Affairs, 164
National Education Association (NEA), 57-60, 62, 70
National Endowment for Democracy (NED), 10, 162, 164-167
National Endowment for the Humanities, 182
National Farmers Union, 54-55
National Fatherhood Initiative, 175-176
National Forest Service, 86-87
National Forum for Black Public Administrators, 142-143
National Foundation for Infantile Paralysis, 109-110
National Institutes of Health, 115, 126, 128
National Low-Income Housing Coalition, 184
National Lung Association, 111
National Organization for Women (NOW), 28-30, 36

National Organization for Women (NOW) Legal Defense and Education Fund, 20, 28
National Park Service, 86-87, 101
National Recycling Coalition, 95
National Rifle Association, 18
National Right to Life Committee, 171
National School Lunch Act of 1946, 62
National Senior Citizens Education and Research Center (NSCERC), 55-56, 82
National Senior Citizens Law Center (NSCLC), 157
National Smokers' Alliance, 125
National Society for the Study and Prevention of Tuberculosis (NSSPT), 111
National System of Interstate and Defense Highways, 86
National Tuberculosis and Respiratory Disease Association, 120
National Urban League, 54-55, 140-142, 172
National Welfare Rights Organization (NWRO), 182
National Wilderness Preservation System, 86-87, 89
National Wildlife Federation (NWF), 87-88
National Wildlife Refuge System, 86-87
National Women's Political Caucus, 18
National Youth Crime Prevention Demonstration Act, 173
Nazi Society for Racial Hygiene, 34
Neighborhood Justice Center, 185-186
Nelson, Sen. Ben (D-NB), 155
Nelson, Sen. Gaylord (D-WI), 95
Nicaragua, 76-77
Nixon, Pres. Richard M., 170
North Korea, 169-170
North, Oliver, 55
Notestein, Frank, 103
Nynex, 21

O'Connell, Brian, 6-8
Office of Education, U.S., 43-44
Office of Management and Budget (OMB), 6
Office of Special Counsel for Immigration Related Unfair Employment Practices, 76
Office on Smoking and Health, Centers for Disease Control, 29
Ohio Developmental Disability Council, 135

Okonski, Kendra, 78
Older Americans Act, 54, 158
Older Women's League (OWL), 36-37
Operation Rescue, 28
Oregon Hill Home Improvement Council, 180-181
Osorio, Ivan G., 2, 53-55, 77
Owens, Governor Bill, 123

Packwood, Sen. Bob (D-WI), 93-94
Paige, Connie, 161
Palestine Liberation Organization (PLO), 169, 178
Parent-Teacher Association (National Congress of Parents and Teachers), 61-69, 180
Parent-Teacher Organizations (PTO), 68-69
Parker, Jay, 172
Paul, Rep. Ron (R-TX), 130
Payer, Lynn, 122
Peace Corps 182
PepsiCo, 39, 140-141
Percy, Sen. Charles (R-IL), 105
Perot, Ross, 4
Pfizer, 102
Philadelphia Association of Community Development Corporations, 181
Philip Morris, 39
Planned Parenthood Federation of America, 34-35, 46, 171
Plumbers and Pipe Fitters Union, 70-71
Political Economy Research Center, Montana, 86-87
Pollack, Ron, 186
Prescription drug benefits, 151, 154, 158, 186
Private schools, 65-66
Project ASSIST (American Stop Smoking Intervention Study for Cancer Prevention), 126-128
Project Inform, 48
Public Justice Center (PJC), 185
Public-choice theory, 9
PTA, 2
PUSH, 9

Quayle, Dan, 80-81

Rainbow Coalition, 183
Rathke, Wade, 182
REACH, 180

Reagan administration, 5, 9, 53, 80, 88, 169, 183
Reagan, Pres. Ronald, 10, 87, 124, 164, 166
Reagan Recession, 80
Recycling, 95-98
Reforestation, 97
Renault, Richard, 155
Renewable Energy Policy Project (REPP), 104
Resource Conservation and Recovery Act (RCRA), 85, 117-118
Reuther, Walter, 74
Rhongji, Zhu, 170
Rice, Constance, 33
Richards, Amy, 22, 25
Richardson, Bill, 163
Richtman, Max, 155-156
Riordan, Richard, 177
R.J. Reynolds, 113
Robb, Sen. Charles, 55
Robertson, Pat, 176
Robertson, Rose Marie, 129
Rockefeller Brothers Fund, 145
Rockefeller, Sen. Jay (D-WV), 167-168
Rohatyn, Felix G., 168
Ronald Reagan Presidential Library 171
Roosevelt, Eleanor, 162
Roosevelt, Pres. Franklin D., 16, 58, 98, 109-110, 153-154
Roosevelt, James, 153-154
Roosevelt, Pres. Theodore, 87
Ross, Walter, 126
Rothbard, Murray N., 26, 44
RU-486, 32
Rudin, Ernst, 34
Rural Development and Finance Corporation, 179-180
Russell, Dan, 183
Ryan, Frank, 111

Samples, John, 2
Sanger, Margaret, 34
Sara Lee, 21
Sarah Scaife Foundation, 172
Saunders, John E. III, 142-143
Schippers, Eric, 125
Schlesinger, James, 168
Schrag, Peter, 177
Scowcroft, Brent, 168
Screen Actors Guild (SAG), 70-71
Sears, Roebuck & Company, 148

204 Tax-Funded Politics

Second Amendment Sisters, 28
Senate Subcommittee on Employment and Productivity, 80
Senior citizens, 152-158
Senior Citizens for Kennedy-Johnson, 54
Senior Community Service Employment Program (SCSEP), U.S. Department of Labor, 54-55
Seniors in Community Service, 141
September 11, 2001, 33, 71-72, 169, 171
Sexual harassment, 42
Sexual Minority Youth Assistance League (SMYAL), 20-21, 48-49
Shanker, Albert, 61
Shearer, Derek, 179
Sheldon, Rev. Lou, 176-177
Sheldon, Phil, 177
Sheridan Group, 134
Sierra Club, 87-90, 93-94
Simon, Bill, 177
Simon, Julian, 90-91, 100-101, 105-106
Simpson, Sen. Alan (R-WY), 4
Simpson, O.J., 33-34
Slaughter, Louise (D-NY), 4
Small Business Administration (SBA), 142
Smart Growth, 181
Smeal, Eleanor, 31-32
Smith, Gov. Al, 193
Smith, Steven Rathgeb, 11
Smucker, Bob, 5
Social Security, 37, 40, 56, 72, 143, 148, 151, 153-157
Socialism, 85-86
Society for Cutting Up Men (SCUM), 13
Soil Conservation Service, U.S., 101
Solanis, Valerie, 13
Solarz, Rep. Stephen (D-NY), 165
Soler, Esta, 28
Sommers, Christina Hoff, 22-24, 26
South Africa, 32
Sowell, Thomas, 172
Spillar, Katherine, 33-34
Statute of Virginia for Religious Freedom, 1
Steinem, Gloria, 21-26
Straus, Anna Lord, 17
Stroup, Dr. Richard, 86-87
Students Against Sweatshops (SAS), 78-79

Stuhler, Barbara, 15
Subcommittee on National Economic Growth, Natural Resources, and Regulatory Affairs, 3
Substance abuse treatment, 73, 142
Summers, Secretary Lawrence, 26
Summit of the Americas, 78
Sumner, William Graham, 44
Sweatshops, 72, 76-79

"Take Our Daughters to Work Day," 24-25
Talbott, Strobe, 171
Taliban, the, 32-33
Taxes, 2, 32, 65, 72-73, 87-89, 148,151, 156-157, 186
Taxpayer Funding of Foreign Elections Act, 10
Taylor, Jerry, 97
Teamsters Union, 70
TennCare, 135
Tennessee Disabilities Council, 135
Tennessee Health Care Campaign (THCC), 135
Terrorism issues, 163
Texas Fatherhood Initiative, 175
Texaco, 39, 102
Third Sector in Transition, 11
Tierney, John, 95-97
Thomas, Justice Clarence, 25, 29, 32, 172
Tobacco/smoking, 29, 67-68, 113, 120, 123-128, 130-132
Toqueville, Alexis de, 9
Trade, 72-79
Traditional Values Coalition, 176-177
Treasury, U.S., 150, 170

Uclaf, Rouseel, 32
Unemployment Compensation Trust, Department of Labor, 55-56
Union Institute of Cincinnati, 43-44
Union of Needletrades, Industrial, and Textile Employees (UNITE), 72-74, 78
Unions, 69-72
United Auto Workers (UAW), 70-71, 74
United Federation of Teachers (UFT), 60-61
United Food and Commercial Workers Union (UFCW), 75-76
United Nations, 17-18, 35
United Parcel Service, 140-141

Universal Health Care Action Network (UHCAN!), 134-135
Universal Health Care Task Force, 135
Urban League, 140-142
Urban League Institute for Opportunity and Education, 142

Van't Hof, William, 133
Vasconcelos, José, 146
Venezuela, 166
Volunteers in Service to America (VISTA), 182
Vouchers, school, 65-66, 151

Wal-Mart, 75
Warhol, Andy, 13
Warner, Sen. John (R-VA), 167-168
Warren, Mark E., 11
Warren, Roland, 176
Wattenberg, Ben, 90
Waxman, Henry (D-CA), 4, 194
Wefald, Susan, 27
Welfare, 17, 40-43, 54, 62, 181-182, 184, 187
Wells, Marguerite, 15-16
Wheeler, M. Cass, 131
White House Office on Faith-Based and Community Initiatives, 174
Wiley, George, 182
Wilkie, Wendell, 162
Williams, Eddie, 143
Williams, Walter, 172
Wilson, Marie, 22, 25-26
Wilson, Pres. Woodrow, 15-16
Wiseman, A. Clark, 96
WMX Technologies, 119

Wolf, Naomi, 22
Women Employed Institute, 38, 40-42
Women in Apprenticeships and Nontraditional Occupations (WANTO), Department of Labor, 39-40
Women on Waves, 31
Women Work! The National Network for Women's Employment, 38-40
Women's Appointment Collaboration, 18
Women's Christian Temperance Union, 99
Women's Reproductive Rights Advocacy Prohect, 18
Women's Research and Education Institute, 43
Woodson, Robert, 139, 172-175
Workers Defense League, 56
Workforce Investment Act of 2000, 81
Working Families Party, 186
World War I, 16
World War II, 17, 162
World Wildlife Fund (WWF), 92-93
Wright, Louise Leonard, 17

Xerox, 140-141

Yablonski, Christopher, 2
Yard, Molly, 29
Yokich, Stephen, 74
Yorkin, Bud, 31
Yorkin, Peg, 31-32
YWCA, 2, 7, 49
Yzaguirre, Raul, 148-149

Zoellick, Robert, 167